THE BEST BUDDHIST WRITING 2006

THE BEST
BUDDHIST
WRITING
2·0·0·6

Edited by Melvin McLeod
and the Editors of the *Shambhala Sun*

SHAMBHALA
Boston & London · 2006

Shambhala Publications, Inc.
Horticultural Hall
300 Massachusetts Avenue
Boston, Massachusetts 02115
www.shambhala.com

9 8 7 6 5 4 3 2 1

First Edition
Printed in the United States of America

⊛ This edition is printed on acid-free paper that meets the
American National Standards Institute z39.48 Standard.
Distributed in the United States by Random House, Inc.,
and in Canada by Random House of Canada Ltd

ISBN-13: 978-1-59030-400-6
ISBN-10: 1-59030-400-4
ISSN: 1932-393X
2006213739

Contents

Introduction

History will trace the founding of Buddhist practice in the West to a handful of great teachers, maybe four or five. They came to America over the course of the last century and committed themselves wholeheartedly to their American students, holding nothing back. One of these pioneers was the late Shunryu Suzuki Roshi, founder of the San Francisco Zen Center, whose legacy and students are well represented in this book. His wife, Mitsu Suzuki, told this story in the twenty-fifth anniversary-issue of *Wind Bell*:

> He would never chat. Once I asked him to stay after dinner and chat with me. "Sorry," he said, "I don't have time to chat." He stood up, crossed his arms, and moved back toward his room. "What do you think about all the time?" I asked. "Buddhism in America," he replied, "whether it will spread in this country, and how." "Is that all?" I asked. "Yes, just this one thing."

Why should the establishment of Buddhism in the West be such a difficult question? Other religions find it more straightforward. Practitioners establish their places of worship and practice their religion, with any converts they might gather, much as they always did. It's different with Buddhism. It grows new and afresh in the native soil of every society it enters. It sheds its previous cultural trappings so its timeless wisdom can take on new, indigenous forms that are skillful and appropriate. Buddhism didn't make China like India, nor Japan like China. Chinese Buddhism is truly Chinese; Tibetan Buddhism is truly Tibetan. American Buddhism will, if it succeeds in its mission, be truly and fully American. What that will mean— the merging of the greatest and most successful materialist culture with the greatest and most penetrating nonmaterialist philosophy— is a challenge and an adventure.

On one hand, this book stands on its own. You'll find in it stories, essays, and teachings that are insightful, thought-provoking, and helpful to your life. All are imbued with a spiritual philosophy and practice that is at once profound yet accessible, powerful yet gentle, radical yet life-affirming. You will be entertained, enlightened, and moved by these examples of the best Buddhist writing published in 2005. But on the other hand, this book is part of something much bigger. The third in an annual series, it's a reflection, and I think an important one, of how Buddhism is developing in the modern world. Buddhism's impact on Western thought has already been considerable—far out of proportion to the relatively small number of actual adherents—but I think we're a long way off from knowing exactly how influential Buddhism is going to be. What we do know is that the development of a genuine Buddhist tradition in the West is an interesting and challenging proposition, and one whose success is by no means guaranteed.

In its encounter with the West, Buddhism is meeting not just with tremendous wealth and material progress, but with science, technology, nearly universal literacy, multiculturalism, psychology, feminism, democracy—all the extraordinary knowledge, wisdom, and neurosis of the modern world. What a fertile—and potentially historic—encounter this could be.

How will Americans change Buddhism? How will Buddhism change Americans? This book tells us some interesting and hopeful things about how Americans will make Buddhism their own.

For me it's the personal stories that stand out most in this year's edition of Best Buddhist Writing. I'm moved and inspired by the honesty and wisdom these writers have brought to life's challenges and difficulties. Such intensely personal accounts are not totally new to Buddhism. One thinks of the Tibetan guru Marpa losing his son in a riding accident, or the death of the Japanese poet Issa's young daughter, about which he wrote:

> The world of dew
> is only the world of dew—
> and yet . . . and yet . . .

Here ultimate truth and relative heartbreak meet in a poignant and irreconcilable tension, as they do in Mariana Caplan's "Death Don't Have No Mercy" and Judith Toy's "Murder as a Call to Love." In other stories like Diana Atkinson's "A Life Cut to Pieces," Polly Trout's "Hair-Braiding Meditation," Lin Jensen's "Maintenance," and Anne Cushman's "What Is Death, Mommy?", the Western traditions of personal narrative and psychological self-awareness reveal the open-hearted quality of Buddhist practice in a way that Asian sources rarely do.

These people have found help in their Buddhist practice. The question that readers of the *Shambhala Sun* most often ask is: How do I bring the Buddhist teachings into my daily life? A number of Buddhist practitioners in America are also helping professionals, and they've made a distinctly Buddhist contribution to challenges such as hospice care, psychotherapy, workplace issues, parenting, and dealing with stress and pain. In this book, you will find such helpful advice in Marc Barasch's contemplation of compassion in America, Nancy Hathaway's Buddhist tips on parenting, and John Welwood's fascinating analysis of where we go wrong in our search for love.

Perhaps the greatest contribution that Western thinkers have made to Buddhism is in their analysis of social and political issues. Buddhism has traditionally dealt at the individual level—it has found the cause of suffering in the mind of the individual and it has sought freedom from suffering in the individual's spiritual practice. To this, Western thinkers such as David Loy have added another layer of analysis, describing how the three poisons—greed, aggression, and ignorance—operate through our social, political, and economic institutions. In "Ego Goes Global," he examines these collective causes of suffering and how we can work together to ease the suffering caused by institutionalized ego.

In "Wash Your Bowls," the poet and Zen teacher Norman Fischer takes us on a complete journey from the traditional to the modern, and from the personal to the global. He shows how the basic insights of Buddhist practice can unfold to inform our lives in twenty-first-century society and finally to guide our choices as citizens and consumers to ensure humanity's future. For as Katy Butler demonstrates in "Everything Is Holy," effective action in the world must be grounded in a sane relationship with our day-to-day lives.

In "Coming to Our Senses," the great exponent of mindfulness practice, Jon Kabat-Zinn, draws inescapable parallels between our personal and global struggles, and shows how only the principles of awareness, caring, and wholeness can heal both. Thich Nhat Hanh, whose essay "A Century of Spirituality" concludes this book, is a great Buddhist teacher with a deep understanding of the ways of the world, which he developed in years at the center of the conflict in his native Vietnam. His rare combination of spiritual profundity and political sophistication makes him an important, perhaps crucial, voice in the world today.

And of course in this book there are teachings, the staple of Buddhism for 2500 years. Yet even here, contemporary teachers both Western and Asian are bringing a rich mix of references and associations to their presentation of Buddhism's timeless truths. His Holiness the Dalai Lama is an avid student of Western science who writes in this book of the great potential he sees in the meeting of Buddhist meditation and Western mind science. American teachers such as Joan Sutherland, Sharon Salzberg, Roshi Bodhin Kjolhede, and Tenshin Reb Anderson draw on their deep experience of Buddhist practice, fleshed out with references to Western literature, psychology, fairy tales, philosophy, and even sports. Conversely, contemporary Asian teachers such as Sakyong Mipham, Ponlop Rinpoche, and the Dalai Lama himself are teaching in a new idiom informed by the concerns of contemporary society. All told, these teachings represent a fertile meeting of East and West that is only going to get richer and deeper in the years to come.

Of course, there are those who worry that genuine dharma may yet be co-opted and corrupted by modern materialism, by the appeal of money, fame, and followers. But genuine Buddhism has been resisting the three lords of materialism (see Carolyn Gimian's teaching on this vital subject) since its inception and it should be able to handle this powerful modern version. All concerned Buddhists must think hard, as Suzuki Roshi did, about how Buddhism will grow on this soil. At the same time, we can have faith in the great power and integrity of the dharma. Another great pioneer of Buddhism in America, Nyogen Senzaki, put it this way in a 1947 poem to his teacher:

> As a wanderer in this strange land forty-two years,
> I commemorate my teacher each autumn.
> Now, on the sixth floor of this hotel,
> He gazes at me as awkwardly as ever.
> "How is the work, Awkward One?"
> He might be saying to me.
> "America has Zen all the time.
> Why, my teacher, should I meddle?"
>
> *Namo Tasso Bhagavato Arahato Samma Sambuddhassa!*
> *[Homage to Him, the Holy One, the Enlightened One, the*
> *Supremely Awakened One!]*

This is the third in the Best Buddhist Writing series and I would like to thank Peter Turner, president of Shambhala Publications, for the honor of editing this series. It has enriched and expanded my understanding of Buddhism in America with all the talent and insight it offers. I would also like to thank Beth Frankl, who edited the first in the series and has returned from maternity leave to edit the third. My colleagues at the *Shambhala Sun* and *Buddhadharma* magazines are companions on this journey we call the early days of Buddhism in the West, and their wisdom is reflected throughout this book. More personally, I thank my wife, Pamela Rubin, and our child, Pearl McLeod, who is my inspiration, and my Buddhist teachers, the late Chögyam Trungpa Rinpoche and Khenpo Tsultrim Gyamtso Rinpoche.

The selection of the "best" Buddhist writing is naturally a subjective process, and it cannot reflect the full range of Buddhist writing out there, from popular books to academic works to teachings for committed practitioners of specific schools. I would like to thank the writers and publishers represented in this book but also to acknowledge the great worth of all the dharma books and periodicals being published. If you enjoy what you read in this book, I urge you to explore the world of Buddhist writing more deeply. If you wish, take this book as your invitation to join the marvelous spiritual, intellectual, and artistic journey called Buddhism in America.

MELVIN MCLEOD
Editor-in-chief
The Shambhala Sun
Buddhadharma: The Practitioner's Quarterly

The Best Buddhist Writing 2006

It's Up to You

Dzigar Kongtrül

Buddhism is a nontheistic religion. On one level, that simply means it's a religion with no deity, God, or external savior. But more broadly, it means there is nothing solid at all we can rely on—no soul, belief, person, community, possession, or accomplishment will save us. All we have going for us is our own intelligence and insight, but if we apply these with courage and honesty, it is enough. The place to begin, says Dzigar Kongtrül Rinpoche, is to look unflinchingly at our own self-deception.

LOOKING IN THE MIRROR

When we look in the mirror, the one thing we don't want to see is an ordinary human being. We would like to see someone special. Whether we are conscious of this or not, we are simply not content to see an ordinary human being with neuroses, obstacles, and problems.

We want to see a happy person, but instead we see someone who is struggling. We want to think of ourselves as compassionate, but instead we see someone who is selfish. We long to be elegant, but our arrogance makes us crass. And instead of a strong or immortal person, we see someone who is vulnerable to the four streams of birth, old age, sickness, and death. The conflict between what we see and what we want to see causes tremendous pain.

The Pain of Self-Importance

We are imprisoned in this pain by a sense of specialness, or self-importance. Self-importance is the underlying clinging we have to "I, I, I, me, me, me, mine, mine, mine," which colors all of our experience. If we look closely, we find a strong element of self-importance in everything we think, say, and do. "How can I feel good? What will others think? What will I gain? What will I lose?" These questions are all rooted in our self-importance. Even our feeling of not measuring up to who we think we should be is a form of self-importance.

We like to see ourselves as strong and in control, but we are more like a fragile eggshell that is easily broken. This makes us feel deeply vulnerable—and not in a good way. This vulnerable self requires protection, armoring, the gathering of forces, and the construction of walls. As a result, we become painfully trapped. We are increasingly fearful of relaxing with things as they are and increasingly uncertain that anything will work out the way we would like.

It takes courage to go beyond self-importance and see who we really are—but this is our path. The point of all Buddhist teachings—formal or informal—is to reduce self-importance and make room for the truth. This process begins with self-reflection.

A Questioning Spirit

The great Indian pandita Aryadeva once said that to merely question that things might not be as they seem can shake the very foundation of habitual clinging. This questioning spirit is the starting point for self-reflection. Could it be that this tightly knit sense of self is not what it seems? Do we really need to hold everything together, and *can* we? Is there life beyond self-importance? These kinds of questions open the door to investigating the cause of our pain.

The actual practice of self-reflection requires us to step back, examine our experience, and not succumb to the momentum of habitual mind. This allows us to look without judgment at whatever arises, and this goes directly against the grain of our self-importance.

Self-reflection is the common thread that runs through all traditions and lineages of Buddhist practice. It also takes us beyond the boundaries of formal practice. We can bring the questioning spirit of self-reflection to any situation, at any time. Self-reflection is an attitude, an approach, and a practice. In a nutshell, it is a way to make practice come alive for us personally.

OUR TRUE FACE

If we look at our habitual mind without deception or judgment, we will see beyond it to who we truly are. Beyond the "self" and what it does or doesn't want, beyond the self that is constantly fighting or tugging at the world, lies our true nature and true face.

This is the face of our natural state, free from the struggle to become what we are not. It's the face of a potentially realized being whose wisdom, qualities, and courage are beyond measure. Seeing both our deeper potential *and* our hindrances, we begin to understand the cause of our suffering—and we can begin to do something about it.

When we practice self-reflection, we take liberation into our own hands. This uncompromising path demands true courage and fearlessness. Going beyond the ordinary notion of self leads directly to the truth of our buddha essence, our true face, and to freedom from suffering.

THE SPOOKINESS OF EGO-MIND

Holding to an ordinary notion of self, or ego, is the source of all our pain and confusion. The irony is that when we look for this "self" that we're cherishing and protecting, we can't even find it. The self is shifty and ungraspable. When we say "I'm old," we're referring to our body as self. When we say "my body," the self becomes the owner of the body. When we say "I'm tired," the self is equated with physical or emotional feelings. The self is our perceptions when we say "I see," and our thoughts when we say "I think." When we can't find a self within or outside of these parts, we may then conclude that the self is that which is aware of all of these things—the knower or mind.

But when we look for the mind, we can't find any shape, or color, or form. This mind that we identify as the self, which we could call ego-mind, controls everything we do. Yet it can't actually be found—which is somewhat spooky, as if a ghost were managing our home. The house seems to be empty, but all the housework has been done. The bed has been made, our shoes have been polished, the tea has been poured, and the breakfast has been cooked.

The funny thing is that we never question this. We just assume that someone or something is there. But all this time, our life has been managed by a ghost, and it's time to put a stop to it. On one hand, ego-mind has served us—but it hasn't served us well. It has lured us into the suffering of samsara and enslaved us. When ego-mind says, "Get angry," we get angry; when it says, "Get attached," we act out our attachments. When we look into the "slavish" arrangement we have with our ego-mind, we can see how it pressures us, plays tricks on us, and causes us to do things that bring undesirable consequences.

If you want to stop being the slave of a ghost, you must demand that ego-mind show its face. No true ghost will show up when it hears this! You can practice this simple meditation throughout the day. Whenever you don't know what to do with yourself, challenge your ego-mind to show its face. When you're cooking your dinner or waiting for the bus, challenge your ego-mind to show its face. Do it especially when ego-mind overwhelms you, when you feel threatened, fearful, or enslaved by it. Just straighten your posture and challenge ego-mind. Don't be gullible, wiggly, or spineless. When you challenge ego-mind, be firm but gentle, penetrating but never aggressive. Just say to your ego-mind, "Show me your face!" When no mind shows up saying, "Here I am," ego-mind will begin to lose its hold on you and your struggles will lighten up. See if this isn't true.

Of course, maybe your mind does have a face and your experience will be different. But if you don't find a mind with a face, you won't take your struggles so seriously, and all of your pain and suffering will lessen.

When we question ego-mind directly, it is exposed for what it is: the absence of everything we believe it to be. We can actually see through this seemingly solid ego-mind, or self. But what are we left with then? We are left with an open, intelligent awareness, unfettered by a self to cherish or protect. This is the primordial wisdom mind of all beings. Relaxing into this discovery is true meditation—and true meditation brings ultimate realization and freedom from suffering.

A Practitioner's Approach to Life

Looking for ego-mind is very important. This is the only way to know that it can't be found. And if we can't find ego-mind, we can't find a self—so how can we take all our thoughts, emotions, and experiences so personally?

I remember my first experience of selflessness. I felt a strong sense of freedom and a deep appreciation of how fundamentally perfect things could be if I didn't let my self-importance get in the way and complicate everything. I felt relieved to bring to light all my useless efforts to maintain a self.

People tend to appreciate nature. We associate the natural world with beauty, that which is pure and untouched. When we see someone cutting trees or digging in the wilderness, it disturbs us. We can realize the beauty of our own inner nature when we stop manipulating everything that crosses our path as a way to fortify a sense of self. This is a practitioner's approach to life.

If you think about it, when we grasp on to a self, how can we possibly practice self-reflection? Everything becomes personal: *our* pain, *our* anger, *our* shortcomings. When we take thoughts and emotions personally, they torture us. Looking at our thoughts and emotions in this way is like rubbing our nose in something unpleasant—what purpose does it serve other than to create more pain? This is not the kind of looking we are speaking of here.

With the view of selflessness, we can enjoy whatever arises in our awareness. We can accept that everything that arises is a result of our past actions, or karma, but it is not who we are.

Utilizing Thoughts and Emotions

Thoughts and emotions will always arise. The purpose of practice is not to get rid of them. We can no more put a stop to thoughts and emotions than we can put a stop to the worldly circumstances that seemingly turn for or against us. We can, however, choose to welcome and work with them. On one level, they are nothing but sensations. When we don't solidify or judge them as good or bad, right or wrong, favorable or unfavorable, we can utilize them to progress on the path.

We utilize thoughts and emotions by watching them arise and dissolve. As we do this, we see they are insubstantial. When we are able to see through them, we realize they can't really bind us, lead us astray, or distort our sense of reality. And we no longer expect them to cease. The very expectation that thoughts and emotions should cease is a misconception. We can free ourselves from this misconception in meditation.

In the sutras it says, "What good is manure, if not to fertilize sugar cane crops?" Similarly, we can say, "What good are thoughts and emotions—in fact all of our experiences—if not to increase our realization?" What prevents us from making good use of them are the fears and reactions that come from our self-importance. Therefore, the Buddha taught us to *let things be.* Without feeling threatened or trying to control them, just let things arise naturally and let them be.

When ego-mind becomes transparent through meditation, we have no reason to be afraid of it. This greatly reduces our suffering. We may actually develop a passion for seeing all aspects of our mind. This attitude is at the heart of the practice of self-reflection.

THE THEATER OF REFLECTIONS

When we're watching a movie in the theater, we can relax and enjoy the show because we know it's an illusion. This magical display that we're watching is the result of a projector, film, light, screen, and our own perceptions coming together. In separate momentary flashes of color, shapes, and sound, they create an illusion of continuity, which we perceive as characters, scenery, movement, and language. What we call "reality" works much the same way. Our ability to know, our sense perceptions, the seeds of our past karma, and the phenomenal world all come together to create our life's "show." All of these elements share a dynamic relationship, which keeps things moving and interesting. This is known as interdependence.

When we look around us, we can see that nothing exists in isolation, which is another way of saying that everything is interdependent. Everything depends upon an infinite number of causes and conditions to come into being, arise, and fall away moment by moment. Because they are interdependent, things don't possess a true existence of their own. For instance, how could we separate a flower from the many causes and conditions that produce it—water, soil, sun, air, seed, and so forth? Can we find a flower that exists independently from these causes and conditions? Everything is so intricately connected it is hard to point to where one thing starts and another ends. This is what is meant by the illusory or empty nature of phenomena.

The outer world in all its variety and our inner world of thoughts and emotions are not as they seem. All phenomena appear to exist objectively, but their true mode of existence is like a dream: apparent yet insubstantial. The experience of emptiness is not found outside the world of ordinary appearance, as many people mistakenly assume. In truth, we experience emptiness when the mind is free of grasping at appearance.

Seeing the emptiness of the phenomenal world relieves us of the heavy notion of things being solid or intrinsic. When we understand that nothing exists independently, everything that does arise seems more dreamlike and less threatening. This brings a deep sense of relaxation, and we feel less need to control our mind and circumstances. Because the nature of everything is emptiness, it is possible to view our life the way we would view a movie. We can relax and enjoy the show.

Enjoying the Show

Watching our mind can be more enjoyable than watching a Hollywood movie. The screen, projector, story, characters, and drama are all within our own experience, and all of samsara and nirvana is part of the show. Such a great theater production couldn't be bought for millions of dollars. Our ticket into this theater is "seeing through": seeing that phenomena do not exist as they appear.

Seeing through appearance—thoughts, emotions, and outer objects—is very important. When we don't see through appearance, we invest that which is fluid, changing, and ungraspable with an existence it doesn't have, and the world seems to either lure us in or threaten us. This makes peace of mind almost impossible.

For instance, something makes us angry and we just have to pursue it, get to the bottom of it, or bring it to some conclusion. We're having an intense conversation, and we just have to make our point. Or we're experiencing confusion and we have to get some clarity. One thought is just bursting to give birth to another. But at some point we need to realize that whether they are relevant or not, these are just thoughts and emotions—insubstantial and fleeting.

What if we could see through our beliefs and fears the way we see through a movie? We could begin to have fun with them, laugh at them, and let them be. Taking them too seriously defeats the purpose of everything we're trying to do on our path. We could do ourselves a big favor by just letting this discursive mind be.

From a Buddhist point of view, letting things be allows them to become what they are, instead of what we want them to be. There is a saying: "Meditation is much more pleasant when it's not fabricated; lake water is much clearer when you don't stir it up"—which means let it be. This is the meaning of self-reflection.

Not Losing Your Seat

The point of the practice of self-reflection is to experience things clearly, without muddying the waters by trying to change or control them. People who believe they can change or control everything are usually in a great deal of pain, because this is simply not possible.

Sometimes practitioners resent disturbing thoughts and emotions or feel they should be exempt from them. Those who have been practicing for many years may wonder, "Why after all this time do I still experience so much mental turmoil? Why is my mind not at peace?" This question reflects a mistaken view of the purpose of practice. No matter how advanced we may be in practice or realization, mind's natural activity does not cease. It's an expression of mind's nature, which is pregnant with possibilities. Instead of resenting mind's vitality, we can use it to deepen and enrich our practice.

The point of practice is to work with both peaceful and unpeaceful states of mind. Generally, we find unpeaceful thoughts and emotions disturbing. If they relate to our well-being, anxiety arises. But it's important to know that this is all very natural. Thoughts are the fruit of our karma; emotions and anxiety are like the juice of that fruit. Experiencing them doesn't necessarily mean you've lost your seat as a practitioner.

When disturbing thoughts and emotions arise, your only choice is to let them unfold naturally. Don't try to control or indulge them. Giving them importance only makes them more "real." Instead, shift your attitude a bit. You will see that this disturbed and anxious mind is just an expression of mind's basic nature—which is emptiness itself, and quite OK. Everything is in a good place, and there is no need for such weightiness or concern. Seeing this brings peace.

Peace comes about when the true nature of things outshines their appearance. A mind that is subtle enough to recognize the true nature of its expressions—to know that this nature is open, unobstructed, and full of potential—is at peace. For this kind of realization, we all need to practice ongoing self-reflection.

Self-reflection is the gateway to freedom. It also brings much greater appreciation and enjoyment. We begin to enjoy spending time with our own mind, and we enjoy reflecting on our experience of the teachings. Like the sun emerging from behind the clouds, the teachings of the dharma become clear. And the blessings of the lineage—those realized masters who have gone before us—enter our hearts and dissolve our habitual relationship with mind.

Then it becomes clear how we must use this life, and how we must relate with ordinary happiness and pain. Since both are expressions of our basic nature, striving to be happy or happier is as pointless as striving to be free from suffering and pain. In order to find peace, we must connect with our life on this very basic level.

This Floating World

Joan Sutherland

*A dream, a bubble, an illusion, a magic show—these are some of ways
Buddhism describes this "reality" we live in. That doesn't mean things don't
exist. It doesn't mean they do. "Existence" and "nonexistence" are both
extreme views; the true nature of reality cannot be conceptualized but only
experienced. The twist, says Zen teacher Joan Sutherland, is that when we
embrace life's dreamlike nature, we experience it with more vividness,
poignancy, and love than ever before.*

One of our Western sutras is the children's round that goes:

> Row, row, row your boat,
> Gently down the stream.
> Merrily, merrily, merrily, merrily,
> Life is but a dream.

The image of a human life as a small skiff on the wide waters of
the world has been around as long as people have had boats, and the
thought that life is a dream is no news flash either. But what does it
mean that there is something happy, maybe even beautiful or con-
soling, in thinking so?

The founding myth of Buddhist tradition—the life of Siddhartha, who became the Buddha—has something to say about this. Here's the story, as I understand it.

"A long time ago there is a green and pleasant land nestled in the foothills of the Himalayas. The queen's name is Mahamaya, which means 'the Great Dream of the World.' One year, during the midsummer festival, Mahamaya herself has a dream: The Guardians of the Four Quarters lift her up and carry her high into the mountains. They bathe her in a lake and lay her on a couch in a golden palace on a silver hill. A beautiful white elephant, carrying a white lotus in his trunk, approaches from the north and enters her right side, melting into her womb. When she awakens, she knows that she has conceived. The priests interpret her dream to mean that if her child follows the householder's life, he will become a great king, but if he follows the spiritual life, he will become a buddha."

(Looking back, people realize that at the moment of this conception, people began to speak kindly to each other, musical instruments played themselves, and every tree burst into blossom.)

"When she is about to give birth, Mahamaya sets out for the place she was born, as is the custom. Along the way, she stops in a grove of trees to rest. She stands on the roots of a great tree, and as she reaches up for a branch to support herself, she gives easy birth to a son who will be called Siddhartha. Seven days later Maya dies and is taken into the heavenly realms, where she watches the rest of his life unfold."

This story begins with a dream rising within a dream: Mahamaya, the great dream of the world, steps from the hubbub of life into her quiet apartment, where she has a dream. She is taken someplace new, someplace she's never been before, to conceive of something never conceived before. It is a blessed moment, a sudden upsurge of beauty and kindness in the world. The following spring she gives birth to another dream, an individual named Siddhartha.

In this passage there is the sense that the world is endlessly imagining itself into existence, endlessly generating the specific and individual things of which it is made. The Chan teacher Great Master Ma used to say that the universe is the samadhi of dharma nature, out of which no being has ever fallen; in other words, the universe is the deep meditative state of the universe itself, which contains all things. But this deep meditation doesn't just hold everything; it actually *becomes* earth, wind, flame, and water, and then mountains, rivers and trees, skin and bones, flesh and blood, as Zen teacher Keizan Jokin added. You and I and the teapot on the table between us are the samadhi of the universe.

In meditation we can fall through the bottom of our individual states into this deep meditation of the universe-as-a-whole, like individual waves sinking back into the ocean for a while. It would be more accurate to say that we don't fall or sink anywhere, but simply remember what is already and always true. And the remembering wave retains its shape: each of us is the ocean in this particular form. Each of us is Siddhartha come into a body: human siddharthas and piñon pine siddharthas and subatomic particle siddharthas.

Human beings, especially ones involved in spiritual practice, often try to abandon the wave in favor of the ocean, as though there is something truer about the vastness of the ocean than about life as a wave. Zen teachers have colorful names, like corpse-watching demon, for people who succumb to this impulse. Our human fate is to move the other way, right into the middle of our lives, and to remember there the salty taste, still in our mouths, of that vast ocean.

This brings us back to how we feel about the dreamlike quality of life. If we believe that the ocean of essential nature is the true thing and that the world of our everyday experience is somehow less true, then the world becomes a veil that obscures our sight, an illusion we have to see through. But if we don't create levels of reality and then rank them, if ocean and wave are aspects of one whole thing, then the dreamlike quality of life might become something that simply is, as far as we can tell. "Life often seems like a dream" becomes a wondering about how things are, rather than a verdict on them.

This world we are born into—this complicated, difficult, hauntingly touching world—is the one whole thing. It is the world we awaken in, and awaken to. Our awakening is made of this world, just as it is. It doesn't come from some other realm like a bolt from the blue, and you don't go to someplace else when you awaken. Awakening is not a destination, and meditation is not a bus ride. Awakening is the unfolding of an ability to see what has always been here. To see, more and more reliably, what is actually in front of you.

Neither the ocean's perspective nor the wave's perspective—sometimes called the absolute and the relative—is the whole truth; each is an aspect of the way things are. There's an old story about a woman who's been meditating very deeply, and she comes to that moment when everything falls away. Her young son arrives home from school, and she stares at him and asks, "Who are you?" We can understand the wonder of that question, asked from the perspective of everything fallen away. It's not about whether she recognizes him—"Who are *you*?"—but, "Who *are* you? Who am I? Who is anybody?" And we can also see that this might be an alarming question for a seven-year-old boy to hear from his mother.

When we've experienced both the mother's and the son's perspectives, at first it's a matter of holding them simultaneously. It's as though, at any given moment, one is the foreground and the other the background, one up front and vivid and the other receding. Mostly, as we go about our everyday lives, what's in the foreground is the realm of place and time, the world where we fall in love and eat peaches and have car accidents. Sometimes, in meditation or just walking down the street on a blustery day, all of that recedes, and for a while what's in the foreground is how timeless and limitless and radiant the universe is.

As our meditation goes along, we might notice that these two perspectives begin to bleed into each other—foreground and background are no longer so distinct, and it isn't a matter anymore of choosing between them. More and more the world begins to feel like one whole thing: one continuous ground, full of life, like white herons in the mist. Where do birds end and clouds begin? How is it that the black bamboo at my gate is eternal in the morning sun, and yet I remember planting it there more than a decade ago? The ageless bamboo planted in 1994—in its shade, the mother in the old story might think, "Oh, my radiant, completely empty son, it's time for dinner; you must be hungry."

There is a grace and a poignancy to experiencing life in this way. The dream of the world becomes a kind of field of awareness. We begin to experience things as rising and falling in that field, like herons stretching and slowly flapping their wings. A hungry child appears in the field. A dream of white elephants. A thought arises. A thought lasts awhile. A thought goes away. What we've experienced as a busy, insistent, and separate self is becoming part of the field of awareness. Not a creature in the field, nor an observer of it, but the field itself, in which everything, even the parts of ourselves we are so familiar with, rise and fall as a dream.

This can be a happy thing, when what rises in our hearts and minds seems no more and no less important than anything else in the field. A woman I used to know would say to her son, "The trouble with you is that you take your life too personally!" What a relief it is when every passing thought or reaction doesn't automatically take pride of place, doesn't need us to bend the world according to its whim.

The first passage from Siddhartha's story ends when he is born and Mahamaya ascends to the heavens. The Great Dream is still mother to what happens, but the rest of the story is the working out of a particular human life. Part of this is coming to see the dreamlike qualities of life in the ways we've been discussing, and then taking another step: *trusting* the dream of life, because this trust is one of the things that helps make the world. Here's how the story continues:

"Many years later, Siddhartha has been practicing such extreme austerities that he's on the brink of death. Sitting in the forest, he faints with hunger. When he comes to, he is alone and disheartened, but suddenly he remembers something from his childhood: He is lying under a rose-apple tree, looking around. For the moment everyone has forgotten about him. He feels no resistance to what he sees, no sense that anything is lacking; there is nothing he wants other than exactly what is happening. He wonders why this image should appear now, and whether that early memory of ease, rather than the harsh discipline he's been practicing, is the way to freedom. 'Are you afraid of this happiness?' he startles himself by asking. The answer is no, but he is too weak to do anything about it.

"Meantime, in a nearby town, a woman named Sujata falls asleep and has a dream. Because of the dream, she goes out to her family's herd and milks a thousand cows, feeding their milk to five hundred cows, and so on down to the last few cows. She mixes this rich milk with rice, puts it in a golden bowl, and walks out into the forest. She has no idea what she'll find, which turns out to be Siddhartha sitting under a tree, just awakened from his faint. Though he is weak, already there is a muted glow about him. She offers him her bowl of milk and rice, saying, 'May this bring you as much joy to eat as it brought me to make.' Siddhartha eats, and Sujata's blessing flows over the harsh landscape of his austerities."

Siddhartha and Sujata make this small moment in the vast sweep of the world by trusting the dreamlike quality of things. They take seriously the images that come to them out of that dream—Siddhartha's in a memory of childhood, Sujata's in her sleep. For each of them, a possibility appears from beyond the territory of what they already know, and they walk out to meet it. They share a willingness to take that walk without being certain that the path will be there under their feet. This is a fundamental kind of trust, and it has nothing to do with the likelihood that things will turn out as we think they should; though we know where the story is going, it might initially have seemed like a setback when Siddhartha's small band of followers abandoned him in disgust because he took food from Sujata.

A meditation practice that trusts in the dreamlike quality of life is like this. We meet whatever happens, come into relationship with it, and take another step. And we do this without the certainty that we are right—indeed, knowing that whatever we choose will in some way be a mistake. But we're willing to take a step anyway, and to notice what happens, so that what we notice becomes part of the next step.

To trust the dream of life is to be at ease with the provisional nature of things. I've been me for half a century now, but that's still provisional; it rose and will fall. How much more so our thoughts and opinions and moods, which come and go like the weather? And what are they compared to the Rocky Mountains, which themselves rise and fall, though much more slowly? And the Rockies compared to the Milky Way? When I sit on my deck on a summer evening, the Milky Way looks like an immense and timeless river of light across the sky, which consoles me in difficult times. But from closer up, it's full of supernovae and black holes and red dwarves; things explode and collide, swirl in and out of existence, and everything is moving unimaginably fast. A Navajo storyteller might say that Coyote stole some bread baking on the coals of First Woman's fire and left a trail of ashes across the sky. They're all just different ways of interpreting the Milky Way dream, bits of the ongoing conversation that is human life.

We're awfully lucky that life isn't a monologue. There is so much that is unexpected and unplanned for, and those are the things that can make all the difference: raising a child you didn't give birth to, helping an elderly neighbor as she's dying, spending time in a foreign country because you fell in love with someone who lives there. Sometimes these things fall like grace from some unanticipated cloud, and sometimes it's more like a meteor plowing into us. But the world is filled with stories of how hardships and difficulties can pull us deeper into life, if we let them; they can bring us heart and soul in a way the easy life never could.

In this dreamscape of a world, heavens and hell realms are a thought or a phone call or a news broadcast away. Children turn into adults you never could have imagined they carried inside them. The sky over the sea is full of pelicans, and then they almost disappear, and now the sky is full of them again, because humans started using DDT and then stopped. On any morning, what happens on the other side of the world can make you weep over your breakfast.

Perhaps, after all, we shouldn't take our lives so personally, shouldn't think of them as the monologue of busy and insistent and separate selves. Perhaps we are made up of landscapes and events and memories and genetics; of the touch of those we hold dear, our oldest fears, the art that moves us, and those sorrows on the other side of the world that make us weep at the breakfast table. The astronomer Carl Sagan used to say that if you really want to make an apple pie from scratch, you have to start with the Big Bang.

It's as though there is a communal dreaming going on underneath everything, a great river of co-creation where our individual dreams, our individual lives, touch and are touched by the dreams of others, and that is how our common world is made. The world is full of meetings between Sujata and Siddhartha. I sat for years in a meditation hall among the redwoods on the California coast. I know that those trees became part of me, that my meditation has, among other things, a redwood flavor to it. And perhaps the redwoods made their own tissue of winter rain and summer light, and the samadhi of all those sitting in that hall.

Needless to say, our co-creations aren't always benign. We are equally capable of making nightmares like ethnic cleansing and impenetrable trances like fundamentalism. And there are the pinched daydreams of gossip and grudges and self-deception. When we run into this recalcitrant stuff, we sometimes fall back on distortions of the ocean and wave perspectives: either nothing matters because it's all empty, or everything is a mess, and that's all that matters. But if we can rest in the dreamlike quality of life, if we find it moving rather than problematic, then the natural view is something like, "Oh, my radiant, completely empty son, it's time for dinner; you must be hungry."

By which I mean, to experience the dreamlike quality of life is to understand that there is something mysterious at the heart of things, something we can't figure out or get control of. It's a mighty big ocean whose surface we skim. If we lean back into that experience, we're more and more at peace with what isn't certain, and less and less in a chronic state of complaint at what W. H. Auden called the disobedience of the daydream. We spend so much time disappointed in life for being life. But as we feel less and less resistance to things as they are, as peace grows in the midst of uncertainty, kindness is not far behind. We're not at war with life so much anymore, and that is a kinder way to be. When we're not fighting with life, or turning away from it, joining in seems to come pretty naturally. Someone is hungry; it's time to make dinner. An election turns out badly; where do we go from here? When we're aware of the dream of life, we know that we're part of its co-creation whether we act or not.

Merrily, merrily, merrily, merrily,
Life is but a dream.

The word *merry* came from roots meaning "pleasing" and "of short duration." This poignant life, so fleeting and yet made entirely of eternal moments—this is the dream we are making together, this is the dream that is making us, and that is the one whole thing.

Searching for the Heart of Compassion

Marc Ian Barasch

Call it love, kindness, compassion, heart—it's the real elixir, the one that transforms life. We all know that—every religion says it—but where do we find it? We all want to give and to receive love, yet our society often seems cold and uncaring. Marc Ian Barasch searches America for compassion in action, compassionate people, and the compassion inside himself that is a natural part of our being.

> I am thankful that thorns have roses.
> —ALPHONSE KARR

Every now and then, I'll meet an escapee, someone who has broken free of self-centeredness and lit out for the territory of compassion. You've met them, too, those people who seem to emit a steady stream of, for want of a better word, love-vibes. As soon as you come within range, you feel embraced, accepted for who you are. For those of us who suspect that you rarely get something for nothing, such geniality can be discomfiting: *They don't even know me. It's just generic cornflakes.* But it feels so good to be around them. They stand there, radiating photons of goodwill, and despite yourself, you beam back, and the world, in a twinkling, changes.

I appreciate these compassion-mongers, even marvel at them. I rarely think that I could be like them. Sure, I've tried to live a benign life, putting my shoulder to the wheel for peace, justice, and Mother Earth (mostly churning out words on a page, bouncing signals off the satellites). I doubt that it's made me much less egotistical (maybe a bit more so). I still have that too-cool objectivity that can suck away my sympathies like an outgoing tide.

But I want to be good. Not that cramped, chiding Moral Majority good (I'll keep my minority status, thanks). Not sticky-sweet, watch-your-insulin-level good. Just deep-down, unfailingly kind. The fact that I'm not, when the world could use so much more kindness, frankly vexes my spirit.

Oh, I'm a nice enough guy. Like most people, I adore my offspring, even when they drive me crazy; love my parents, despite the corkscrew of childhood; dote on my siblings (though there is that scrapbook of old slights); treasure my friends (even if they sometimes let me down). Conventional wisdom wouldn't fault me for saving the best stuff for my nearest and dearest and giving the rest of humanity the leftovers.

Thus it is, say the sages, that the harvest of kindness—of kindredness—is winnowed down to a precious few grains. For at the center of all spiritual traditions is the beacon of a truly radical proposal: Open your heart to everybody. *Every*body.

What *is* compassion, that x-factor that every faith (the founders, if not the followers) exalts as a supreme virtue? When the Dalai Lama says, "My only religion is kindness," and the Pope calls for a "civilization of love," it can't be just mealy-mouthed piety. Kindness and love are powers unto themselves, able to transmute even the most relentless enmity. Nelson Mandela once remarked he befriended his jailers, those grim, khaki-clad overseers of his decades of hard labor in a limestone quarry, by "exploiting their good qualities." Asked if he believed all people were kind at their core, he responded, "There is no doubt whatsoever, provided you are able to arouse their inherent goodness." If that sounds like wishful thinking, well, he actually *did* it.

When I was in my twenties, my Buddhist teacher tricked me into taking a vow of universal compassion. Using some spiritual sleight-of-hand I've yet to unravel, he made it seem I could aspire to a tender concern for everybody, even putting their welfare before my own.

Fat chance, I'd thought. But in his wily way, he had framed this vow—the bodhisattva's promise to live for others—as a case of enlightened self-interest. It was not, he told me, a matter of wearing a one-size-fits-all hair shirt. I was taking the vow for my own good. It would give me some leverage to pry loose, finger by finger, the claustrophobic monkey-grip of ego; give the heart a little breathing room. By treating others generously, I might find them responding in kind. I felt I was being made privy to an ancient secret: *To attain your own human potential, be mindful of everyone else's.*

At some point in my vow ceremony, a deceptively casual affair held in a rocky field, it had felt as if my vision suddenly cleared. I'd glimpsed, like a sky swept clean of clouds, everyone's innate okayness. Years later, I still marveled at the spiritual chutzpah of the liturgy: *However innumerable are beings, I vow to save them all.* It was vintage Buddhist bravado—a pledge to empty all the world's oceans using only an eyedropper. Hardly knowing what I was doing, I had planted myself in a millennia-old tradition that claims you can love all without preconditions, exclusionary clauses, or bottom lines; that says life isn't *quid pro quo,* but *quid pro bono.*

To my surprise, the vow hadn't made me feel obligated, but liberated from my own suffocating strictures, from the narrowness of my concerns. It was as if I'd been waiting for a signal, a green light to step onto the crosswalk to the opposite curb; some goad to be compassionate not out of blind craving for virtue, but because it seemed the only genuinely interesting thing to do with my life.

Just forming the intention to make myself useful felt salutary, like some fast-acting antivenin to my snakebit business-as-usual. I had assumed life was about magnifying myself (for the greater good, of course), but now that seemed like the wrong end of the telescope: It made everyone else look small. I soon took a job running a residential therapeutic community in exchange for room and board, surprised at my ability to care for the walking wounded. I stopped thinking so much about how others had let me down, broken my heart, failed to anticipate my needs, or take my oh-so-unique sensitivities into account. I began striving to see—and even nourish—other people's possibilities, receiving in return those surprise concoctions that the human spirit dishes out when it feels accepted and at its ease.

But there came a point on my journey when I'd stumbled badly and fell far: a dire illness, an interminable recovery, penury, loneliness, full-on despair. Friends clucked in sympathy but stepped gingerly over the body. Family didn't do much better. I had a soul-curdling realization: the people you love (and who ostensibly love you) may not be there when you need them most. I got through it—the kindness of strangers and all—but I was soon back to squinting at people through my cool fish eye, seeing their preening vanity, their intellectual shortfalls, their ethical squishiness. It took time until I realized such shortsightedness takes a toll—let alone that there was anything I could do about it.

Finding my way back to meditation helped. Nothing like getting a good, long look at myself (and funny how much I looked like everyone else). I noticed how often my social trade-offs were more about getting than giving; how many of my thoughts revolved in geosynchronous orbit around Planet Numero Uno. Inner work is a warts-and-all proposition; it gets harder to kid yourself. Still, my teacher had insisted one thing was certain: despite seeing all the ego's pitfalls and pratfalls, real bodhisattvas make friends with themselves. Everyone, he said, possessed some worth past quantifying or qualifying, some value beyond judgment or fine-tuning—and that included oneself.

To love our neighbor *as ourselves*, after all, is the great injunction of every religion. But what does loving yourself *mean*? It's one thing to say it; another to know it in your bones. Do I talk to the mirror, whispering sweet nothings? tenderly imagine a little homunculus inside me and pet it, tickle it, scratch it behind the ears? The spiritual consensus seems to be that it's like learning to love anyone: you start by getting to know them. The side benefit to this is that to know yourself is also to know the person sitting next to you and the one halfway around the world. "Read thyself," wrote philosopher Thomas Hobbes. "Whosoever looketh into himself . . . shall know what are the thoughts and passions of other men."

Still, having looketh'd into myself, I can't say I loveth all I see. I *have* read myself, and there in oversize type it says: petty, suspicious, greedy, vain, jealous, lazy, stingy, dull (and that's just on the page; there's more between the lines). That I also reckon myself to be magnanimous, conscientious, loyal, thrifty, brave, and intermittently humble is beside the point. It's not enough to offset scourging self-judgment with a roll call of compensating pluses. We have to take ourselves (and each other) whole. The Dalai Lama points out that the Tibetan term for compassion, *tsewa,* generally means "love of others," but "one can have that feeling toward oneself as well. It is a state of mind where you extend how you relate to yourself toward others." If it's true that what goes around comes around, compassion is about nothing if not love's tendency to circulate.

And radiate. Alexander Pope (poet of the "eternal sunshine of the spotless mind") envisioned compassion as a series of concentric circles rippling outward:

> . . . Self-love but serves the virtuous mind
> to wake,
> As the small pebble stirs the peaceful lake;
> . . . Friend, parent, neighbor, first it will
> embrace;
> His country next; and next all human race.

It sounds great. It *is* great. But for many of us, there's a nagging doubt that this whole compassion routine could edge into self-effacement—into loving others *instead* of ourselves, giving away the store until our shelves are bare. The usual formula is first to stockpile some extra self-esteem—*then* you can afford to be generous. That isn't quite how the nineteenth-century religious philosopher Søren

Kierkegaard saw it. The command to love thy neighbor, he wrote, had but one purpose: "as with a pick, [to] wrench open the lock of self-love and wrest it away from a person." (He said it approvingly, but . . . oh, great, now compassion will burglarize us.) What about looking out for number one? Isn't it prudent to follow that flight attendant's advisory: *First place the mask over your own nose and mouth, tightening the straps to begin the flow of oxygen?* We're of no use to anyone if we're passed out in our seat from hypoxia.

It's a hard balance to strike. If I am not for myself, who will be? But if I am only for myself, what am I? There is a growing sense in our society, left, right, and center, that the balance has woozily tipped; that our obsession with seamless self-contentment ("What I love about Subway is it's all about *me!*") has occluded our ability to love each other. Our cultural default setting has become "get your own needs met." Our psychosocial mean temperature, suggested one recent article, is "people-friendly narcissism." Our therapeutic model focuses so much on strengthening the ego-self that it omits what some dissident psychologists call the self-in-relation. One group of mostly female psychologists has proposed "openness to mutual influence" as a more reliable barometer of mental health than self-esteem.

But *self-esteem* is our all-purpose buzzword, a stock phrase in therapists' offices, corporate training modules, even elementary school curricula. This is fine on the face of it: After all, what's the alternative—self-loathing? Psychologist Abraham Maslow coined the term itself in 1940 after observing a monkey colony in a Madison, Wisconsin, zoo. He was fascinated by the cockiness of the troupe's dominant alphas and the social benefits they accrued, so reminiscent of socially successful people. His concept of self-esteem, then, had its origin not as simple self-affirmation, but as the alpha's great cry of triumphal self-love: I *Am* Somebody—and You're Not. (Maslow's first stab at a terminology was "dominance-feeling.") This self-esteem was more akin to that sense of self that made Sinatra sing about how swell it was to be king of the hill.

What Maslow failed to stress was the social dimension. Even in a primate colony—especially so—no ape is an island: Modern prima-tologists point out that an alpha animal, contrary to its reputation as solitary lord of all it surveys, is thickly enmeshed in a social webbing, dependent on the reciprocities of group life. Maslow's paragon of the "self-actualized" person ("authentic, individuated, productive," with "a surprising amount of detachment from people in general") begins to sound less like a social creature than a self-pollinating flower.

Taking potshots at Maslow may be a little unfair. At a time when psychology was obsessed with what goes wrong in the psy-che, Maslow championed the things that go right. He was an exu-berant advocate of human potential when most shrinks spent their fifty-minute hours chronicling pathology. And he did posit that self-actualization would inevitably lead to responsibility for others. But his emphasis on personal growth as the be-all helped spawn a national cottage industry devoted to building a better me, some enhanced self-to-the-tenth-power with its full entitlement of psy-chospiritual fabulousness. Not such an awful idea, I suppose, but as the song goes, Is that all there is?

I dropped in on a human potential workshop recently. Plenty of talk about self-empowerment and self-realization, self-efficacy and peak performance, but compassion didn't rate a second billing on the marquee. It made me wonder what sort of selfhood we're seek-ing: the self that "gets its needs met" but is never fulfilled? Or the self that abundantly gives yet is never emptied? Instead of self-discovery, what about *other*-discovery, our real terra incognita?

I wonder, too (as a pragmatic question, not a moral one), if this pedal-to-the-metal pursuit of happiness really does make us any happier, or if we have the whole thing backward. "The American way is to first feel good about yourself, and then feel good about others," notes the Benedictine monk Thomas Keating. "But spiritual tradi-tions say it's the other way around—that you develop a sense of goodness by giving of yourself."

I've been an Audrey Hepburn fan since I was a boy with my first major movie-star crush, all the more when I discovered that the adorable, to-die-for gamine of *Breakfast at Tiffany's* was also a great humanitarian. I once came across a lost nugget of her philosophy while waiting in the dentist's office. A fashion magazine had asked her for her beauty tips, and she'd written back:

> For attractive lips, speak words of kindness.
> For lovely eyes, seek out the good in people.
> For a slim figure, share your food with the hungry.
> For poise, walk with the knowledge you never walk alone.
> If you ever need a helping hand, you'll find one
> at the end of each of your arms.

This homily, a sort of St. Francis Prayer for the Maybelline Set, is a graceful rebuttal to the fetish of self-improvement. Instead of being all about me, it's about us; instead of getting and having, it's about giving and then giving some more. St. Francis himself went beyond mere charity. The son of a rich clothier, he gave up wealth and privilege to dress in rags and hang out with lepers. This was taking kindness to an extreme few of us would find attainable, let alone remotely appealing. But compassion has a certain down-and-dirty quality and a more than casual familiarity with the soul's darker, draftier labyrinths.

At its root meaning of "to suffer with," compassion challenges our tendency to flinch away from life's too-tender parts. I know this much: when I acknowledge my own pain, I am much less squeamish about drawing nearer to yours. I seem to acquire my compassion piecemeal, hurt by hurt. After a bad sprain and time spent on crutches, I became more sympathetic to the locomotion-impaired—the lame and the wheelchair-bound, those who hobbled on canes and walkers.

Perhaps Thomas Aquinas was not so far off when he claimed, "No one becomes compassionate unless he suffers." I take this less as a mandate for medieval masochism than an indecorous call to embrace our own authentic experience. If we're not at home with the depth of our feelings, we're likely to skirt the deep feelings of others.

Do we love ourselves/others only when we/they are feeling fine? (Or as a rural proverb has it, "Do you only care about your cow when it's giving you milk?") I've become suspicious of the unblemished life. Maybe the heart must be broken, like a child's prize honeycomb, for the real sweetness to come out. Although something inside us yearns to walk on air, never touching the ground, compassion brings us down to earth. It has been likened to the lotus, whose exquisite, fragrant blossom grows out of the muck and mire.

The Buddha, the jewel in the lotus himself, didn't start out in the mud. He was raised like a hothouse flower, living the cosseted life of a pampered young prince. His royal parents, fearing a prophecy that he would grow up to become a spiritual teacher instead of a king, confined him within high castle walls, surrounded by every luxury, in a kind of Hindu 90210. The lame, the sick, and the down-and-out were banished from sight. It wasn't that his parents were afraid their son would be shocked by the sight of suffering (after all, he was to be a battle-hardened feudal monarch), but that he would *respond* to it. They were afraid, in other words, that their son might become compassionate.

One day the prince secretly ventured outside. He stumbled first upon a diseased beggar, then a dead man. The walls that had separated him from the world-as-it-is crumbled. Indeed, the castle might be thought of as a sort of metaphorical ego-structure: Don't we often try to secure happiness by fortifying ourselves against imperfection? When the Buddha proclaimed his first noble truth, *dukkha* ("dissatisfactoriness"), he was pointing to the dissatisfaction of this ego-driven existence. A traditional image from the Sanskrit is an oxcart wheel that wobbles because its axle is out of kilter: To be self-centered is to be off-center from life itself. In the end, the Buddha's enlightenment was to accept everything and everyone as they are; to sit down, as it were, for the full meal, and stop trying to eat around the broccoli.

Though his teachings acquired an aura of detachment in the Western mind (my own included), the image of some solitary quest for higher consciousness misses the point. When I first took my

vows and embarked on the Path, I assumed that after X years of diligent meditation, I'd be a wise man with a small secret smile, wafting
clear and calm through my own inner space, in some permanent altered state. Loving-kindness would be a spin-off technology from
my private moon shot, like Tang or Teflon. But after some time spent
trying to attain escape velocity, I noticed that most spiritual teachings regard compassion as the main event—the path to enlightenment, the way to slice through self-deception, the means and the
motive to relinquish small thoughts for Big Mind. "Spiritual practice
is not just about feeling peaceful and happy," a Buddhist lama once
told me, "but being willing to give up your own comfort to help
someone else. Unless there's some sacrifice for others, it's just meditation by remote control!"

I recently saw a film about a morose, beaten-down man whose job
in a Las Vegas casino was to bring gamblers calamitous bad luck.
Known in the trade as a "cooler," when he drew near, the dice became frigid, the cards grew a layer of hoarfrost, and the queen of
hearts wept icy tears. But then he fell in love, and the world turned
topsy-turvy. Everywhere he went, slot machines that had spit
lemons now pealed with ecstatic jackpots, the dice were too red-
hot to handle, and baccarat tables practically sprouted crocuses.
Even murderous goons and heartless goombahs were stirred to
noble deeds. It was a wonderful evocation of that love that flouts
the law of averages, beats the house odds, and finally breaks the
bank.

   I have a few friends who embody this brand of beneficent love
some researchers refer to as "generativity." I'd first gotten to know
Alicia and Paul (not their real names) when I was teetering at the
edge of a private cliffhanger. They'd heard I was hurting, and though
they barely knew me, they'd shown up one day with a check that
pulled me back from the brink. No strings, they'd assured me as I
stammered my thanks. I didn't have to do good with it, reciprocate
in any way tangible or intangible, or even, they joked, have dinner
with them. Just be, they said. It wasn't just the sum, several months'

food and rent, that startled me, but the clear sense I got of the givers' unencumbered hearts.

Over the years, we've become close friends. Alicia and Paul live on a hilltop bordered by redwood forest with their three kids, a cockatoo, an ancient desert tortoise, a once-feral cat, a snake, and a pet white rat, all of whom gather around their large breakfast table each morning and seem to get along famously. The family is both well-off and deeply well-intentioned. They save swatches of rainforest; they build schools and teach in them; they take political refugees into their home; they plant community gardens, digging in the dirt. The last time I saw her, Alicia had just received her massage certification so she could give dying hospice patients the tenderness of her touch.

I sat in their kitchen one recent morning, looking out on a vista that was almost absurdly breathtaking: clement, mist-shrouded valleys undulating like bumps in a green carpet rolling up to the edge of a silver sea. Paul wandered in for breakfast. Soon, so did a pet rooster, its spurs clicking regally over the ochre tiles until, abandoning all dignity, it leaped onto his lap. "It's spooky," he said. "Even our animals are nice." He wasn't bragging, just bemused. With his straw-blond hair and a ruddy, open face, Paul's surfer-dude placidity yields only occasional glimpses of the shrewd businessman who secured the family's fortunes. He clearly adores his kids, who are all stalwart, funny, and, for tweeners, preternaturally considerate. He doesn't see himself as particularly compassionate, he tells me, just lucky—lucky to have made enough money to be able to give some away; lucky to have met his wife.

He credits Alicia with giving him the compassion 411. "Philanthropy's not that hard. Learning how to be kind to people—that's more elusive. Alicia's sort of a genius in that department."

I can attest to it. She makes you feel so favored—as if you'd done something extraordinary by simply existing—that you can't help but osmose a little of whatever she has and try to pass it along. Alicia, I'd always assumed, was one of those from-the-cradle love-bugs, born with some extra endowment of solar warmth.

"You've got to be kidding," she says. If anything, she insists, she was "born sad, not sweet," an anxious, self-enclosed kid. It was her mother, a "kind of saintly" woman with an eighth-grade education, who got through her shell. "She flat-out taught me compassion. She told me that life's greatest joy was to 'pull the beauty out of people,' because that makes your life beautiful, too. She was rock-solid in her devotion to other people. She'd be there for that super-annoying person no one else wanted to be around, take care of the one who'd landed in the biggest mess. She adopted every single fuckup in my family, and a fair number of passing strangers." At age eighty-five, her mother still corresponds weekly with dozens of people in varying degrees of muddle and distress, people who, Alicia says, "count on her letters to help them hold on."

"I'm not at all like her," Alicia claims. "I'm much more critical of people. Mom kept saying the secret was just to take a genuine interest in others—just ask them questions, want to know how they are, really. I'd try that and it would feel good, so I'd do it some more. Step by step, I got to see how wonderful that sensation is of serving others." Alicia also credits her kids ("They taught me how to nurture—but that's nothing unusual, right?"), a few books, and sundry gurus. But she says it wasn't until she met Tommy that it all came together.

He had dropped by one day to visit a friend who was doing some construction on their house. Tommy had been told he had less than a year to live: AIDS. He had no money. No place to stay. "Well, it just seemed so obvious," says Alicia. "Not just to say, Gee, I'm so sorry, good luck, but *duh!* you can stay *here.*" Alicia and her family and a group of friends agreed to divide up the tasks. "I assigned myself to care for him physically, give him massages, that kind of thing. And I found I just loved it. When you see the suffering a person's enduring, there's no way you can't respond. It takes you beyond yourself. Suddenly all those judgments you'd make if you just met them at a party evaporate. You're stripped down to two people doing their best to partake of this mystery."

Tommy had been walking with a cane when they first met him. Six months later, he was a quadriplegic. "But God, was he fun! He had this sparkly, devilish, bad-boy quality. Even when he was really sick, he'd want to go down to Baja and throw some big soiree, so we'd organize this whole elaborate caravan of his friends and our friends and IVs and wheelchairs and just *do* it. You think you've loved before, but this kind of thing opens your heart a thousand times. Tommy seemed to get more and more transparent the closer he got to death, and it enfolded you. I was with him when he died, when that transparency just turned into light."

Her weekly hospice work grew out of that experience. Alicia at fifty still has that lean, blond, freckled California-girl look, her shoulders tan and muscular from paddling in the surf. It's easy to imagine her large, strong hands kneading the failing flesh and comforting the moribund. But aren't there times, I press her, when you wonder why you're putting yourself through this; when you think of other things you could be doing—times you feel repulsed?

"I would have thought so," she says. "But the worse it got, somehow the more I felt attracted. After all the surgeries, the bodies look like battlefields. You feel the loneliness of that person whose skin is falling off, who has tubes coming in and out of everywhere. And still, behind this war-torn shell, you feel the incredible strength of humanity. It may sound strange, and corny, but there's nothing more heavenly than connecting with that."

Alicia's no sentimental pushover. She says she has a "fierce" side. She describes one of her charges who was "frankly an asshole, and the fact that he was dying hardly softened that one bit. He ticked me off something terrible. I had to draw the line: I'm not just a rug to be walked on, and I'm not doing you a favor if I let you." But she's learned to do something when she feels cornered: to "clear away evaluation and just rest someplace that doesn't have all those opinionated voices in it. When you do that, then out comes this love that melts people—not melts who they are, but who they *aren't*. Finding that is just like finding yourself. It makes you feel great." She laughs. "I swear, it's a totally *selfish* thing."

While we've been talking, the phone has been ringing. And ringing. Somebody wants something. Alicia gets up to answer. "If we can't help each other, what's the point?" she says. "Everything else gets kinda old after a while."

Now, I'm not trying to sell you on Alicia and Paul as Mother Teresa and Mahatma Gandhi. They've had rough patches like any couple; they're spiritually unfancy folk. They enjoy their bounty with a contagious *joie de vivre.* You could quibble that, sure, it's easy to open your heart in the lap of luxury; but I've met insanely wealthy people who are more miserable than Midas.

Besides which, I know another family that's just like Alicia and Paul's, except they're living a gritty existence barely above the poverty line. If 90 percent of life is showing up, they go the other 20. Their door is always open, even if the weathered porch is sagging in. There's always a pot of chili on the stove. If you drop by, their easy affection embraces you (and you, and you, too). Their small living room feels crowded with conviviality. You can stay a few nights on the fraying couch if cat dander and dog hair don't bother you too much. They take care of jobs and kids and ailing grandparents and friends' troubles and community causes, and when I ask them how they do it, they say, "Do what?" Folks like these have basically eliminated any option of pretending I don't know what we can be for each other. I know for a fact I could stand to be kinder, more generous, fiercer in cleaving to the good, true, and beautiful. It could be worth a shot. I've been pondering something John of the Cross wrote: "Where you find no love, put love, and you will find love." Maybe he had some idea what he was talking about.

One evening, I gathered a random assemblage of people to chew the fat about love. Heady types mostly, some with sharp elbows, so they were a little cautious at first. "There's no remedy for love," said a poet, lamenting its "misconception and intrigue." But after they'd proved to each other they weren't soppy romantics, they admitted there was more to the story.

"Love dismantles the whole judgment thing," said one, a lawyer. "The sluice gates open, and more water flows over the dam. When that happens, love's a verb—you can love anything."

"When we're in love, we're a love *factory*," a woman said. "We're churning out so much, we have tons extra to give away."

"Whenever you love," opined a political activist, "you're undermining consumer culture. Who needs all that *stuff* when you have other people?" He gave a little smirk. "Like they say: Accept no substitutes!"

"Love is like the great pulsating orb in old sci-fi movies," someone effused toward the end of an increasingly well-oiled evening. "The one where no matter how many missiles you fire at it, it just absorbs them all and keeps getting bigger and bigger!"

After they tumbled out into the night, noticeably buoyed, I thought about that last one. *Doesn't* love encompass everything you can throw at it? Doesn't the whole human repertoire spiral out of and circle back to love? Even justice, Martin Luther King, Jr., once said, is only "love correcting that which revolts against love." It may have been the evening's wine talking, but suddenly everything seemed to have *something* to do with love. The same love-molecule, like water, everywhere, in every form: boiling into steam as passion, or freezing into glistening hate, or just flowing, upstream and downstream, into every crack and crevice, irreducible.

Don't know how to maneuver with your husband, wife, boyfriend, girlfriend, boss, employee, parent, child, friend, enemy? Love! Everything else is just a finger in the dike, holding back an ocean that, ironically, you could happily drown in. Sometimes I think, trying to get it through my own thick seawall of a skull, that compassion means only this: When in doubt, just love.

By the next morning, the effects of the evening's mild bacchanal had worn off; but I still half-believed it.

Hair-Braiding Meditation

Polly Trout

Love is beyond time and space. It has no set form. It's in the small moments and ordinary hopes of life every bit as much as in the grand gestures of saints. Here's a lovely aspiration by Polly Trout. What's your prayer as you go about your life, caring for the people you love?

May I be filled with loving-kindness. May I be well. May I be peaceful and at ease. May I be happy.

May my daughter, who wants a billion tiny little braids this morning, be filled with loving-kindness. May she be well. May she be peaceful and at ease going to school with a billion tiny little braids.

May her best friend, who got a billion tiny little braids put in her hair at Club Med Ixtapa last week, be filled with loving-kindness. Also her mother, may she be peaceful and at ease. And the woman the mother hired to do all that cornrowing, may she be well. May she be happy.

May I be filled with loving-kindness as I put in these billion tiny little braids.

May I be peaceful and transcend greed. Also, may I go to Club Med Ixtapa next season, when the beach will be even more inspiring due to my newly enlightened and greed-free state. May I be happy.

May my coworkers be filled with loving-kindness as they wonder why I am late for work as I make these billion tiny braids. May they be peaceful and at ease.

May my daughter not notice that these braids are not nearly as cute as her friend's braids that got done professionally in Ixtapa, or if she does notice, may she be peaceful and at ease about that, please for God's sake.

May my toddler, currently trying to vie for my attention as I make these tiny braids for her big sister, be filled with loving-kindness. May she be peaceful and at ease.

May my mother, who did this for me when I was five, be filled with loving-kindness. May she be peaceful and at ease. I wonder why I never thanked her for that.

May I remember this day, sitting with my daughter, braiding her hair, late for work again, peaceful and at ease, happy.

Maintenance, Seeing, The Questioner ⟫

Three short essays by Lin Jensen

If we're lucky, we experience life as intersecting arcs of disintegration and clarity. In other words, with age comes wisdom—but only when we accept our own impermanence with honesty and clarity. Otherwise, age can bring bitterness and disappointment. Zen teacher and essayist Lin Jensen is one who is aging wisely. He does not deny loss—its sadness is real—but he knows that impermanence is the greatest of all teachers. Here are three essays on lessons he has learned: to accept, to see clearly, and never to stop questioning.

Maintenance

These words are being written from a room in a house that has recently become for me a temporary residence. The walls and ceiling of the room are covered in rare and beautiful vertical-grained Douglas fir, all heartwood, rescued from a fire-burned ridge in the Santa Cruz Mountains of northern California. The windows and doors are framed of clear, kiln-dried redwood. The floor is laid with Spanish-red paving bricks underlain by an inch of mortar, small-mesh wire, thirty-pound felt, and a tight sub floor. Each brick, 3,460 of them, was lifted by hand and grouted in place by Karen and me. Every wall and ceiling board, every inch of trim, was milled and cut and nailed in place by the two of us. From the first spade-full of rocky earth torn loose to allow for its concrete footing, to its cabinets and bookshelves that now hold all the personal possessions either of us owns, this house was built by we who were to live in it and who would come in time to know it as "home."

But now, only seven years since the Plumas County building inspector signified that our work was finished and that Karen and I could move in, a sign has been posted at the entrance to our drive declaring to all who travel Plumas County Road A-23 that the house we built is for sale. I can see the sign from our kitchen window. It is about four feet square, tacked to a post and cross-arm and, though it faces away from me toward the road, I know its message by heart: Lynn Welch Realty, twenty acres, custom solar home.

When Karen and I retired, she from a hospital pharmacy and I from teaching and carpentry, we had thought to live out the remainder of our lives on these twenty acres, in this house, within walls grown as familiar to us as our own aging images in the mirror. But now, whenever I return from some outing with a load of groceries or gas for the snow blower or anything else, Lynn Welch Realty is there to remind me that I am once more a person in transition.

When buyers come to look at our home, we point out everything good about it: the yard that Karen landscaped so beautifully, the vegetable plot with raised beds, the compost bins, the garden shed, the woodshed where cords of firewood are stacked. We fairly glow with enthusiasm, so naturally we are sometimes asked why we are leaving. When confronted with this question, I offer up the obvious and plausible response that a recent injury to my spine prevents me from continuing the heavy work of maintaining the place.

What I don't tell the questioner is how much I regret not doing the things that need doing and that Karen and I have always done together. I don't tell how the demands of our mountain life measure with distressing accuracy the exact extent of my daily inadequacies, and of the loss that this evokes in me. I tell of it now because I want to show how loss itself cancels the source of its own distress.

My knowledge of the self-healing qualities of misfortune came with a shocking injury to my spine that left me lying helplessly in bed with legs so useless I was reduced to crawling to the bathroom in order to reach the toilet. Throughout those days, I could hear Karen moving about in the other rooms, hauling in armloads of firewood, shoveling snow away from the outside doors, and digging her way to the woodshed so that she might haul in wood again, and then mopping her own muddy tracks off the floor. I could hear her cooking and washing and carrying kitchen waste to the compost bin and doing these things over and over again. Beyond all this, I had no option but to watch her care for my needs as well, bringing me water and food and tablets of codeine and Vicodin, endlessly bringing me these things day after day, night after night, week after week. And still in the early morning, when she herself was hopelessly exhausted, she would try just this once more to rub the pain away.

I could do nothing to ease the burden on her. And I knew (for I had been explicitly told) that when the surgery I was awaiting had restored me to my feet, much that I had always done I would never do again: "No weights over twenty-five pounds, no repetitive movement of an extended duration; no twisting, compacting, or sudden bending of the spine." I would never again do any sustained carpentry or turn clover under in the garden or drag up a few bales of hay for mulching or split wood. I would never backpack or turn a somersault or jump to the ground from even the most modest height or run the length of half a block. I lay in bed looking up at the ceiling Karen and I had nailed in place, and I felt once again the familiar fear of losing myself, of not knowing who I was or how and where I might ever be found again. Nailing ceilings, one nails a wood tongued-and-grooved board in place while standing on planks laid across sawhorses. A partner helps secure the board while the nailer bends backward pushing the groove hard onto the tongue with one hand and driving the nail in with the other. I would never nail another ceiling. The life I had lived for all these years was impossible now and I had no option but to let it go. And in that yielding I saw more clearly than ever before what sorts of ceilings and walls I'd been building all these years.

I saw that I had tried to construct my life as I had built this house, with some fixed and lasting sense of myself nailed securely in place. I saw that no life so constructed could be held secure against the exigencies of time and circumstance, that I must inevitably exhaust myself in futile maintenance of such a structure. A lifetime of certainties fell about me in disrepair. I could no longer conceptualize who I was, and in that very loss the healing was found.

Knowing we must move on, Karen and I recently drove over the mountains to see if Chico, California, might be a place for us to live. The town has a state university, and Karen thinks she would like to go back to school for a while. Of course, there's much adventure in an excursion like this, yet at times we both felt a little forlorn. The motel room was unfamiliar, its papered walls not those of our own making. The toilet was sealed sanitary with a strip of paper, a precaution some stranger had taken on our behalf. The towels smelled of detergent we were unaccustomed to. And when we sought out the weather channel on a TV so awkwardly hung as to be viewable only while lying on the bed, the meteorologist bore a face we didn't recognize.

But we persisted in our intent and were able to join a small group of local residents on a wildflower outing to nearby Table Mountain. On the mountain we walked with the others on a windswept plateau where tiny flowers of yellow and blue hugged the rocky earth. Karen and the other women talked among themselves, and when they turned down along a little stream toward a falls, I was drawn uphill to see what species of sparrow it was that moved so low among the grasses. The birds turned out to be lark sparrows. In my trailing after them, I found myself on a prominence that lay an unobstructed horizon about me on all sides. I turned slowly, 360 degrees. In all that space there was nothing, not even a trace of the very steps that had brought me there, to suggest where one might go next. I understood that I could, at that moment, walk in any of all possible directions.

We invent ourselves that we might know who we are and what we are to be. But the consistency we seek in these inventions can't be maintained against the fabulous inconsistency of actuality. Sensing this, we clutch at cherished constants ever more urgently. The builder of the house of ego can never rest, for he is ever at work to control outcomes and limit alternatives. His structure makes its appeal to our longing for the familiar and the safe, but in the end, he delivers only diminishment. I am weary of maintenance.

SEEING

Twenty years ago, Mother was seated at the kitchen table. I was seated beside her, near enough to touch her if I were to reach out. It was the second day of my visit. Father, who always treated me as a guest upon first arrival, was settling once more into his customary routine and had gone outdoors to sweep leaves off the drive. Mother was taking advantage of his absence to talk to me about a book she had been reading and some ideas in which Father had little interest.

Her face was turned from me toward a window that opened on the backyard so that as she talked I watched her in profile. The sun from the window lit up her face and hair. She was absorbed in what she was saying, punctuating her words with crisp little bobbings of her head and emphatic hand gestures. I recall that she asked my opinion on something, the content of which I have long forgotten or never knew, because it was exactly then that I realized I was seeing my mother as if I had never seen her before. Her hair, gray now in her late sixties, the wrinkles radiating from the corners of her eyes and around her mouth; her lips, thinner than they once were, pressed together in the pauses between sentences; the sharp insistence of her gaze when she turned to inquire for my response— nothing about any of this was new to me. Yet for the moment these features seemed divested of all my forty-four years' experience of her. I needed to recite to myself that this woman was Lucy Beatrice Jensen, that she was my sixty-six-year-old mother whom I knew to be, in every detail, exactly the person that sat opposite me.

She was suddenly still, as though holding her breath in anticipation of what was to come. The eyes behind the lenses of her glasses were questions. I took up her hand, as though it were something I had just found. Mother said, "Yes, I'm growing old." I understood that she referred to the liver spots that had appeared on the backs of her hands. But that was not it; I had long been aware of such changes. How could I explain to her, or to myself for that matter, that in all her familiarity she was utterly new to me at that moment?

My mother, eighty-six now, still lives. I have known her for sixty-four of her years. Yet this tiny episode of two decades ago, little more than a single minute, persists. It has a reality that refuses to be ignored. It resists all my ideas of it. So for most of the twenty years since Mother and I sat down to talk, that brief moment with her at the kitchen table has stuck in my mind like a buried splinter that refuses to be dug out.

There is a seeing that occurs before thought, which means, of course, before recognition. And though as yet momentarily nameless, the object seen is not featureless. It is in fact more nakedly and vividly present in all its detail than it can ever be after the intervention of thought. All of us naturally see in this elemental way; to do so is unavoidable. It's just that we fail to notice its occurrence, and the reason for this failure is that our natural sense of seeing is overridden by our ideas regarding the objects of our sight. A sudden splash of yellow and orange, singular and unprecedented, is so readily and habitually converted to the categorical generalization of a rose that all we end up seeing is our idea of a rose rather than the living rose itself. Anything that looks familiar to you, even if it is the face of your own child, is not truly being seen. If you were really seeing your child, the features of her face would appear as if for the first time. Our perception of the familiar is an idea about something, a generalization intending to fit many occasions and thus never really fitting a single occasion at all. Still, there's always that fresh instant of seeing before even the simplest thought intervenes. If you notice this, it's possible to cultivate eyes that see beyond thought regardless of how busy your mind might seem to be.

Adjacent to "The Avenues" neighborhood of Chico is a cemetery with wide lawns, ancient valley oaks, and a few maples whose fallen leaves paint the ground in the shortening days of late October and November. It's a stretch of ground as intimate to me now as any I've ever known, and yet more and more often these days it appears to my eyes as to those of a stranger. At such moments, the landscape seems to reach for me before I can reach for it. The blossoming myrtle tree, the scrub jay pecking at the lawn, the sprinkler splashing water on the gravestones, the oak with its limb broken away, a squirrel motionless on an elm trunk, leaves scattering on the wind, children running on the far lawn of Chico Junior High, a vapor trail spread high above the Sacramento Valley—all this coming upon me fresh and nameless, without the familiar qualities I attribute to things. I have entered a visual universe where even the most marginal objects come to me with the same living insistence I felt at my mother's kitchen table all those years ago.

The present moment is swifter than thought. My body, in its intrinsic and native power of sight, has always understood this. It reads life directly and is teaching me now to do so as well. It has loosened my hold on things that they might move, as they must, along the sequence of the moment. It has shown me that this sycamore rooted to the banks of Chico Creek on this blustery afternoon in mid-October cannot be held in place beyond the instant of my seeing it here any more than its yellowing leaves can be held from their fall to earth. I know now that the only sycamore I can hold on to has its roots sunk nowhere but in my thoughts of it.

I have not risked seeing the world as it actually is. My eyes have snatched at things, picked and sorted them, until there was little left to see but an arbitrary arrangement of my own thoughts. Between classes at Chico State University, students by the hundreds crisscross the quad on their way to various destinations. Watching them, I have discovered that most of them look down, their eyes controlling the short patch of ground into which they forever walk. Others stare ahead with such singleness of purpose that I marvel they do not collide with each other. Only a few have eyes that risk the present moment. These few know one another on sight.

I soften the edges of intent that I not reside within the fixed and narrowed center of my will. The eye that sees forever opens on the fullness of itself where edges join the center and sight receives things as they are.

Five hundred miles south of Chico, my mother lives alone now that Father has died. I will visit her soon and I will give her a hug. In the meantime, I must settle for the mother I hold here in my mind. But there is no such mother, and when I make my visit I will see that this is so. The mother I hug will only be herself, a fact my own mirror now teaches me daily where, search as long and hard as I will, I cannot find the person I thought I was.

THE QUESTIONER

"What is it that Buddhists want to learn," he questioned, though no one had asked him to question anything. We were supposed to be listening to the dharma talk Susan was giving, her explanation of some aspect of Buddhist teaching. Besides, his question had nothing to do with Susan's talk. It was all very strange.

It was Thursday night at the weekly session of the Chico Zen Sangha, our group that comes together to meditate weekly. We had settled into a circle to hear Susan's talk, when Karen noticed this young man outside who seemed to want to come in. So she asked him, and he came in. He was tall, graceful, and poised, and he carried himself with an air of quiet purpose. He found a place in the circle and sat down on the floor cross-legged with the rest of us. He looked as if he'd been sitting meditation his whole life.

Susan got out her notes and put on her reading glasses. Her topic, she informed us, was gossip. I believe she intended to make reference to the Buddha's teachings concerning "right speech"—but I never found out because no sooner had she got started than our visitor spoke up. He interrupted Susan in mid-sentence and he announced to us that he was in possession of a "Toastmaster's International Certificate of Completion." He had the document in hand so we could all verify it. I was trying to make out the wording from across the circle when, with a sort of measured solemnity, he said, "I have been sent to ask this question with eloquence and dignity: What is it that Buddhists want to learn?"

None of us thought to ask who sent him, but I've since come to accept the fact that he was, in some sense, "sent." At any rate, being a resilient group, we set out to tackle his question. I suppose we thought that we could give him a few answers and then Susan could get back to her planned talk.

Susan tried first. She offered him something somewhat pat like, "We Buddhists want to learn the Four Noble Truths and the steps of the Noble Eightfold Path." She added something to the effect that these teachings were central to the Buddhist Way, and then she resumed her talk—but she'd barely gotten her notes back in order when the questioner interrupted her again. "What is it that Buddhists want to learn?" he repeated. Apparently he hadn't bought the noble truth and eightfold thing; he was looking for answers.

I tried: "We Buddhists are seeking the true nature of self." I thought that was pretty good, but when he responded again with, "What is it that Buddhists want to learn?" I could see for myself that I'd merely uttered words. Whatever it is that Buddhists "want to learn," it can't be passed off as "seeking the true nature of self."

We tried other things. We fed him assertions about impermanence, compassion, the dissolution of ego. We kept this up until it became increasingly clear that this question of his, invariably repeated, was the only element of honest discourse going on at the Chico Zen Sangha that night.

He'd stumped us. With an innocent insistence like that of a curious child who really wants to know, this graduate toastmaster had quickly brought us to our limits. "What is it that Buddhists want to learn?" Though we'd previously thought we did, we didn't actually know what it is that Buddhists want to learn. We were beginners after all.

I made one last effort to restore familiar circumstances. "Would you be willing to just listen to the talk that Susan has prepared for us?" I urged in as conciliatory a tone as I could muster. "Perhaps you'll get some answers from that." His response: "What is it that Buddhists want to learn?"

Karen, who'd gotten us into this in the first place, came to our rescue and got us out. "Meditation," she announced. With that, we all retreated to the comfort of something we figured we knew how to do right. Sitting there in proper cross-legged posture, I felt the chagrin of not knowing how to explain even the simplest, most basic thing about Buddhism. It was a lesson that the questioner, with eloquence and dignity, had come to teach.

I'm glad to have gotten that lesson. The questioner brought me to doubt whatever certainties I was holding that night, his unanswered question demonstrating once again the inadequacy of even the most unassailable "truth" to explain the great mystery of existence. His visit to the Chico Zen Sangha released me once more into the freedom that resides in knowing that I don't know.

The Dragon's Mind and the Power of Nonself

Sakyong Mipham Rinpoche

We normally equate power with ego, but this is a myth. It is precisely when we are defending our sense of self that we are at our weakest, ensnared by our own illusions, attachments, and constant calculations of what is for and against us. Actually, it is the mind of nonself that has the greater power. It is vast, wise, and unmoved by narrow concerns. Sakyong Mipham tells us how we can bring the dragon's mind, this powerful mind of nonself, into our lives.

When my friend Jon and I were running in the Scottish Highlands one day, we came into a valley and saw a big dog. We started strategizing how we were going to avoid being attacked. Should we run? We were already running. What about climbing a tree? There wasn't a tree in sight. As we approached the "dog," we realized it was just a large stone. We laughed at ourselves and kept running. We had created an object in our minds and then responded to it with fear. We were afraid of our projection, which had stemmed from ignorance. The minute we saw our mistake, the fear dissolved. Our relief came from seeing how things really were. Seeing things as they are is *prajna*, a Sanskrit word that means "best knowledge." This intuitive wisdom is the self-existing confidence of the dragon.

The tiger, the lion, the garuda, and the dragon represent the four kinds of confidence of the ruler. The tiger represents the contentment that comes from discernment; the lion, the joy that comes from discipline. The winged garuda symbolizes the equanimity that arises from going beyond attachment to hope and fear, and the dragon represents the wisdom that sees the elemental reality of all situations. Developing these qualities results in strong *windhorse,* which is confidence in basic goodness, the awakened nature of everything. Strong windhorse increases life-force energy and leads to success in all activities.

The dragon is a symbol of rulers and master meditators. It represents ultimate wisdom, confidence, and power. There is something inscrutable about the dragon, something that cannot be understood. It has the form of a serpent, yet it flies. There are many stories about dragons, but who has seen one? The Tibetan word for thunder is *drukdra*—the sound of dragons. Like thunder, the wisdom of the dragon wakes us up. It shatters conceptual mind and uproots our insecurity.

The dragon says, "I dance and play in the depth of your own mind. Let me out!" The dragon mind is fathomless. It cannot be read. It rests naturally in the Great Eastern Sun—the wisdom of prajna. With prajna, our mind goes beyond the limits of space. The Shambhala teachings describe the dragon mind as "space that cannot be punctured by an arrow." The dragon is deep wisdom that looks precisely at everything. It sees how we're always trying to make appearances into "things," projecting a concrete world onto a fluid process. We say, "I have a self. I exist," but there is no self in the way we perceive the self. Just as I mistook a rock for a dog, we are always mistaking our ever-changing experience for a solid self or "me." As we continue to sit quietly, meditating and contemplating, we begin to understand that our own wisdom is always trying to awaken us to this truth, which is as elusive as the breath, or as the dragon itself.

We can start by contemplating what the Buddha said: the self we imagine to be solid and continuous is really just a gathering of ingredients—heaps. It is the conjunction of blood, bones, memories, emotions, thoughts, and perceptions. When we experience this conglomeration of elements, ignorance says, "I think I'll call this 'me.'" We are creating an illusion and giving it a name. Not only is the illusion transparent and dreamlike, but the things we make it with are the same. It's like watching clouds form into the shape of a dragon. We know it's not a dragon. We know the clouds themselves are not really solid. But when we see that form, we give it a name—something recognizable.

The moment we mistake the collection of heaps for "me," attachment arises, fear arises, pride arises—and we believe in "me." This projection forces us to perceive the whole world in a certain way. We think, "I'm real, and so are they," and therefore it follows, "If I'm real and they take something away, I will get mad." We suffer from that ignorance. Suffering is the reverberation of not knowing selflessness, the virtue of the dragon.

In his first teaching after his enlightenment, the Buddha made this very point. Life is painful for the basic reason that we are self-obsessed. Sometimes we think, "If I didn't feel angry and jealous, then I would have peace." In fact, negative emotions are simply the embodiment of thinking of a self. Every time we feel irritation or attachment, we are experiencing self-absorption.

If we contemplate this, we will see that it's true. Anger, desire, jealousy—all negative emotions are rooted in attachment to "me." They are fighting a losing battle, for there is no "me." If there is a self, where is it? Contemplating selflessness reveals that looking for "me" is like trying to find the horizon. It looks like a straight line, and from afar it's a definite geographical reference point. But if we're asked to pinpoint it, we'll only go in circles. We'll never find it. We'll just find moods that come and go. Those moods are also selfless; they come and go because they are on unstable ground. There is not another self, apart from the self we try to hold together with the pride of our view, seeing ourselves as separate from—and maybe slightly better than—everything else. The bewilderment from which this pride arises is always telling us a lie. We're making a cloud into a mountain. Without this confusion, there is no belief in a self, for there is no self-infatuation.

Even when we speak of selflessness, the mind goes to "me." We think, "I'm selfless," but everything is selfless. Saying "everything is selfless" is like calling that stone "dogless." It might give the impression that a dog was there at some point, but it never was. It was our idea of a dog that was there. Similarly, we say that everything is selfless, but the self was never there. There was only our idea of a self. When we realize that we have always been selfless, what is missing? The conceptual mind that centralizes into "me" and then projects a world out there that is solid and separate. Who we think we are and what we think of the world is a concept that we are creating with our mind. We create a concept in our mind and we believe that concept. Our belief in a self is the most obvious example of this fundamental ignorance.

The wisdom of the dragon asks us to contemplate why we are trying to make things so solid. What is it we're trying to hold together? The chair is not saying it's a chair, nor are our arms and legs and chest saying, "I'm me." Our mind is weaving the elements of our body, feelings, sense perceptions, and judgments into a solid entity called "me." "Me" is a mental fabrication. There is no "me," and that's okay. Seeing this and losing the idea of "me" is the point of liberation. What is liberated? *Lungta*—windhorse—and the wish-fulfilling jewel of wisdom and compassion.

Because negative emotions are rooted in ignorance, it's sometimes hard to know when we are bound by their influence. To see them we need prajna, which grows from the mindfulness and awareness of the tiger. It is enriched by the discipline and joy of the lion. With the sharp eyes of the garuda, it recognizes when negativity has thrown us off balance. When we blame, cling, compete, or complain, prajna sees these signs of self-fabrication. It knows what we need to do when they arise: generate compassion and courage, the fortitude to overcome fear. Fear is just lack of prajna. Prajna and compassion are the ultimate *drala*—blessing energy—because they burn through negativity like a laser. The result is great bliss, a mind that has risen above the mistake of the self.

When my own teachers would ask me to look for my self, in the beginning I thought, "What a silly question. I'm right here." When I tried to figure out exactly where "here" was, it became a little tricky. I had assumed a "here." My body might be sitting in a chair right now, but where is the body I had when I was three? Where is the self I thought I was yesterday? And where is my mind? Westerners think the mind is in the head, Tibetans think it's in the heart. In looking for my mind, I discovered that it seems to be in many different places. Sometimes it is drinking a glass of water, remembering swimming in the summer, feeling the breeze. In this contemplation, I observed that the self is more elusive than I thought. Thus began my journey into discovering that my experiences are not as real and solid as I had assumed. Questioning that assumption is what my teachers wanted me to do.

My teachers then instructed me to contemplate appearances— all the things I could see, touch, smell, hear, or taste. Which of those things is not generated by mind? The conclusion I drew was that if my mind weren't here to experience these appearances and—if what they were saying is true—generate them, then I would have no way of knowing if something is not generated by the mind. My teachers wanted me to realize the power of the mind and how it generates our whole environment. We think that there is a self, and that everything else is separate from it. But there is no self, and nothing is separate from selflessness.

When I ask people to contemplate selflessness, they sometimes react as if I've asked them to put their house on the market or give away all their money. If there were a self that existed in the way we think, discovering selflessness would be like putting our house on the market. But in the Buddhist tradition, the discovery of self-lessness is called "completely joyful." It's not called "the raw end of the deal," or "I'd rather go back to bed," or "This is scary and depressing."

I remember rising from my meditation seat one day and being struck by the transparency of the world's appearances. This was not like being in some kind of dream or god realm. It felt like a balance between groundedness and fluidity. I could no longer solidify every thought, every word, every appearance, because the transitory quality of my self and everything around me—the lack of substance—was so vivid. My mind felt buoyant and joyful, because it was open, free from concept.

When we separate ourselves from the world and imagine that "me" has to conquer it, we are paupers who think that there is something to subjugate, own, or manipulate. Because we are objectifying the world, we see it as a threat and we defend ourselves against it. With the virtue of knowing selflessness, we are pulling the rug out from under the world's ability to terrorize and confuse us.

Surprised by Joy

Sharon Salzberg

A great Buddhist teacher, old and infirm, was meeting with a Western
student for what both expected would be the last time. The Westerner
leaned forward to receive the teacher's final transmission, the culmination
of years of advanced practice. The teacher whispered to him, "Be kind."
Here, Insight Meditation teacher Sharon Salzberg tells how we can develop
this greatest of all attributes, the one that brings joy to ourselves and others.

When we see how quickly life disappears—how even the longest
life span is over in a flash—we realize how important it is to create
the conditions that help us move toward true happiness. The bravest
thing we can do, which is the beginning of an awakened life of kindness, is to question our assumptions about what we are capable of,
what brings us happiness, and what life can be about.

Many factors make developing kindness challenging. We may
feel competitive and find a tad of satisfaction when someone is a little down. We might genuinely care but be afraid to get involved. We
might find ourselves dominated by a feeling of helplessness or a
sense that anything we offer would be insufficient. We might be confused about the right thing to do.

If we are willing to take a risk anyway and consciously practice
kindness, we learn that, in contrast to the messages we hear from
the world about how to be happy ("Buy more," "Compete more

strongly," "It's a dog-eat-dog world"), a more refined happiness comes from feeling joined, from a sense of belonging—both to this life and to one another. We need to hone our own sense of purpose. We need to understand what will help us realize happiness more steadfast than any temporary pleasure, acquisition, or fleeting triumph.

In addressing happiness, the causes of happiness, and how to practice those causes, the Buddha taught simplicity and the path to liberation.

First we look at our vision of life and of ourselves in relation to one another. This is something that is not fixed or determined but can grow and expand as we perceive things more acutely, or see them from a different angle. I saw this several years ago, when I had been quite sick all winter. I had bronchitis, and every time I began to get better I'd have a relapse. Finally, I began to recover.

I was living in New York City at the time, and walking down the street one day, I heard a woman's voice saying, "I was very sick all winter." Naturally intrigued, I turned around and saw a woman handing a street person some money. She went on talking to him: "I had pneumonia, and every time I started to get better I'd have a relapse. Now I am finally really getting better, and I just wanted to share the joy."

I was taken aback. Realizing that I had walked right by that man without a thought of sharing the joy of my own renewed health, I wondered whether I should go up to him, hand him more money, and say, "You won't believe this, but I was really sick all winter too, and I'd like to share some joy as well."

I ended up not doing that, but I felt I'd learned something from that woman. The decision whether or not to give a street person money is complex, and there is no single answer to suit every situation. What made this such a forceful lesson for me was that I had walked right by that man without any thought that his life had anything to do with mine. Without that view, there was no impetus to relate to him—through noticing his sorrow, or thinking of sharing my own joy.

Life can and does turn on a dime. One little rotation of the wheel of fortune, and we're no longer feeling on top of life and impervious to change. Kindness doesn't mean saying "I, who have everything together and am invulnerable, am standing way over here, looking at you way over there, and since our lives don't touch except in this tiny, peripheral way at this moment, I am going to just toss you some money."

We all share the urge toward happiness, and no one leaves this earth without having suffered. Thus we can look at others and see something not only about them, but about ourselves as well.

Often this insight extends only so far. Then something may happen—a confrontation, a new relationship, a dawning view of the intricacy of a person's life—and we find our perspective broadening. A friend of mine was a wonderfully empathic therapist. One day a man came to see her, beseeching her to be his therapist. She found his political views alienating, his feelings about women difficult, and his behavior quite annoying. In short, she didn't like him and urged him to find another therapist. However, because he very much wanted to work with her, she finally acquiesced and took him on as a client.

Now, because he was her client, she tried to look with compassion instead of disdain or repugnance at his unskillful behavior and the ways he shut himself off. She began to see all the ways in which his life was difficult. Soon, even though she continued to see his unpleasant behavior, she found herself feeling that she was his ally. Her goal became his release from suffering, which would also affect those around him. As she put it, he had become "hers." Even though I don't believe she ever came to like him or approve of many of his views, she came to care about him.

Hearing this story, I began to think of the role of the bodhisattva. In the Buddhist tradition, bodhisattvas aspire to enlightenment, dedicating their transformed minds and actions to the liberation of all beings. When we aspire to be a bodhisattva, everyone becomes "ours," in a way. Our goal becomes the release from suffering of all beings, and so we view ourselves as working on behalf of everyone. Even when we take strong steps to keep someone from acting harmfully, we do this, to the best of our ability, without rancor or contempt. Developing this perspective is a great challenge, and it is also a great opportunity to bring about the unique happiness that compassion can offer.

What Is Death, Mommy?

Anne Cushman

Because of death, human hearts are always broken. Because of death, we are sad and tender and full of love. Because of death, we live. For every parent, love and heartbreak meet when their child asks what happens after people die. Anne Cushman wonders what a Buddhist mother answers.

My four-year-old son's preschool teacher, Toni, was dying of lung cancer.

I'd known that she was fighting it a year earlier, when I first enrolled Skye in the Peaceable Kingdom, the wonderful little Montessori school that Toni ran on the bottom floor of her hillside home.

But month after month, she showed up in her classroom every weekday morning—as she had for over thirty years—sitting at the end of a low table on a child-size chair, her spine ruler-straight and her gray hair cropped short, greeting each child with a warm smile and a firm instruction to "put on a smock and choose some work to do." Just after Christmas, though, after a particularly rough bout of chemotherapy, she went upstairs and went to bed. She didn't come back down.

"Toni is resting," her assistant, Sarah, explained to the children.

But after she had been gone a few weeks, Skye came to me one evening in the kitchen as I was stir-frying tofu and broccoli. "Toni is never going to get better. She's never going to come back to school."

"Did Sarah tell you that?" I asked.

"No," he told me. "I just figured it out for myself."

"We don't know for sure that that's true," I told him, trying to choose my words carefully. "But she is very sick. Does that make you sad?"

He nodded. "It does."

Skye had come to the Peaceable Kingdom as a three-year-old refugee from a larger, more chaotic preschool, where he had spent his days sitting alone on a chair in the corner, singing to himself and watching the other children squeal and play. He was a precocious but eccentric child who could converse with adults about relativity but couldn't figure out how to play blocks with another little boy. Toni took him under her wing—as she did all the children—teaching him math and reading while training him step by step in the fundamental rules of social engagement: "Skye, go ask Baxter, 'Can you show me where to hang my coat?' Now say, 'Thank you, Baxter!'"

A native Frenchwoman and strict disciple of the Montessori method, Toni had faith in the power of social conventions, and her rules quickly penetrated our own home, too. Within a couple of weeks, Skye was watching me disapprovingly as I sneaked a piece of pasta with my fingers before placing our dinner plates on the table. "At the Peaceable Kingdom Montessori School," he reproved, "we aren't allowed to start eating until everyone is sitting down and a grown-up says, 'Bon appetit.'"

Skye's first questions about death had started long before Toni got sick, as he encountered dead bugs, dead flowers, the half-eaten mouse our cat deposited on our doorstep, a crow we found in the garden with maggots crawling in its eye sockets.

One day a hummingbird flew into our sunroom window and broke its neck. "Does everything die?" he asked as we buried it under a lavender bush. "Will I die, too? Will you?"

I hadn't prepared any good answers in advance. As a California

Buddhist mom, I didn't have a culturally agreed-upon story to tell him, like the one I had learned as a child in Catholic school: that when you died your soul went to heaven to live with Jesus. When it comes to discussions of the afterlife, Buddhism—at least the secular, intellectual brand I'd been studying here in the West—didn't really have any answers I thought would be reassuring to a three-year-old. ("Well, sweetie, it all has to do with the chain of interdependent co-origination . . .") Unlike some brands of Buddhism, the paths I'd studied didn't emphasize reincarnation, at least not in any literal sense, and I had trouble telling him a story I didn't believe myself. But I wanted to tell him something that would make him feel safe.

"Nothing really dies," I told him. "It just turns into something else. Everything is always changing form. Do you remember the pumpkin that rotted into the earth in your garden? Tomatoes sprouted where it used to be. This bird will go back to the earth and turn into lavender flowers and butterflies."

"When you die, will you turn into a flower?" he asked, looking a little worried. "Maybe," I said, patting the earth down over the hummingbird. He thought for a while, then asked, "But will the flower know that it used to be Mommy?"

He'd gone right to the heart of the central koan, the question of the persistence of consciousness. This was what had always bothered me, too, about New-Agey stories that tried to gloss over the finality of death. After all, if you don't remember that you used to be a shepherd in medieval England or a princess in ancient Egypt, what difference does it make? All I could say was what would come to be my mantra when it came to questions of the afterlife: "I don't know."

When Toni had been absent for over a month, Skye paused one evening as he was bouncing naked on my bed after his bath. "I'm going to assume that Toni's dead," he told me.

"Oh, Skye-berry, she's not dead." I wrapped a towel around him and pulled him into my lap. "She's just very sick."

"But she's going to die."

I pressed my face against his damp hair. "She probably is."

"Will the worms eat her body?" he asked.

"Yes, they probably will." I wondered if I was a Bad Mommy. Maybe I should make up a nicer story than this: "No, no, sweetie, worms don't eat people, they just eat crows." But Skye's dad and I had always prided ourselves on telling him the truth, as best we knew it.

"But she won't feel it," he said thoughtfully. "Because she will be dead. How long will it take her to go back to the earth and turn into something else?"

"Oh . . . about a month? Maybe a few months?" I felt myself getting into deeper and deeper waters. What kind of images of his beloved teacher was he creating in his head?

"Oh, that's way too long." He shook his head. "I think maybe . . . a day. And then she'll turn into a cat."

All on his own, it seemed, Skye was generating from scratch the theory of reincarnation, the story that—whether or not you literally believe it—captures an eternal truth: that nothing is separate from anything else, that all life is inextricably interwoven from generation to generation. He smiled at me. "So if I see a cat coming up to me and saying 'meow, meow,' I'll know it's Toni."

A few weeks later, Skye and I drove to Lake Tahoe so he could play in the snow for the first time. It was just the two of us, a special mommy-son solo adventure before I left for my first meditation retreat since he was born. After a day of sledding, snuggled under a blanket by the fire, he asked me, "When children die, do their mommies die with them?"

The question took my breath away for a moment. Skye doesn't really understand, yet, that he had an older sister—my first child, Sierra, who died at birth. "Sometimes they do, but not always," I said. I stared at the flames, remembering Sierra's sweet round face, the fire of her cremation. A month after she died, I dreamed I went to visit her in a damp basement, where she was crying, "Mamma! Mamma!"

Skye shook his head. "No, that's not right!" he said. "You're wrong about that! A mommy wouldn't let her kid be dead all by himself!"

"You could be right," I said. Certainly, some part of me had died with Sierra. Sometimes I am able to see her in the lavender bushes and the butterflies and Skye's plump lips and long fingers, so much like hers. Most days, that's not nearly enough.

"So if I die, you will die with me." Skye leaned his head against my shoulder. "So it will be OK. We won't be lonely. And we can talk to each other in dead language."

A few weeks later, we were sitting on the couch together, reading his current favorite bedtime story—"Will You Be My Friend?"—a sweet story about a bunny and a bird who live in an old apple tree. The first time we'd read it, he had burst into tears in the middle, when the rain blew in and ruined Bird's nest: "What will she do?" he wailed, his face crumpling. But now that he knew it had a happy ending, he wanted to hear it over and over.

When we finished, he said, "I wish I could live in an apple tree. Maybe I could die and turn into a bird!"

"Maybe you could just pretend to be a bird," I said, trying to steer the conversation away from death. But he wouldn't be deflected.

"Sometimes," he said, looking worried, "they take your body and burn you up. They don't even let you turn into something else."

"Who told you that?" I asked.

"Mary." Mary is his beautiful and beloved babysitter, a Buddhist vegan belly dancer with a silver ring in her nose and deer tracks tattooed on her calf, who has taught him to bake bread, grow tomatoes, sing folk songs, and identify wildflowers and edible plants. Mary is passionately devoted to the Whole Truth: She also told him, apparently, that eventually the sun would explode and burn up the whole earth. ("But we don't have to worry," he reassured me. "It won't happen for a long time, until all the people on earth have died out.")

"Well," I said now, "even if they burn your body, you still keep changing into something else. The ashes will change to something else. Remember the fireplace ashes we put in your garden? They'll be lettuce this summer."

He nodded. "So even if they burn me up, I'll still turn into an animal, or maybe another boy, or something."

He sat for a while, obviously puzzling something out. "So . . ." he said. "Before I was a boy . . . before I was even a seed inside you . . . was I something else? Like an animal? Or another boy? Or was I just a boy right from the beginning?"

Possible answers flashed through my mind: Before you were born, you were your father and mother, getting stoned to Brian Eno in a college dorm room twenty years ago, and laughing till it hurt. You were your granny and granddad, dancing at an officer's hop in Mississippi in the middle of World War II. You were a baby girl named Sierra, who your mommy and daddy loved so much they had to make a new one right away. But before I could find any words:

"I think, probably, I was just a boy right from the beginning. That's what I think," he said. "That was a really good story. Is it time for bed yet, or do I have time to listen to 'Steal My Kisses' on iTunes?"

In early March, in the middle of the spring rains, Toni died.

When I told Skye, he looked worried, but didn't cry. "How do you know?" he asked.

"Her daughter called and told me."

"But how do you really, really know for sure?"

I suggested to Skye that we could light a candle and some incense, and send love to Toni. He looked at me like I was losing my marbles. "Mommy," he explained patiently, "Toni's dead."

"But we can still send love to her spirit," I said. "That's the part of her that lives in our hearts, and will never die."

He nodded. "That's the part of her that will turn into something else," he said.

At school, each of the children had a different theory about where Toni had gone. Max said she had turned into a giraffe. Lulu said she was a star. Colin insisted that she had gone back to France.

Toni's husband is making a garden in their front yard, where he will scatter her ashes under a Japanese maple. The children are planting sunflowers and daffodils there.

It's spring now, and the wild irises are blooming, just as they were six years ago when Sierra died. The baby quail are marching through our yard again, and the cat is stalking them. I can't give Skye any real answers about where Toni is now. But I hope he will always be able to see her in the red maple leaves and the golden faces of the sunflowers; and I hope, as he grows up in a world where nothing he loves can be held on to forever, that that way of seeing will be of some comfort to him.

Everything Is Holy

Katy Butler

Enlightenment is sometimes called "crossing over to the other shore."
But that doesn't mean enlightenment is about escaping from the world.
The other shore is nowhere else but right here; what changes is how we
understand its nature. Here's how Katy Butler came to see her Buddhist
practice not as separation but as full immersion in the sacredness of
nature and her daily life.

Every Wednesday morning, when I can afford the time, I park at the foot of the valley I live in and climb Mount Tamalpais, my holy mountain. It is more sacred to me than any temple, and as powerful a place of practice. My path is as ritualized as the stations of the cross. I take a wooden footbridge over a stream and climb through second-growth redwoods and past blackberry bushes, now sere and brown in the winter cold. My worries come with me: I chew on a conflict with my eighty-year-old mother, a disastrous visit home.

I climb steep railroad-tie steps to Cowboy Rock. My glutes and lungs burn, driving me into my body. I pant. I sweat. I take off my fisherman's knit sweater, machine-loomed in England and bought at a local mall. Then up past the county water-tank and the dozen expensive houses built where the Flying Y Ranch used to be.

At ten o'clock, I breach a ridge and enter a vast bowl of unpopulated hills. Car sounds die away. Finches twitter in the chaparral. I follow the trail beneath a bay laurel, upswept by the winds into a clinging topiary. A madrone shows its red bones. "Mountains," the Zen master Eihei Dogen told an assembly of Japanese monks in 1240, "are our Buddha ancestors"—our primordial teachers. Inside my brain, an invisible hand turns the volume knob down.

Now I am moving deep into the sock of the valley—the only visible human. Except for a ribbon of yellow-lined asphalt below me, there is no sign of human making. Beyond the last hills lies the Pacific.

An hour later I round a ridge and the peak of the mountain reveals herself, rising. I remember Mirabai, the sixteenth-century devotional poet who abandoned her aristocratic family and wandered India, singing, "I worship the mountain energy night and day." The trail switchbacks take me down deeper. An hour after noon, I stop at a flat, thick wooden bench in a grove of old-growth redwoods that the loggers left behind. Here I sit zazen, robed in silence and filtered brown light. The natural world restores my soul. It soothes me like a mother. I rest my head on it and lay my burdens down before it the way some Christians rest their heads on the cross.

California is not my native home. I was raised in Oxford when England was recovering from the Second World War. The country had been a coal-burning industrial power for more than a century, but compared to the way Americans live today, we lived almost as frugally as Thoreau at Walden Pond.

Eggs and butter and meat were rationed. Shoes were polished and repaired. A big black dray horse named Flower clopped down our street twice a week, pulling a cart from which my mother chose vegetables to cook with dinner. Our cramped brick row-house had no central heating, and white furry mold grew up the walls of the cellar.

People took buses or walked everywhere. Even after our family bought a car, my father was one of thousands who mounted bicycles and flooded the city at rush hour like swarming bees. My mother, who had no outside job, knitted sweaters and darned socks in the evenings before the fire. She had a washing machine but no dryer. Before she hung the laundry up to dry, she cranked it through the rollers of a mangle to squeeze the water out. Nobody called her "ecological" or understood that her daily work was an expression of respect for the natural world. But she was as frugal and attentive as the cook in a Zen monastery. One of her favorite phrases was "elbow grease."

One day when I was very young, she stopped the car on a road through a great beech woods. It was autumn. All the leaves were golden yellow. The branches of the beeches met high above our heads, making an arched and open cathedral. The very air was yellow with the glory of the trees.

My mother turned off the ignition and put the keys in her pocket.

"We are going to build a house for the fairies," she said, and opened the door.

We walked into the glowing woods. At a hollow place at the foot of a tree, my mother knelt down. She brushed away leaves and stuck forked twigs into the ground. She balanced sticks across the clefts, making roof-beams, a ridgepole, and then rafters.

I propped beech leaves against the sides and set them along the roof—they were broad-bladed, like flattened spears, and their points made a jagged line along the peak. We put moss in the front garden, and round white stones to lead the fairies to the door.

My mother was an agnostic, a rebel, and a lover of modern architecture. She had nothing good to say about reverence. But that day she led me to something she could not give me and built something close to an altar.

My parents were nominally Anglicans, and on Sundays, when I grew older, they sent my brothers and me to the church of St. Michael and All Angels. There, in the basement Sunday school, I glued images of martyred saints onto cardboard. I was told that God was everywhere and saw everything, and I imagined him as a series of transparent shower curtains embedded with multitudinous fish eyes, moving in every wind.

At night, I'd kneel by my bed and beg for a sign of His reality. But God was silent—at least in the forms that I expected Him to speak—until Saturday, when I would ride my bike to green fields bordering a stream and lie facedown in the mossy grass, letting the green energy rise up into me.

There, I had an inkling of a wholeness beyond the logic of my family. I didn't have to work for it. All I had to do was put myself in a position to receive. Green things continued to feed what I call my soul long after I abandoned hope of ever seeing the luminous fish eyes of God waving in the transparent wind. I worshiped holy water and holy dirt long before I called it prayer.

When I was eight, my family moved to America and my parents built a Bauhaus-inspired four-bedroom house overlooking a lake in the suburbs of Boston. America amazed us: the supermarkets, with row on row of perfect, pesticide-kissed fruit; the oil furnaces in the basements of big houses, blasting hot air into every room; the ice cream parlors with their banana splits and three-scoop ice cream sundaes; the giant milk-fed children; the enormous superhighways and big cars—all summing up what my mother called America's "higher standard of living."

In due course my father got a better job and a bigger house and our family acquired many little machines: a television, station wagon, lawnmower, second car, blender, coffee grinder, microwave, rice cooker, toaster oven, hair dryer, air conditioner. Friends of my parents moved into a new development where clotheslines were forbidden.

We didn't think we were trying to satisfy endless craving. We didn't see a connection between what we bought and the destruction of wild places we loved. We just wanted to be warm, safe, fed, and comfortable. We did not know that something in the human brain never hears or whispers "enough." We were part of a liberal, affluent society that believed that "the greatest good for the greatest number" was mathematically translatable into "the greatest number of goods for the greatest number."

We knew nothing of Buddhism. We'd never heard of a then-obscure British economist named Ernest Friedrich Schumacher, who, in a 1966 essay called "Buddhist Economics," suggested another path, especially for developing nations: the greatest possible human enjoyment from the smallest quantity of goods.

The Buddhist ethos of right livelihood, E. F. Schumacher argued, could be extended to an ethos of right consumption. He argued against elaborately sewn, soon-to-be-outmoded suits and in favor of the loosely draped medieval robes of the monk—always in fashion! No ascetic, he argued for a middle way in material matters—in favor of enjoyment and against craving. Happiness, his work suggested, was not typified by the ice cream sundae wolfed down alone in front of the television, but by a cookie and a cup of green tea, brewed in awareness and sipped at leisure with friends, while watching the rising moon.

When I was twenty-eight and working as a newspaper reporter in San Francisco, my roommate and I went on a camping trip in the Ventana wilderness inland from Big Sur. On a whim, we drove down a long dirt road to a hot springs resort deep in a knifelike canyon in the Santa Lucia Mountains. The place turned out to be Tassajara Zen Mountain Center, and by chance I ran into an old San Francisco friend who had become a resident there. He arranged a cabin where we could spend the night, and the next morning before dawn he led me to the zendo.

Two and a half hours later, I came out into an early morning light in a state of clarity I'd never before known. Something I had not known was still alive inside me had been listened to, and I had faith that it would someday find its voice.

I spent the whole of the next summer there.

As we walked up and down the canyon to clean cabins, chop vegetables, light kerosene lamps, and sit in the airy wooden zendo, we were soaked in the natural world. Crickets, streams, silence, and the rising force of the surrounding mountains permeated everything we did. I still wonder if Buddhism would have grabbed me the way it did if I'd first encountered it in a city.

One morning in the zendo I saw a lizard crawling along the shoulder of a man's black robe. Another evening in the zendo, we prostrated ourselves over and over in the Full Moon Ceremony, and I climbed a hillside afterward in the astonishingly bright light of the full moon.

In the library, I came across Dogen, who brought an invigorated form of Ch'an (Zen) from China to Japan in the thirteenth century. His work was dappled with natural images: the moon flooding the water with light; a water bird paddling and leaving no trace; a vegetable leaf transformed into the golden body of a Buddha; mountains flowing, mountains walking, mountains traveling on water. "The color of the mountains is Buddha's body," he wrote. "The sound of flowing water is his great speech."

The Christian theology I'd been raised in had posited a hierarchical "great chain of being" with God on top, humans in the middle, and all other creatures and plants arrayed systematically below. Dogen suggested a radically democratic "flow of being" in which we humans could be instructed by the ten thousand interpenetrating and flowering things of the natural world. In Dogen's view, each thing flowed without effort from form to form: from cloud to rain to stream to cloud and back again; from corpse to rot to compost to earth to flower. These were not metaphors for transience, reincarnation, no-self and interdependence, but manifestations of them.

"Walls and fences cannot instruct the grasses and trees to actualize spring," Dogen wrote. "Yet they reveal the spiritual without intention, just by being what they are. So too with mountains, rivers, sun, moon, and stars."

When the summer was over, I drove back to the city and started meditating each morning in a basement zendo near the freeway. I spent hours each day meeting deadlines on a computer under fluorescent lights downtown. Something wordless that had risen up in me in nature—a yearning for beauty and an ecstatic gratitude for life—had helped pull me back into religious life and into a new religion. Now I lost touch with it again. I saw no connection between the awe I'd felt in the mountains surrounding Tassajara and the chanting and bowing I did in an urban Buddha hall each morning.

Awe seemed out of place in my city practice and city life. A fellow student told me he saw Buddhism as a philosophy and a practice, not a religion. He couldn't understand why we bowed at all. Like many of the people I knew who practiced within the Vipassana tradition, he wanted simply to count the breaths, sweep the body, examine the workings of the mind, and practice walking meditation. His strain of American Buddhism, growing within a secular, consumerist urban culture, seemed rationalized, almost denatured, spun clean in a centrifuge. I kept hiking and meditating, but saw only my meditation as a form of practice.

Like Christianity, Buddhism is one of the great abstract second-generation world religions. Its overarching principles are universal and portable, not bound to culture or place. But in place after place, both Christianity and Buddhism have been enriched by animism's fertile, complicating stains. In Europe, Christian holy days were pegged to pagan festivals that brought a ragged joy into a religion flavored with self-denial; churches were built at the sites of wells and hills sacred to indigenous religions. Likewise, nature worship permeated Asian cultures before the Buddha was born.

Natural images abound in the early Buddhist sutras: Shakyamuni was born under a tree; he awakened on a cushion of buffalo grass in the light of the morning star; he touched the earth in response to the temptations of Mara; and he held up an Udambara flower to enlighten his disciple Ananda. He delighted over the beauty of the rice fields. He told his monks to meditate at the foot of trees.

A decade ago, I went on a tour of Japanese temples as a travel writer for *Vogue*. Signs of Shinto nature worship were everywhere. In fields, folded white papers hung on shocks of rice to draw the attention of nature spirits. In the mountains, I walked under torii gates to a clearing in a cedar grove and found a small altar hung with red lanterns and guarded by two stone foxes. The trunks of cedars rose, as smooth as masts, far above my head, and then opened into a canopy of feathery branches. I was standing at the bottom of a hundred-foot-high column of filtered light. The shrine did not create the sacredness of the place, but simply drew attention to it.

This was my wordless introduction to folk Shinto, Japan's indigenous, pre-Buddhist religion. It has no founder, no dogma, and no scriptures—just rituals tied to the natural world. It honors a world spontaneously brought into being by the hard-to-translate *kami*—spirits of nature embodied and embedded in everything beautiful and therefore sacred: a rock, a lightning bolt, a waterfall, a grove.

"Do not be attracted by the sounds of spring or take pleasure in seeing a spring garden," Dogen told his disciples in thirteenth-century Japan. "When you see autumn colors, do not be partial to them. You should allow the four seasons to advance in one viewing and see an ounce and a pound with an equal eye." But outside his monastery gates, rice farmers were welcoming the spring with Shinto festivals and giving thanks for the harvest in autumn, knowing full well that the seasons would turn and come again.

I picked up a broom, entered the little enclosure, and swept the shrine free of fallen leaves.

A few days later, in the mountains near Yoshino, I watched two young monks chant the *Heart Sutra* in a small temple built over a stream. They were followers of an ascetic and syncretic Shinto-Buddhist mountain tradition called *Shugendo,* which venerates snakes and waterfalls as well as buddhas and bodhisattvas. Blowing on conch shells, they exited the temple and walked up a series of stone steps, bowing at dozens of small altars. They bowed equally to peaceful stone bodhisattvas lined against a rock face running with water, and to a huge dragon-headed metal snake twined around a Shinto spear. I followed them, bowing, the two halves of my religious life finally coming together.

It is usually three or four in the afternoon when I retrace my way off the mountain, leaving the redwood grove and moving through bays and grasslands, passing a red-tailed hawk swooping across the bowl of the hills. Car sounds return. I descend past the rich houses of Flying Y Ranch and Cowboy Rock, into the valley of my daily life. I put my sweater back on, and start thinking about dinner. I start the car and drive home, to our dishwasher, coffee grinder, microwave, computers, and panoply of electric lights. The joy of my day on the mountain has fueled my efforts to live a saner life. It somehow helps me meditate for the rest of the week.

At home, I pick up the phone, call my mother, and reconcile. Then I take Dogen down from my bedroom bookshelf and read "Instructions to the Tenzo," a practical guide for the head cook at a Zen monastery. Its severe tone seems at first to have little in common with the mysticism of his *Mountains and Waters Sutra.* Lose not a grain of rice, he says. Take care of the monastery's rice and vegetables "as though they were your own eyeballs." And when you boil rice, "know that the water is your own life."

I try to obey. At dinner, I put the newspaper aside, light candles, and eat with full attention. "Innumerable labors brought us this food," goes the meal verse we chanted at Tassajara. "We should know how it comes to us." I try to remember where everything I use comes from and where it is going. I feel a mixture of guilt and gratitude. I try to regard everything I handle—my rice, my sweater, my vacuum cleaner—as if they were my own eyeballs.

I blow out the candles. I clean the table and stove using super-cleaning microfiber cloths that require only hot water rather than chemicals. I apply elbow grease.

These forms of attention are more mundane and difficult for me to practice than the ecstasy I often feel on the mountain. Yet they too express a reverence for the natural world and an understanding of interdependence, just as my mother did when she squeezed water out of her laundry in England, and as Mirabai did when she worshiped the mountain energy night and day. Ultimately, Dogen says, housewifery and ecstasy are not that different. "Taking up a green vegetable, turn it into a sixteen-foot golden body," he challenges me.

My altar holds not only a Buddha, but a seashell, a metal cricket, a snake, and an image of Mary. Likewise, my religious practice now is a hodgepodge of nature worship and Buddhist meditation and twelve-step programs, and I cannot make it all sound logical or consistent. When I'm tired or lonely and want to be numb, you can often find me driving alone up Highway 101, feeding the hunger that isn't hunger, stopping at Whole Foods and Costco and Trader Joe's, loading up on Brazilian papayas and toilet paper from the forests of the Northwest and my favorite yogurt from Greece. Sometimes I think I'm in the realm of the gods when in reality I'm acting like a hungry ghost. I forget that there is something in the brain that never hears "enough."

Yet I don't want to become so ascetic, taking no pleasure in a spring garden, but rather to open my heart and my senses to the vivid love I have for the natural world. The paradox is that when I open myself fully to pleasure, I use and waste less.

The next morning at breakfast, I light the candles, bow over my food, and chant. I eat a bowl of oatmeal and half a papaya with a squeeze of lime. I dig the spoon into a bowl of smooth Greek yogurt. I let it roll off my tongue. It is not only asceticism that will save us, but delight. All the universe is one bright pearl, wrote Dogen. Everything is holy.

The Mystic and the Cynic))

Peter J. Conradi

Inside every spiritual practitioner, says Peter Conradi, wrestle the mystic and the cynic. "After extended meditation," he says, "the joyous mystic is ascendant; in periods of idleness the depressed, anxious cynic wins." Conradi, biographer of the British novelist Iris Murdoch, tells us about a long meditation program he attended (like "being invited outside your life to understand the principles that secretly govern it," he says) and the place of joy and sacredness it led to.

All "stories" are problematic. And there is something odd, perhaps fake, about making the meditative path into a "story." Iris Murdoch's first novel has a hero who knows, too, that all stories are lies. A later novel again asserts that "the spiritual life . . . has no story" (*The Unicorn*). Yet we value novels because of their stories: only through stories can we get at the truth.

The spiritual life has no story because it has no hero; and meditation, while someone must perform it, has in some sense no subject. *Thoughts without a Thinker* is the title of one book on the topic. Meditators will thus say that they have been "sitting" or "practicing" rather than "meditating."

Shedding one's biography, or skin, is one point of meditation, which, if this can be begun at all, can only happen through a journey down into all the contradictory "stuff" from which one appears to be made, where Yeats taught us that all ladders start: "In the foul rag-and-bone shop of the heart."

One of the greatest living Tibetan meditation masters—Khenpo Tsultrim Gyatso—is often compared to the "Lord of Yogis Milarepa," whom he resembles in both substance and style, and whose songs he has taught from. He has no fixed abode, a few possessions, has practiced for years in solitude, sometimes sealed in darkness.

He was on meditation retreat, perhaps for life, in a cave in Eastern Tibet when alerted to Chinese violence in 1959, and willingly broke his retreat to flee to India with a group of nuns whom he took under his wing. He was once asked by his students to tell them a story about the many three-year retreats he is believed by then to have completed. He recounted, in two sentences, the happiness he once felt, watching the sun come up.

After a honeymoon period when the new meditator is in love with practice, it usually becomes clear that "going Buddhist" is neither a quick fix nor a one-shot deal. Those who believe that it takes many lifetimes to perfect oneself can find necessary patience in the idea of reincarnation. (Though one writer friend says it seems an unpleasant trick: "Just when you think you've got through with the business of living and dying, they recycle you as an earthworm.")

In the meantime, a willingness both to see through your stories and to meet repeated disappointments is sometimes said to be the best way to proceed. Some get discouraged by the sheer demandingness of this—the long hours of meditation, or the devotional aspects—and may step back for a while.

What you believe and live by, judges you. The heroic style of the age is blackwashing, not whitewashing. One symptom is Christopher Hitchens's *The Missionary Position,* his demythologizing of Mother Teresa's life's work—jacket-puffed as "hilariously mean." Hitchens's friend Martin Amis has written that Indian mysticism means the ability not to see Indian poverty. Our taste for bad news is inexhaustible, our best books—Lorna Sage's wonderful *Bad Blood,* Sebald's magnificent *Rings of Saturn*—always gloomy. As with Dostoevsky's *Notes from Underground,* nothing is so quick at awakening our disgust and active spite as any hint of idealism or transcendence.

The meditator can split into two contradictory people. One, an ordinary unregenerate impatient jaded materialist, sees humankind as a fortuitous and pointless blend of minerals and star-gases in a dead universe, and life as self-interested, without meaning. He is a cynic, which is to say a disappointed romantic. For him the spiritual path is pretentious, a kind of vanity. His favorite opening line is Beckett's *Murphy*: "The sun shone, having no alternative, on the nothing new" with its echo of Ecclesiastes ("Nothing new under the sun"), though he scorns all that is lyrical or elegiac.

His favorite adverb is Martin Amis's "unsurprisingly." He fears his own disappearance, both in death, and in meditation. He resembles the hero in Sartre's novel *Nausea,* for whom the world exists in superabundant threat to his own sense of being. This stubborn hero is all too familiar, to the point sometimes of seeming almost to be a part of me.

Yet this is not the whole story. An alternative persona has a child's capacity to lose itself in a condition of extreme wakefulness, attentive to what it sees and hears or does, "engrossed in a world of play." The perceptual field expands and shows a new world: the mystic finds the meaning of life within love. There is no final victor in the war between these two embattled personae, and meditation is one site where they repeatedly encounter one another.

After extended meditation the joyous mystic is ascendant; in periods of idleness the depressed, anxious cynic wins. They speak different tongues. The world appears very differently to each, with its own internally coherent logic. They seem zoologically distinct species, each addicted to his own cherished truths.

The mystic, however, does not see *more* than the cynic: he sees less. What is subtracted is what is self-involved. With that crucial subtraction, the world and all that it contains becomes vivid and marvelous and moving. The cynic suffers less impersonally. He is anxious, and depressive. It is remarked of some who are dying that they record their wonderment at never before having felt so intensely alive. The meditator would like to feel aliveness without being obliged to wait for this final moment. The terror of a world without sacredness is the greatest terror. The meditator remembers that life itself is sacred; the cynic forgets this.

Why do many persist with meditation, given the many pitfalls? Perhaps they become less anxious, or develop a more spacious quietness, energy, and contentment, or a better heart, and feel that such qualities answer a private yearning: a simple romantic belief—in the best sense—that developing compassion matters. Buddhism emphasizes the essential workability of all situations, and for the meditator obstacles might turn into challenges. Seeing fellow practitioners discover resourcefulness is inspiring.

Retreat practice is one place where such processes seem for a while accelerated and visible, and most Buddhist paths involve some form of retreat, solitary or communal, or some alteration of both.

En route to my first month-long group retreat in August 1985, I reflected that I hated boarding school: why did I put myself through replications of its conformity and absence of privacy, such as once spending a year working on a kibbutz, and now a long communal retreat?

Month-long group retreat is described, perhaps optimistically, as the "best present you can give yourself." It resembles being invited outside your life to understand the principles that secretly govern it.

Friends who have recovered from a stroke recount how "cobbled together" their sense of self can suddenly come to seem. We are not what or who we think we are: we think ourselves into being. Nor is our world quite as solid as it sometimes looks, or rather, as we try to make it. The mind tries to solidify and freeze experience, to turn what is intrinsically fluid into a fixed story.

Month-long group retreat is sometimes also described as coming home to complete simplicity, a healing surrender to the contingency of things. (There are said to be three Buddhist lies, the first of which is "I enjoyed every minute of my month-long group retreat." The second is, "I'm not jealous—despite the fact that my partner has gone off for the night"; the third, "The talk will begin promptly at eight o'clock.")

This first month-long group retreat happened near Drogheda, Ireland, in a red-brick ex-orphanage whose nineteenth-century Church-of-Ireland nurses had bullied and patronized Catholic single mothers. A mean-spirited, depressing list of house rules from around 1890 hung on one wall. Although most who meditated there loved the house and were heartbroken when it had later to be sold, I felt unhappiness enduring like wet-rot: it was always damp. It rained each and every day. Most slept in dorms. I slept in a tiny tent with a bottle of illicit hooch for a nightcap and emerged, umbrella-forward, when the bell sounded at 6:30 A.M. into a Somme of mud each morning.

There were days indoors when everyone seemed to be wading, metaphorically speaking, through deepest mud, too, and the going was hard. Close by on the same estate a twelfth-century tower survived from a ruined castle, at the rickety top of which the demanding so-called "preliminary" practices happened. These start with 108,000 full prostrations, a surrender that can make you physically fit but also make you encounter your emotional volatility (the number 108 has special significance to Tibetan Buddhists).

Poisonous yellow ragwort beset the common approach-path, the water supply was so limited that both baths and the flushing of the lavatories were rationed, and quarreling farmers abounded. I was unsurprised that the place later turned into a themed hotel for Gothic Horror weekends. A gentle landscape undulated toward the ancient iron-age burial site of New Grange.

In nearby Drogheda Cathedral the withered black hand of the Blessed Oliver Plunkett, martyr of sacred memory, sat mesmerizing in its glass case, a relic to be worshipped. We were twenty miles from the border, and the Troubles too. We joked that suspicious locals might say of us, "Who knows whether them feckers is *Catholic* Boodists or *Protestant* Boodist?" (I overheard one visitor whisper to her friend, "They don't *dress* like Noodists," and be answered, "Not *Noodists,* eejit: *Boodists.*")

Our house rules had their own rigors, which included a ban on alcohol, drugs, musical instruments, and non-Buddhist books. There was often a rule of silence, so you adopted mime except when doing kitchen work, where not speaking might cause dangers, and even there speaking was "functional"—"Pass the salt"—no chatter. We meditated for an hour before breakfast, then three hours before lunch, did house chores followed by a free hour, then three hours "sitting" before dinner, and an hour or two afterward. There was one wholly uninterrupted three-hour meditation session, unannounced, at the end of the month, a "tradition" that has since languished. The previous year the retreat leader, from Germany, clearly kept people meditating too late. From an empty shrine room, he eventually tracked down the practitioners sensibly, mutinously quaffing pub Guinness miles away. We were luckier in 1985: the going was easier.

Meals were eaten in silence, in the style of Zen monks, using a demanding ritual called *oryoki* that was, in prospect, terrifying. It was said that Trungpa Rinpoche, the Tibetan Buddhist teacher who founded the community, observed his early students sitting well in meditation and then raiding the icebox to eat like lower beings. He introduced oryoki as a bridge between meditation and "real life." This precise eating practice requires a choreography to develop mindfulness and awareness.

You are served, seated uncomfortably cross-legged only on your flat under-cushion, in quadrants, and the opening and closing of the lacquered set of nesting bowls with their blue ritual cloths have an exact decorum to each single movement, as has the manner in which it is served (with generosity) and, in principle, eaten (with elegance, without greed). Nothing is wasted.

The opening chants are so long that the food is invariably luke-warm by the time you eat it. You use chopsticks. Chants aside, meals are entirely silent, and communication on being served is by *mudras* (hand gestures) betokening "Only a small quantity" or "Enough" of each of three dishes. Then you clean your own set with hot water and drink the slops. After a week, fear went and was replaced by delight in high comedy. Each individual revealed himself nakedly in how he related to food: greedily, nonchalantly, or in ignorance.

It was soon hard to stop laughing. Watching thirty adults from half a dozen countries earnestly meditate seemed a good joke. Laughter came, too, from listening to good but solemn talks on "Obstacles to Meditation and Their Antidotes" (laziness, wildness, etc.), "The Nine Points of Resting the Mind," and "The Six Marks of a Dharmic Person" (cutting down too many activities, passionlessness: there was plenty of passion on the retreat, but clinging to passion is not enjoined). Laughter came from the realization that nobody truly hides except from himself; it came unbidden at many points in the day, and irritated some German friends, though others minded *foux rires* less. Some wept in letting go of a lifetime's tension instead, seeming to express the grief of beings everywhere.

But the effect was the same, a kind of letting go into the discipline of the day, and of moving through a pain barrier like Alice disappearing through the looking glass.

On the far side of "pain" was a new world full of unexpected space and detail. You entered it by discovering that what you had feared as pain was not pain at all, or rather, was purely impersonal, a characteristic of how things always were, but which you had fortified and defended yourself against for nothing. There was less need to insert a sense of self into the pain as a signature. "It suffers," rather than "I suffer," the Buddha said. Life was slowed down, and the volume turned up.

The journey between these two was marked by claustrophobia, by bodily aches and pains, by witnessing the compulsive and stale nature of much fantasy, where nothing fresh could happen. The tension of silence gradually changed into relaxation and relief. Here was a precious commodity, lost and rediscovered.

You arrive with the speed of the ordinary world, so collisions occur, from which something is learned. The ordinary judging/censorious mind holds the world at bay; the accepting, relaxed mind welcomes the world as it is; and it is easier to ask changes of one's world if one is willing first to see it as it is. Willing it to differ changes nothing. One older woman arrived whose naked aggression pained many. It was revelatory to find the courage to confront her—after 9:30 at night, when ordinary speech was sometimes permitted—and then to learn to like her, too. Normally it is not always clear what emotion belongs to whom, and it is possible to feel somebody else's shame as if their frailty were yours. Some sorting out seemed to have happened. Yet there were communal moods, too, both of elation and sorrow.

Benedick, in *Much Ado About Nothing,* seeing his own flightiness, announces, "Man is a giddy thing; and that is my conclusion." The mind is giddier even than one suspected. You fall in love at sunrise, dislike the same person at lunch, feel indifferent at tea, and are in love again by dinner. You watch the tendency of mind to make "a mile out of an inch." It makes an Iris Murdoch novel look understated. Since one is hollow, some humbleness follows. Here were new incentives to think about "emptiness."

I had no idea that a day had so much time packed into it. On a ten-day retreat soon after, I was astonished to witness a dishcloth fall in slow motion. Doubtless it had always fallen at the same speed. My mind had slowed down to meet it.

Extended meditation discloses an experience of profound aloneness, and yet, in the middle of an intensely solitary and silent journey, a strong sense of community and genuine intimacy develop, and the birth of some compassion. Patience is said to be the key to all: the hardest of virtues especially to one ordinarily styled to win the competition for the most impatient person in the room or the planet. Patience is based (we are told) on physical relaxation. Not that it reveals a new world, but rather that it reveals the old world anew, so one sees what one's busyness earlier concealed. When Iris inquired about it later, I said, "You fall in love with everyone, even with those you hate"—a sense of unrequited yet unhungry love—and she laughed, then said, "So you sat on the ground? That's good."

Sometimes friends ask, "Is Buddhism escapist?" The Buddhist might answer that there are aspects of our existence worth escaping, in the sense of losing, or going beyond: neurotic misery; the uncomfortable egoistic anxiety delineated by the First Noble Truth, which often drives us and at the same time keeps us asleep; those mental habits that freeze experience and lead us into error, hatred, and greed, and that, writ large, threaten warfare and global ecological disaster.

"But isn't meditation life-denying, in the sense of joyless?" the questioner persists. If there were no happiness, no one would continue. "I am not afraid of such pleasures," the Buddha said. It seems, on the contrary, life-affirming, disclosing "our most intimate and secret life, its freedom, its abundant creativity, and its joy." On the contrary, it is our secular culture that, because it is death-denying, is by the same token life-denying and joyless. Fear of dying, and indeed of living, turn out to be closer than one had thought.

One night I pondered the old needling questions that can rightly elicit only what George Meredith called "a dusty answer": "How is there a world, something rather than nothing? . . . What *sense* is there to be found?"

A story I had heard when living in Poland for two years, a story touching some deep nerves, came back unbidden. When asked "Who are you?," a Warsaw friend's housekeeper replied that she did not know. She knew only that her mother was rounded up for deportation in Warsaw's *Umschlagplatz* around 1943.

By this stage in the war it was understood that this meant a cattle truck to the gas chambers of Treblinka, and most knew how soon and in what manner that journey would end. In the square the terrified, ill-nourished women from the ghetto passed their babies over their heads one to another set of upraised hands—as I saw it in my mind's eye, with care, though presumably also with haste—toward a high wall enclosing them. They were thrown over to the far side, where pious Catholic Polish women waited and caught, collected, and brought them up as Gentiles.

This tale haunted me, as if it contained the key to understanding something else. This woman did not know who she was. She knew only that she was the child of two kinds of courage: that of a forever nameless mother who had let her go, and that of a foster mother who held and cherished her.

Her story was scarcely universal. Yet it seemed to shed its own strange light. There might never be final answers to the old questions. But meanwhile the qualities both mother and foster mother alike showed on that singular day were as palpable as life itself: both had lived in the challenge and intensity of the moment, rather than among imponderables. There are sources of terror, but courage, generosity, and compassion are real too.

Meditation can (but need not) unlock joyous states, better even than the joy of sex with someone you deeply love. Because one is, albeit momentarily, in the truth, a state of compassion so hair-triggered that you can watch one grown man shed tears on one side of the meditation room while a second, witnessing him from the other side of the room, visibly feels for the first. . . . Yet you are absolutely your own person, and you like yourself and you have the power to bless and to be blessed. Self-consciousness and embarrassment go; a grace of certainty replaces them. How can that be? You belong to yourself, as if for the first time, and then notice how naturally that self feels for others. Everyone, it seems clear, carries her or his own wisdom, though they have not yet always understood this. . . .

You are in love and brokenhearted, but without any drunken or blind need, the exact opposite of depressed. If you are drunk at all, it is on looking at others and their beauty. Those who have meditated for a month look beautiful, ten years younger, newly fledged. You can recognize them in a meditation center. It is said that they appear processed by discipline, both mindful and aware. . . . You need nothing and nobody and have discovered (for a spell) how to be quiet and still and that much speech is superfluous, unmindful, and you are in love with the world and all that it contains, and see how valuable, fragile, and painfully moving that world is, like a cosmonaut witnessing for the first time the little globe journeying nakedly, vulnerably, bravely through open space, with its infinitely precious serendipitous cargo.

You are quietly and as if as never before certain of your own mortality, and that of others, not resenting "the contract" under the terms of which all humans suffer and labor. There is gratitude instead, and a sense of power. For example, the power to glimpse Yeats's understanding that the soul is "self-delighting/self-appeasing, self-affrighting" and then the power physically to touch—to those brought up in stuffy English boarding schools, a real discovery.

At a last-night bonfire party on the retreat an Irish friend recited Prospero from memory and was asked to repeat and repeat the whole speech by others, most of whose first language was not English (Dutch, German, French), listening spellbound, as the sparks flew upward into the night sky:

> Our revels now are ended. These our actors,
> As I foretold you, were all spirits and
> Are melted into air, into thin air:
> And like the baseless fabric of this vision,
> The cloud-topped towers, the gorgeous palaces,
> The solemn temples, the great globe itself,
> Yea, all which it inherit, shall dissolve
> And, like this insubstantial pageant faded,
> Leave not a rack behind. We are such stuff
> As dreams are made on, and our little life
> Is rounded with a sleep. . . .

A friend, a tough-looking postman, observed humorously of his fellow meditators, "I don't know why I'm crying; *I've hated them all for the whole month.*"

I imagine the scorn of a cynical friend and want to say to him that this joy is not stupid or soft but tough and intelligent even if short-lived. It fades and the beginner wants it back. If there is intelligence within cynicism (and there is), there is also soured romanticism. The cynic's secret hope is that his is not the whole story; his secret fear that it is. His is *not* the whole story, though giving up cynicism is frightening: it protects from feeling.

I tried to explain all this later to Iris, repeating, "You fall in love with everyone, even with the people that you hate," and she laughed, and then thought carefully in her customary way, and watched as the dog watches, and replied gently and firmly, "That's good."

The Great Doubt

Roshi Bodhin Kjolhede

Perhaps the most important difference between contemplative and fundamentalist religion is the role of doubt. Doubt in this case doesn't mean disbelief but the open, questioning mind that is the opposite of fundamentalism's solidity and certainty. Doubt plays a particularly important role in Zen, which seeks enlightenment not in answers but in the questioning mind itself. This doubt, says the American Zen teacher Bodhin Kjolhede, is the very means by which we express and deepen our faith.

In Yasutani Roshi's "Introductory Lectures on Zen," recorded in *The Three Pillars of Zen,* he outlines the three essentials of Zen practice: faith, doubt, and determination. A footnote in the text reminds the reader that "in Zen, 'doubt' implies not skepticism but a state of perplexity, of probing inquiry, of intense self-questioning."

Outside of the Zen school of Buddhism, doubt is seen as the very enemy of faith. Early Buddhist doctrine lists it as one of the Five Hindrances, along with desire, aversion, sloth, and restlessness. Among these, doubt, meaning skepticism or unbelief, is considered the worst since it incapacitates the mind. It raises questions that can cripple one's efforts: "What is the point of this practice? Why am I doing this? Where's it getting me?"

But in Zen, faith and doubt don't conflict; they co-arise. If we have faith that the world is in some way ultimately perfect, then how can we not wonder why there is so much suffering in the world? If we believe what Shakyamuni realized through his great awakening that all beings are intrinsically enlightened, how can we not be perplexed at the evidence that contradicts the statement, namely, the greed, hatred, and delusion that is endemic in human beings? Skepticism would lead us to conclude that the Buddha must have been wrong. When our faith is intact, however, it generates the need to resolve the contradiction between what we believe and how things appear.

The doubt that co-arises with faith is, like faith, an innate part of our nature, yet it changes form in the course of our maturation and development. Questioning first reveals itself when the child begins speaking, as early as age one and a half; before that, it couldn't be articulated, even in the mind. Until language is acquired, we experience the world as undivided, devoid of "self" or "other," "right" or "wrong," "inside" or "outside," "now" or "then." Once we learn "I" and "me" and other pronouns, and "Mama" and "want," we find ourselves, like Adam and Eve, banished from Paradise. The experience of simple oneness yields to a world of differentiation. The two-year-old tests his new powers of bifurcation, fascinated especially by the "No!" that affirms his incipient sense of self.

With the arising of what Buddhism calls "name and form," then, comes verbal questioning, a uniquely human response to phenomena. In children it is often simple inquisitiveness, an eagerness to learn about things—their attributes and values and the relationships among them. The "what," "where," and "why" questions of children sometimes seem endless and can get exasperating. But because they arise from such pure not-knowing, they can also be startling, even dumbfounding. A member of our sangha was asked by her granddaughter, "Who thought up dying?" There are also the comical questions. At one of the earliest weddings I performed, when I was still doing the service in my priest's robe, I entered the room of guests (to the strains of Pachelbel's Canon), proceeded to the altar, and turned to face everyone for the entrance of the bride and groom. At that moment, from the back of the room, a little girl's high-pitched voice rang out, "Mommy, why is he wearing *pajamas*?"

As we mature, our natural childhood perplexity shows itself less. What happens to it? No doubt, as we hear more and more explanations and other answers, we wonder less. We're told about the natural world and people, and the way things work—all vital information, of course, for our functioning in the world. We do need to learn and remember the nature of real dangers and threats, how to work and get along with others, and to manage our affairs. But along the way we also accumulate mental freight we don't need. Parents, teachers, and siblings transmit as basic knowledge concepts with which they themselves were inculcated: assumptions about the world, and ways of classifying and ranking people, opinions, judgments, and religious dogma. Anxious to make sense of the world, as children we soak up what we're told. The mind-sets we absorb most deeply are also the least visible to us, thus remaining unexamined.

Through schooling, our knowledge grows exponentially. We amass a prodigious body of facts, ideas, and principles, and come to see this as "the way things are." But the more information computers enable us to harvest about the world, the more demonstrably complex, mysterious, and even chaotic our world is revealed to be. Thomas Edison, who must have had a keener and more probing mind than most of us, once declared, "We know a millionth of one percent of anything."

As we're heaping up data about the world, we're also steadily molding a self-construct about our abilities, liabilities, bodies, personalities, intelligence, and relative worth, all gleaned from what others tell us and how they respond to us. It is a sculpture without substance. It has some validity to it, since we do have some relatively enduring traits and tendencies. But to the extent that we see this self as fixed, it is a fiction. Moreover, the older we get, the more we are likely to assume—erroneously—about the world and ourselves. Much of this amounts to nothing more than "subjective emotional consciousness," as the ancient Chinese masters called it. We become blinded by what we "know," and like vast cities blazing in artificial light every night, our minds are left with less and less of the darkness that inspires wonder. No wonder our natural inquisitiveness fades.

There is no point in lamenting this filling of the mind; it is an inevitable part of childhood development. Nor does it occur only in technologically advanced cultures. Even primitive peoples come to acquire mental structures that determine how they interpret reality. In *The User Illusion,* Tor Norretranders recounts how a Pygmy guide became disoriented when an anthropologist took him out of the Congo forest, where he had spent his entire life without the experience of judging the size of objects at great distances. The Pygmy looked out over the plain at a herd of buffalo in the far distance and identified them as insects. When driven by jeep to see the buffalo up close, he became increasingly frightened and then bewildered, ascribing the transformation of the "insects" to witchcraft. "Believing is seeing," a Buddhist might note.

As children move into adolescence, their questions become weightier, gravitating toward their crystallizing sense of separate identity. They question matters of responsibilities and rights— "Why do I have to . . . (go to bed so early, do the dishes, etc.)?" "Why can't I . . . (wear, have, take, go to see, etc.)?" Such questions are protests, yes, but they also signify a sharpening sense of oneself and one's limits. The teen's self-concept has now solidified enough for her to feel apart from the world, but not enough to feel secure. (As long as we imagine we are apart from the world, how secure can we ever feel?)

As the adolescent is coming to feel more at odds with the world, he finds himself in possession of a developing new faculty: critical intelligence. Brandishing this new weapon, he finds faults everywhere: with parents, siblings, friends, teachers, school, church, society, and the wider culture—and, of course, with himself. The individual's criticism of people and things reveals a growing ability to discern what is false, and without this no questioning is possible. But without faith in something that is beyond both self and other, our critical faculties may be used merely to reject, and this leads us to the ordinary, negative doubt of unbelief.

Skepticism itself, however, may be a cover for unrealized faith. Philip Kapleau was one of the first American teachers of Zen. When he was young he was the founder and first president of his high school's Atheist Club. Conversely, what passes for religious belief may be devoid of the doubt that confirms true spiritual faith. A recent survey of American teens ages thirteen to seventeen summarized their faith as "wide but shallow," finding that although a majority of them "believe in God and worship in conventional congregations," their religious knowledge is "meager, nebulous, and often fallacious." The study points to the prevalence of blind belief, which, to use a Buddhist expression is the "near enemy" of true faith. This "knowing" forecloses genuine questioning.

When the mind is girded with even an inchoate faith, the person can use her critical intelligence not just to criticize or deny, but to question. The potential targets of our condemnation can then be subjects of inquiry: "What makes him so mean?" "Why can't Mom and Dad get along?" "How do I take care of myself without being selfish?" Two especially loaded questions aimed at religious dogma are: "In what sense are children 'sinners'?" and "Did Adam and Eve have belly buttons?"

The normal trajectory of human doubt shows the questioning of childhood and adolescence sputtering out as full maturity sets in. It can't seem to survive the growing weight of our belief systems, the pressures of adulthood. Before that, however, our various perplexities may, as if in a last stand, coalesce around a single, ultimate question. Among the most common of these are: "What is the meaning (or purpose) of life?" "How do I live in Truth?" "Who am I?" "Where did I come from before I was born, and where will I go after I die?" Such potent questioning signifies a breathtaking spiritual opportunity, and the last time that most people—unless they take up meditation—will gaze unflinchingly at the naked mystery of being. Few of those who are gripped by ultimate questions have them persist long enough to effect an overturning of the mind. One for whom this did happen was Flora Courtois, who as a college student in the 1940s came to spontaneous awakening after several months in which she was consumed by the question "What is reality?" As a sixteen-year-old, Ramana Maharshi, who became one of the greatest spiritual masters of the twentieth century, suddenly was overcome by a fear of death that plunged him into the deepest doubt: "What really is it, then, to die?" In just half an hour his self-inquiry brought him to profound enlightenment.

Such spectacular eruptions of faith-doubt, whether in adolescence or later, are exceedingly rare. Most young people who are not walking in lockstep to their parents' religion seem to navigate their way through faith and doubt as did the character in one of Nathaniel Hawthorne's novels who "can neither believe, nor be comfortable in his unbelief." It is hard to imagine, though, that the questioning unique to our species can ever be extinguished. At times of adult crisis, the parent who may have once dismissed their children's existential questions as pointless, and the clergy who reflexively offered church doctrine in response to such queries, may find their former doubt resurfacing.

When someone close to us dies, in our grief we may for the first time find ourselves seized by religious or philosophical questions: "Where did she go? What is the meaning of it all? Why now, why her?" Or, in the case of a violent crime, "Why would a just God permit this?" These or other probing questions may well up after a diagnosis of terminal disease or a divorce or even losing a job. Our assumptions, expectations, or hopes are left shattered, and we *don't understand.* Such profound perplexity may erupt in the face of stunning evil as well. For Philip Kapleau, it took four months of courtroom testimony at Nuremburg to provoke the doubt that, supported by faith, drove him to the meditation mat. His previous understanding of human nature and cosmic order had been torn, leaving him in the darkness of doubt.

What further evidence suggests that doubt, coupled with faith, is integral to our true nature? The whole history of human achievement! It is most obvious in the realms of discovery and invention. Leif Eriksson, Lewis and Clark, and Amelia Earhart all had faith that there were new lands beyond their horizons, and with this came the questions "Where?" "What?" and "How?"—and the need to find out. What else but an inquiring mind working in tandem with faith enabled Jonas Salk to find the polio vaccine, Madame Curie to discover radium, and James Watson and Francis Crick the structure of DNA? It was faith in the yet-to-be-realized, yoked to questioning, that drove Chester Carlson to invent the copy machine, Sigmund Freud psychoanalysis, and George Washington Carver his three hundred uses of the peanut. Late in his life, Albert Einstein, recounting what he went through in developing his theory of relativity, used words that echo the classic spiritual journey. He recalled "the years of anxious searching in the dark, with their intense longing, their alternations of confidence and exhaustion, and their final emergence into the light."

These are just a handful of the most illustrious cases of faith-doubt actualized. But we can see the same force at work in far humbler ways. It fuels the investigations of journalists ("What's going on here?"), detectives ("Who did it?"), physicians ("What's wrong?"), social workers ("What's to be done?"), and teachers and parents ("How do I reach him?"), as well as all the rest of us when we're probing, pondering, and puzzling in the faith that we can know: "What's the answer? What am I missing? What's the way out?" In every case the questioning, arising out of not-knowing, is generated by faith, either in an underlying order to the world or in a basic soundness, balance, and wellness of the body-mind.

Zen doubt refers, of course, to an *inner* process. Both "wondering" and "perplexity" suggest this introspective quality more clearly than "questioning" (the same distinction is highlighted in Spanish, where "to ask or question" is *preguntar*, whereas "to wonder" is the reflexive *preguntarse*, "to ask oneself"). But "questioning" better conveys the active engagement of the mind that is implied in the word *doubt*. (When applied to a Zen koan, it has been compared to "turning the soil" rather than just watching and waiting.)

Dynamic inner questioning seems to work differently than any other type of mental functioning. When allowed to gain traction it empties the mind, erasing thought-clutter. Anyone who has the experience of falling into deep perplexity will recognize this effect. For example, upon having misplaced one's car keys, the effect is most dramatic when you know they must be within a particular room. Yet you've looked there, thoroughly, and more than once. Wondering turns to increasingly intense perplexity, until finally you come to a complete stop, utterly lost in doubt. Such is the centripetal force of doubt yoked to faith. Brain-imaging techniques may someday confirm the uniqueness of this mode of brain functioning.

While nothing, then, engages the mind like a question, that questioning can be evoked from outside us. Those in marketing know that to compete for the attention of readers in certain niches, one of the best strategies is to introduce the product or service in question form. We see this on the covers of the popular magazines arrayed along supermarket checkout lines: "Is Madonna Pregnant?" "Will Brad and Jennifer Split Up?" Most of us really don't know for sure, and publishers have learned that we may be prompted to wonder just enough to buy the magazine. Promotional mailings use the same device, their creators knowing that they can count on only a fraction of a second of the recipient's attention, at most.

Zen teachers are in marketing, too, faced with the task of "selling water by the river." Through their own direct experience they know the titanic potential of focused questioning. They know that the capacity to wonder is a priceless human endowment, but that for most of us it sinks under the weight of conceptualization and other conditioning that tends to thicken as we grow older. They also know that Zen practice will reverse this process of mental coagulation and yield a more youthful openness. They face a question of their own, then: how to activate the dormant perplexity that is embedded in the human condition itself. We alone of all creatures have self-consciousness, the ability to conceive of our existence and our inevitable death. Who among us, then, could not harbor questioning in his heart? Who could not wonder, at least unconsciously, at the mystery of our very being?

Among the resources used by the Ch'an masters of the Sung dynasty were the stories and dialogues of their predecessors, who tossed out confounding responses to their own monks in an effort to stir them to awaken. They collected these records and called them *kung-an* (Jap.: *koan*) or "precedents." The genius of the koan as a meditative device lies in its ability to mobilize the student's latent doubt by bringing it to a focus. It functions as does a magnifying glass under the sun. Natural sunlight is relatively diffuse, but upon passing through a magnifying glass, its warmth can be transformed into a spot of fire in seconds. In the same way, the koan has the power to gather together the relatively weak and sporadic perplexity of the student into a single, burning question—a *doubt-mass*—that empties the mind and leads to awakening more quickly than any other method.

Throughout history, Zen masters have repeated the same formula:

> The greater the doubt,
> the greater the Awakening.
> The smaller the doubt,
> the smaller the Awakening.
> No doubt, no awakening.

What the masters meant by "doubt" didn't always involve koans. After all, koans were not used for the first five hundred years of Zen, a golden age in which there were probably more deeply enlightened masters than in any period since. How many of them, we have to wonder, were driven to realization by their own spontaneously erupting inquiries, like those of Ramana Maharshi and Flora Courtois? Or was their faith so great, and their minds so pure, that their attainments came without questioning? In any case, most of us must rely on the koan to "raise the doubt sensation" and bring our largely unconscious questioning up to consciousness.

A koan usually contains in its very wording a contradictory element that cannot be resolved with our ordinary, discriminating mind. This alone would make it puzzling. But even a koan with no linguistic paradox becomes puzzling simply through our seriously engaging with it. With the koan *Mu* ("Not," "No"), for example, most teachers do not recommend pondering the original dialogue between Chao-chou and a monk. Rather, just putting one's whole mind into the question "What is Mu?" or even just "Mu" will eventually raise the doubt-mass. This happens as the apparent split between the koan and oneself becomes increasingly dubious—and perplexing.

Every koan is a unique expression of our essential nature, just as every flower, every stone, every insect is. To work effectively on a koan, one must have faith in his ultimate identity with it, and that in working on it he is really working on himself. With this faith comes the conviction that he can resolve the contradiction implied in it—for example, "Mu and I are not two, yet it still seems separate from me." These two convictions together form the faith-ground out of which doubt arises.

Theoretically, the same dynamics of koan work could evolve while one is persistently inquiring into the nature of any supposed object, whether physical or mental: an image, a candle flame, a sound, a cloud, a tree, a partner, an idea. When Isaac Newton was asked how he discovered the law of gravity, he replied, "My mind never ceased thinking about it." By focusing all our questioning on one thing, we become more intimate with it even as it becomes still more puzzling—until eventually the doubt shatters, bringing about a radically new understanding of it.

The essential point is that illusion cannot survive intense scrutiny pursued to the end. The most fundamental illusion of all, separation, dissolves. We can't cling to our delusions while sincerely inquiring into the koan. "Knowing" and questioning are mutually exclusive. And the more thoroughly we probe the koan, the sooner the "known" world of self and other dissolves, revealing—what?

If doubt is essential to Zen practice, how does it operate in breath practice, or in *shikantaza* ("just sitting")? Questioning plays no role in these practices. Strictly speaking, a question must be articulated somehow; it cannot exist in the absence of words.

In koan-less practice, doubt is implicit rather than explicit. Like faith, it must be there; otherwise we wouldn't be sitting. But with no actual questioning in the mind, doubt here is to be understood more loosely as a sense that something needs to be resolved. Our sitting testifies to a dissonance between our faith and our experience. It may be, for example, that faith in the inherent unity of phenomena is at variance with one's experience of disunity; faith in the basic completeness of people is at odds with one's perception of their shortcomings; faith in the immanent silence of things is at odds with one's experience of disquiet. In all such examples the perception of incongruity creates a spiritual tension that one seeks to resolve through sitting.

Just as the innate human impulse to question reveals itself in exploration, invention, investigation, and other kinds of inquiring pursuits, so we can see non-questioning doubt at work in worldly aspirations. It may be most obvious in the drive for mastery, whether in athletics, music and art, body work, or academics. Those who dedicate themselves to these and other disciplines are yearning to resolve the disparity between what they believe they are capable of and what they have already achieved. Why else would a world-class tennis player, pianist, or chess player go on training eight hours a day? Questioning, as such, is not involved in these pursuits, but they are bristling with doubt in a movement toward resolution. Unlike zazen, however, they do not lead to ultimate liberation.

In non-koan zazen, doubt- or faith-doubt reveals itself not through questioning but rather as a *looking.* Not just looking *at,* but looking *into,* searchingly, and with bare attention. Doubt here implies looking while not knowing—peering out of darkness into darkness. It is what Wittgenstein meant when he urged, "Don't think, look!" This is the same place to which koan practice leads us, the realm of nonabiding, "holding to nothing whatever but dwelling in *prajna* wisdom." In this realm of no-form, mind as spacious as the blue sky, the world of phenomena is born anew. If, as Socrates said, "Wisdom begins in wonder," it also ends there. Life becomes wondrous.

Studying Mind from the Inside

The Dalai Lama

The true nature of mind, says His Holiness the Dalai Lama, is beyond any concept or physical form. Therefore it cannot be studied solely by the third-person methods of Western science. Mind must also be studied through a rigorous observation of our own subjective experience, which equally meets the norms of the scientific method. In this, Buddhism, a 2500-year science of the mind, excels.

The joy of meeting someone you love, the sadness of losing a close friend, the richness of a vivid dream, the serenity of a walk through a garden on a spring day, the total absorption of a deep meditative state—these things and others like them constitute the reality of our experience of consciousness.

Regardless of the content of any one of these experiences, no one in his or her right mind would doubt their reality. Any experience of consciousness—from the most mundane to the most elevated—has a certain coherence and, at the same time, a high degree of privacy, which means that it always exists from a particular point of view. The experience of consciousness is entirely subjective. The paradox, however, is that despite the indubitable reality of our subjectivity and thousands of years of philosophical examination, there is little consensus on what consciousness is. Science, with its characteristic third-person method—the objective perspective from the outside—has made strikingly little headway in this understanding.

The question of consciousness has attracted a good deal of attention in the long history of Buddhist philosophical thinking. For Buddhism, given its primary interest in questions of ethics, spirituality, and overcoming suffering, understanding consciousness, which is thought to be a defining characteristic of sentience, is of great importance. According to the earliest scriptures, the Buddha saw consciousness as playing a key role in determining the course of human happiness and suffering. For example, the famous discourse of the Buddha known as the *Dhammapada* opens with the statement that mind is primary and pervades all things.

The problem of describing the subjective experiences of consciousness is complex indeed. For we risk objectivizing what is essentially an internal set of experiences and excluding the necessary presence of the experiencer. We cannot remove ourselves from the equation. No scientific description of the neural mechanisms of color discrimination can make one understand what it feels like to perceive, say, the color red. We have a unique case of inquiry: the object of our study is mental, that which examines it is mental, and the very medium by which the study is undertaken is mental. The question is whether the problems posed by this situation for a scientific study of consciousness are insurmountable—are they so damaging as to throw serious doubt on the validity of the inquiry?

Although we tend to relate to the mental world as if it were homogenous—a somewhat monolithic entity called "the mind"—when we probe more deeply, we come to recognize that this approach is too simplistic. As we experience it, consciousness is made up of myriad highly varied and often intense mental states.

There are explicitly cognitive states, like belief, memory, recognition, and attention, on the one hand, and explicitly affective states, like the emotions, on the other. In addition, there seems to be a category of mental states that function primarily as causal factors in that they motivate us into action. These include volition, will, desire, fear, and anger. Even within the cognitive states, we can draw distinctions between sensory perceptions, such as visual perception, which has a certain immediacy in relation to the objects being perceived, and conceptual thought processes, such as imagination or the subsequent recollection of a chosen object. These latter processes do not require the immediate presence of the perceived object, nor do they depend upon the active role of the senses.

The question is, What defines this diversity of phenomena as belonging to one family of experience, which we call "mental"? I remember most vividly my first lesson on epistemology as a child, when I had to memorize the dictum "The definition of the mental is that which is luminous and knowing." It was years later that I realized just how complicated is the philosophical problem hidden behind this simple formulation. Today when I see nine-year-old monks confidently citing this definition of consciousness on the debating floor, which is such a central part of Tibetan monastic education, I smile.

These two features—luminosity, or clarity, and knowing, or cognizance—have come to characterize "the mental" in Indo-Tibetan Buddhist thought. *Clarity* here refers to the ability of mental states to reveal or reflect. *Knowing*, by contrast, refers to mental states' faculty to perceive or apprehend what appears. All phenomena possessed of these qualities count as mental. These features are difficult to conceptualize, but then we are dealing with phenomena that are subjective and internal rather than material objects that may be measured in spatiotemporal terms. Perhaps it is because of these difficulties—the limits of language in dealing with the subjective—that many of the early Buddhist texts explain the nature of consciousness in terms of metaphors such as light or a flowing river. As the primary feature of light is to illuminate, so consciousness is said to illuminate its objects. Just as in light there is no categorical distinction between the illumination and that which illuminates, so in consciousness there is no real difference between the process of knowing, or cognition, and that which knows or cognizes. In consciousness, as in light, there is a quality of illumination.

Western philosophy and science have, on the whole, attempted to understand consciousness solely in terms of the functions of the brain. This approach effectively grounds the nature and existence of the mind in matter, in an ontologically reductionist manner. Some view the brain in terms of a computational model, comparing it to artificial intelligence; others attempt an evolutionary model for the emergence of the various aspects of consciousness. In modern neuroscience, there is a deep question about whether the mind and consciousness are any more than simply operations of the brain, whether sensations and emotions are more than chemical reactions. To what extent does the world of subjective experience depend on the hardware and working order of the brain? It must to some significant extent, but does it do so entirely? What are the necessary and sufficient causes for the emergence of subjective mental experiences?

Many scientists, especially those in the discipline of neurobiology, assume that consciousness is a special kind of physical process that arises through the structure and dynamics of the brain. I vividly remember a discussion I had with some eminent neuroscientists at an American medical school. After they kindly showed me the latest scientific instruments to probe ever deeper into the human brain, such as MRI (magnetic resonance imaging) and EEG (electroencephalograph), and let me view a brain operation in progress (with the family's permission), we sat down to have a conversation on the current scientific understanding of consciousness. I said to one of the scientists: "It seems very evident that due to changes in the chemical processes of the brain, many of our subjective experiences like perception and sensation occur. Can one envision the reversal of this causal process? Can one postulate that pure thought itself could affect a change in the chemical processes of the brain?" I was asking whether, conceptually at least, we could allow the possibility of both upward and downward causation.

The scientist's response was quite surprising. He said that since all mental states arise from physical states, it is not possible for downward causation to occur. Although, out of politeness, I did not respond at the time, I thought then and still think that there is as yet no scientific basis for such a categorical claim. The view that all mental processes are necessarily physical processes is a metaphysical assumption, not a scientific fact. I feel that, in the spirit of scientific inquiry, it is critical that we allow the question to remain open, and not conflate our assumptions with empirical fact.

A crucial point about the study of consciousness, as opposed to the study of the physical world, relates to the personal perspective. In examining the physical world, leaving aside the problematic issue of quantum mechanics, we are dealing with phenomena that lend themselves well to the dominant scientific method of the objective, third-person method of inquiry. On the whole, we have a sense that a scientific explanation of the physical world does not exclude the key elements of the field being described. In the realm of subjective experiences, however, the story is completely different. When we listen to a purely third-person, "objective" account of mental states, whether it is a cognitive psychological theory, a neurobiological account, or an evolutionary theory, we feel that a crucial dimension of the subject has been left out. I am referring to the phenomenological aspect of mental phenomena, namely the subjective experience of the individual.

Even from this brief discussion, it is, I think, clear that the third-person method—which has served science so well in so many areas—is inadequate to the explanation of consciousness. What is required, if science is successfully to probe the nature of consciousness, is nothing short of a paradigm shift. That is, the third-person perspective, which can measure phenomena from the point of view of an independent observer, must be integrated with a first-person perspective, which will allow the incorporation of subjectivity and the qualities that characterize the experience of consciousness. I am suggesting the need for the method of our investigation to be appropriate to the object of inquiry. Given that one of the primary characteristics of consciousness is its subjective and experiential nature, any systematic study of it must adopt a method that will give access to the dimensions of subjectivity and experience.

A comprehensive scientific study of consciousness must therefore embrace both third-person and first-person methods: it cannot ignore the phenomenological reality of subjective experience but must observe all the rules of scientific rigor. So the critical question is this: Can we envision a scientific methodology for the study of consciousness whereby a robust first-person method, which does full justice to the phenomenology of experience, can be combined with the objectivist perspective of the study of the brain?

Here I feel a close collaboration between modern science and the contemplative traditions, such as Buddhism, could prove beneficial. Buddhism has a long history of investigation into the nature of mind and its various aspects—this is effectively what Buddhist meditation and its critical analysis constitute. Unlike that of modern science, Buddhism's approach has been primarily from first-person experience. The contemplative method, as developed by Buddhism, is an empirical use of introspection, sustained by rigorous training in technique and robust testing of the reliability of experience. All meditatively valid subjective experiences must be verifiable both through repetition by the same practitioner and through other individuals being able to attain the same state by the same practice. If they are thus verified, such states may be taken to be universal, at any rate for human beings.

The Buddhist understanding of mind is primarily derived from empirical observations grounded in the phenomenology of experience, which includes the contemplative techniques of meditation. Working models of the mind and its various aspects and functions are generated on this basis; they are then subjected to sustained critical and philosophical analysis and empirical testing through both meditation and mindful observation. If we want to observe how our perceptions work, we may train our mind in attention and learn to observe the rising and falling of perceptual processes on a moment-by-moment basis. This is an empirical process that results in firsthand knowledge of a certain aspect of how the mind works. We may use that knowledge to reduce the effects of emotions such as anger or resentment (indeed, meditation practitioners in search of overcoming mental affliction would wish to do this), but my point here is that this process offers a first-person empirical method with relation to the mind.

What occurs during meditative contemplation in a tradition such as Buddhism and what occurs during introspection in the ordinary sense are two quite different things. In the context of Buddhism, introspection is employed with careful attention to the dangers of extreme subjectivism—such as fantasies and delusions—and with the cultivation of a disciplined state of mind. Refinement of attention, in terms of stability and vividness, is a crucial preparation for the utilization of rigorous introspection, much as a telescope is crucial for the detailed examination of celestial phenomena. Just as in science, there is a series of protocols and procedures that contemplative introspection must employ. Upon entering a laboratory, someone untrained in science would not know what to look at and would have no capacity to recognize when something is found; in the same way, an untrained mind will have no ability to apply the introspective focus on a chosen object and will fail to recognize when processes of the mind show themselves. Just like a trained scientist, a disciplined mind will have the knowledge of what to look for and the ability to recognize when discoveries are made.

It may well be that the question of whether consciousness can ultimately be reduced to physical processes, or whether our subjective experiences are nonmaterial features of the world, will remain a matter of philosophical choice. The key issue here is to bracket out the metaphysical questions about mind and matter, and to explore together how to understand scientifically the various modalities of the mind. I believe that it is possible for Buddhism and modern science to engage in collaborative research in the understanding of consciousness while leaving aside the philosophical question of whether consciousness is ultimately physical. By bringing together these two modes of inquiry, both disciplines may be enriched. Such collaborative study will contribute not only greater human understanding of consciousness but a better understanding of the dynamics of the human mind and its relation to suffering. This is a precious gateway into the alleviation of suffering, which I believe to be our principal task on this earth.

A Saint Beyond My Understanding ◝

George Crane

On a trip to Mongolia, George Crane is overwhelmed by the suffering of the weak and the inhumanity of the powerful. Are indifference and neglect simply part of human nature and social Darwinism our fate, he wonders? And the do-gooders are suspect in their own way. Then he meets Ani Thubten Jinpa and the children she cares for.

Millie's Espresso, a light-filled room with Gobi Desert photographs on the walls, sleek wood tables and chairs, and a stainless Italian espresso machine, a Rancilio, was on the second floor above the Internet café, just off the main drag. It was the favored meeting place and hangout among the sizable consulate, UN, NGO, and expat community in Ulaanbaatar. At Millie's, not only could you get a decent cup of espresso—I've tasted worse in Paris—but information, rumors, and a damn good plate of *huevos rancheros* from a menu that offered an odd mix of American, Mexican, and Cuban food.

The café's proprietor, namesake, and social director was the elegant Million Skoda, whose circuitous route to Ulaanbaatar began in 1964 when she left Ethiopia to study in the United States. There she married an American and had two children. In 1997, her husband, a water and sanitation engineer, was stationed in Mongolia to work on a UN project. When Million arrived, there was no good coffee, just instant, and so she, looking for something to do, opened her café.

Earlier that September, three weeks before leaving New York, I had received a letter from Mongolia by way of London that had been forwarded by my British publisher. It was dated May 12, 2001. Written in purple ink on graph paper, in a careful hand, it had been in transit for just under two and a half years.

A picture was enclosed—a Western Buddhist nun with one baby hanging around her neck and shoulders, another curled in her arms, and twenty more surrounding her. Wiry and trim. Steel-gray hair cropped to a short crew cut. A brilliant smile. Ani Jinpa's eyes, even off the photo, sparked joy. An ecstasy that saints can find even in suffering. And she had read my book *Bones,* she wrote. This on a week when things were not going well. On a day that I felt like grade-A shit. A fraud. It seemed odd. Out of context. I thought, old Barnum had it right. You can fool some of the people all of the time and most of the people some of the time. But the Venerable Thubten Jinpa?

. . . In other news . . . lies are the truth of the human soul.

Ani Jinpa had included an e-mail address. I immediately sent off a reply, telling her when I was due to arrive in Ulaanbaatar and explaining why my response was so late in coming. My e-mail came back as *address unknown.* The only other address in the letter was PO Box 219 in Ulaanbaatar.

Dear George Crane:

I am an Australian Tibetan Buddhist nun working in Mongolia. (Outer.) In fact I think I'm the only Western TBN in Mongolia. We work here with homeless and abandoned babies and children.

With the thought to buy a gift for the only Australian Buddhist monk in Mongolia, I went to the nearby second-hand bookshop and found a perfect copy of your book, which I restrained myself from reading first.

Now that I have just regretfully turned the last page. I did not want to leave the wonderful Tsung Tsai or your lovely prose.

Thank you for such a beautiful book about enduring faith in people and a monk's profound faith in the Buddha's teachings.

Are you coming back . . .
Will you write more . . .
Yes [ ] Yes [ ]
Please tick both boxes.

. . .

bearing Buddha
constantly in mind
I gave up grief
and illusion . . .

A perfect teaching—I have it on my wall. Thank you for it.
Much love,
Ani

Ani was easy to find. I asked Millie, who seemed to know every foreigner in the country. "Ask him," she said, pointing to a very tall fellow leaning over a plate of eggs.

I asked. He knew. John, a Brit working for one of the NGOs operating in-country, knew her. Had helped her raise money.

"I just called her this morning," he said.

He gave me her number. I called.

"Ani Jinpa?"

"Speaking."

"Ani, it's George Crane; I got your number from John. You wrote me . . ."

"George Crane? The writer. *Bones of the Master* Georgie?"

"The one and the same." I laughed, "I'm in Ulaanbaatar. I'd love to meet you. To talk to you."

"Oh yes. We must. What about tomorrow? Lunch? Join the

children and me for soup at the nunnery. We begin serving at two. Come early. I've so much to ask you. How's Tsung Tsai? No, wait—" She stopped herself, her voice girlish and excited. "*Tomorrow*. Before lunch. After lunch. Tomorrow we can talk. Tomorrow is soon enough."

I got directions. "Tomorrow then," I said. "I'll come around noon. I look forward to it."

"Yes," she said. "Just wonderful. The conditions are ripening."

Thubten Jinpa's Dolma Ling Nunnery and Mahayana Buddhist Center, formerly the Chinese monastery Dari-ekh, was located on the city's edge, hidden deep within a maze of narrow squalid alleys that were the nomad slums. These walled-off shanty communities were an anomalous collection of ragged, out-of-context *gers* (yurts) and squalid shacks cobbled together from the capital's garbage, from industrial remnants of every conceivable sort, from burned-out buses to rotting boilers and oil tankers.

The elegant utility of the *ger* was lost in these asylums for the outcasts, the dispossessed, the homeless; the now useless, the weary and the broken; the burned out and drugged out; the sick and the dying—the hopeless, vacant of everything except despair and insanity. For a nomad imprisoned in this place and time, where every social and cultural contract has been destroyed, to be untouched by madness would in itself be madness. Delusional. Catatonic.

I'd arrived by taxi early, first having to bribe the driver with an extra bill to drive me into those back-alley slums. Ani Jinpa, looking just as she had in the photo she'd sent, was waiting at the gate. She was tall and slim, with crew-cut steel-gray hair. She radiated energy—a dervish spinning, a force of nature. She was one of those people who are bigger than life; she filled space. She was in control, on a mission, whether serving soup, tending children (she was a nurse before she took her vows), raising money, or battling bureaucracy.

The Chinese Dari-ekh Monastery was abandoned early in the Soviet occupation and was near ruin when Ani came to Ulaanbaatar for a short visit. She saw need and stayed. In the decade since, Ani had carved out of that dilapidation a temple, nuns' housing, class-rooms, graveled pathways, and a courtyard with scraggly young trees.

"In time . . . ," she said, looking with eyes that saw what remained to be done. Saw how it could be. In time.

Her pride and joy was the new, one-story 1,500-square-foot white stucco community center with its red-tiled roof. "This is what I really want to show you . . . just finished last month . . . the dining room, kitchen, and infirmary."

She opened the door to warmth. The new coal furnace and boiler had been fired up for the first time that morning and were still being tinkered with when I arrived.

"Ah, we have heat." She shivered and rubbed her hands together. "Hot water to wash the children. They have to wash before lunch. Dysentery is such a problem. The biggest killer, particularly among the very young. They eat garbage, you know. They hide it in their pockets, under their clothes; I try to keep them from adding it to the soup."

Ani slept in a small whitewashed room behind the kitchen that also served as the infirmary. There were cabinets for the medical supplies, an examining table, a window looking out across the courtyard through newly planted twigs of trees to the restored tem-ple. The only signs that she lived there were a metal military-issue footlocker, a backpack leaning against the wall, a chair by the win-dow in which to sit and read or rock children, and a narrow, thin futon mattress on the floor. Drawings by and Polaroids of her chil-dren were taped to the wall. These were, I guess, the sum total of her possessions.

Across the hall, she pointed, there was a bathroom; a sink, a bath for the babies, and for younger children, showers.

"This little one," she pulled one of the photos off the wall. It was a classic; a picture of just a dynamite little kid mugging, full of her-self, teasing, wagging her tongue at the camera—her eyes are fear-less. "*Dolma* we call her, was found wandering alone, almost two years ago now. She was, best guess, about four years old. Coal black.

Obviously had never had a bath, clothes so filthy they stuck to her—she probably had never been out of them—we just cut them off. Her hair also. The last layer of rags, practically fused to her skin, had to be soaked off, peeled away in the bath. The first four soaks the water turned to mud. Her skin was pocked with sores and cankers. How she survived, I can't imagine. But look at her now."

The white-tiled kitchen was equipped with four-burner stoves, a refrigerator, an incongruous restaurant sprayer over a stainless double sink, preparation tables. An alcove opened onto a bright and airy dining room where eight wooden tables and benches could seat thirty-two children for soup with meat and vegetables, bread, and milk tea.

"I officially feed fifty children a day, but most days it's closer to sixty."

"What's your budget?"

Ani Jinpa took a breath to calculate. "Five thousand U.S. a year," she said at last. "Sometimes a bit less."

I did a little calculating myself. "Less than fifteen bucks a day? For sixty? How?"

"I have suppliers . . . connections," she said with a conspiratorial wink and a twinkle that indicated she said less than she knew. "But corruption is almost universal; corruption and despair are choking this country," she continued. "Every year we have to make an appearance before some bureaucrat, some committee head, some secretary of something or other, and justify what we're doing here. Which means they want to know what's in it for *them.* How much can *they* get?"

It was just twelve-thirty, and already the children, plus a few pregnant and nursing mothers (whom Ani also feeds and cares for), had begun to gather, huddling together at the nunnery's gate, along with an old man, a tough-looking pug with a battered and broken face. Ani pointed in his direction. "That one's spent most of his life in prison. For murder. He told me he killed someone in a fight. He's seventy and takes care of two young children. His wife is eighteen."

Ani sighed as she took in the scene. "Look at them," she said, again pointing out the window overlooking the street and speaking in such a low voice that it was difficult to make out her words. Her voice changed now, its tones and cadence more suitable for speaking to a young child. "They come early. Always so early. *So* early. And they have such patience. Such grit. They're so stoic. Quiet. Never complaining." She crossed her arms, hugging herself and rocking from side to side as if comforting a baby. "But the wind . . . it's so cold. In rain, snow. I thought if they at least had a place to stand out of the weather."

She stomped her foot and turned away from the window. "I'm going to build a waiting room. We must begin tomorrow. The carpenter has already drawn up the plans. *Tomorrow,*" she said sharply, determined. "Tomorrow, without delay. The money will . . ." She nodded to herself, to the beneficent universe, and there was no contradicting her passion, her certainty. "The money will just have to . . . I'll *get* it. Somehow."

Ani Jinpa circled the table with one of her Mongolian workers, who held the big dented pot as Ani ladled. Another followed, pouring tea and serving bread, two slices each. They all waited. Their washed hands folded. Quiet. Not one of them moved until their bowls were filled—and not paper bowls and plastic spoons either, but crockery and stainless. That's Ani's idea. She wants them to feel as good as possible about themselves, permanent and important. They eat quickly. Nothing is wasted. Not a drop. The bowls are licked clean. Filled with milk tea and licked again.

"How's the soup?" Ani asked.

"Good but a bit salty," I said, trying for politeness.

Ani closed her eyes and leaned her head forward, chin on chest. "I know," she said, sighing. "I know. I'm working on the cooks. Trying to get them to use less salt. It's better now. But still . . . they use so much salt. If I put salt on the table they'd use more. Mongols love salt. High blood pressure and kidney failure are endemic here."

"It seems the least of their problems."

"It is."

• • •

The need in Mongolia is overwhelming. Easy to see. The number
of homeless children is unknown, but it's in the many, many tens
of thousands. In a country with a total population of 2.3 million,
there are an estimated 200,000 malnourished children. "An optimistic number," says Ani, shaking her head sadly. "A very optimistic
number."

The official population of Ulaanbaatar is 820,000. The actual
population may be closer to twice that number, if one counts the un-
counted homeless, the nomads forced off the steppe by poverty's
push. They've sold everything, finally even their *ger,* to survive. In
the short time I walked the streets, I was most often followed by
clouds of street kids begging or selling small bags of sunflower seeds
to scatter to the wind and the pigeons—offerings, gifts for the Buddha. Some so young they fried the soul, stripped away the opaque
membrane that stands between us and compassion. Because what I
saw there of the human condition was too raw, too hard, too horri-
fying for us to justify our lives of comfort and possessive greed, too
terrible to let us continue to think that we are *good* people, a noble
species. We are, all of us, damaged goods.

Here homeless, parentless children as young as four years wandered the streets, babies cradling even younger babies in their arms.
They crawled up in the morning from the underground, the network heating tunnels beneath the street where they slept, huddled
like moles in the dark, hibernating against the long freezing winters.
One thing you quickly learn in Ulaanbaatar is to watch your step,
looking down always, for there is not a manhole cover left in place
on the sidewalks and streets of the capital. They have all been removed for ease, for quick escape, coming and going. Children, occasionally whole families, crawl out from the underground with
morning, continuing their hunt for scraps of garbage, for hand-
outs—for survival and hope. And of course there is almost no hope
for these children. Most of them, still babies, will die; they will die of
every ill known to humankind—of malnutrition, of pneumonia, of
influenza, of colds, of dysentery, of infection, of neglect.

They will die as native peoples have always died. Of genocide. Of cultural mass murder, pushed off their land and out of history by progress, by humanity's inexhaustible hunger for power, for land, for more stuff. They have died and will continue to die. Indians, Africans, Tibetans, nomads—it doesn't matter the country or tribe or race; they will die.

It is Darwinism carried to its logical extreme. The survival of the fittest—that is, survival of the most powerful. It is humanity's repulsive underbelly—prejudiced, superstitious, oppressive, caste-ridden, corrupted by wealth and political power. That we are collectively guilty of murder is the truth; that we are nothing but barbarians, all of us unfit to be called civilized, that too is the truth. Our civility is but a thin façade covering the absolute cruelty of a demented, cannibalistic species—that is nature's truth. We've got the ideas, the ethics all right, but our minds can't control our nature, what's written in the primitive code of life: *Win. Survive at all costs. Damn the consequences.*

China will continue to do to Tibet what America did to her native cultures, what the Europeans did to the Africans, what Russia did to the Mongolians, and what the new Mongolia continues to do to its remaining nomad peoples. What the powerful do to the weak. Period. Etcetera. There is no hope.

But then there is Thubten Jinpa. Ani, who seems unexhausted by the miseries of human life: war, disease, decay, filth, poverty, starvation; the continual, insistent demand for sympathy and personal concern that would harden all but a saint's supply of compassion.

Mostly I don't like saints. Or trust them. They are the same as we are. Barbarians. Sinners also. In the end everything will be found to be true of everybody. Saint and villain are one.

But then there is Ani Jinpa. She is a saint beyond my understanding.

She Who Hears the Cries of the World

Christina Feldman

Libraries are filled with Buddhist philosophy, but it all comes down to two things: wisdom and compassion. And they in turn come down to just one thing, selflessness, experienced by the mind and heart respectively. Compassion, the heart of selflessness, is symbolized in Mahayana Buddhism by the bodhisattva Avalokitesvara, known in Chinese as Kuan Yin. She is the one who hears the cries of the world and vows to ease the suffering of beings, and Insight Meditation teacher Christina Feldman says we can follow her example.

In the first century A.D. in northern India, possibly in what is now Afghanistan, one of the most graceful and powerful texts in the Buddhist tradition was composed. The text that is now known as the *Lotus Sutra* has as its central theme the celebration of a powerful and boundless compassion. It describes compassion as the expression of a liberated heart that pervades all corners of the universe, relieving anguish, pain, and suffering wherever it touches. It speaks about the spirit and the commitment of the bodhisattva Avalokitesvara, the Lord of the World, dedicated to liberating all beings from struggle and sorrow. When the *Lotus Sutra* was translated into Chinese in 400 A.D., the name *Kuan Yin,* or "One Who Hears the Cries of the

World," emerged, an embodiment of compassion that continues to occupy a central place in Buddhist teaching and practice.

Over the centuries, all the great spiritual paths have created symbols, have written poems and songs, about the innate beauty of the human heart. It doesn't matter what our spiritual, political, or social background is, we all long for tenderness, understanding, and safety. What gives meaning to our lives is to give and receive the care, sensitivity, and love that nourish our spirits. When we are young and when we are old, we depend on the compassion and care of others. When we are ill, hurting, or afraid, it is compassion that restores and shelters us. When all of our certainties, defenses, and supports are stripped away, it is compassion that heals us. Compassion is the greatest of all gifts that you can offer to or receive from another. An old Zen monk once proclaimed, "O, that my priest's robes were wide enough to gather up all the suffering in this floating world."

In temples, monasteries, and homes around the world, people begin their day by reciting the bodhisattva vow:

> Though the many beings are numberless,
> I vow to save them.
> Though greed, hatred, and ignorance rise endlessly,
> I vow to end them.
> Though the path is vast and fathomless,
> I vow to understand it.
> Though enlightenment is beyond attainment,
> I vow to embody it fully.

These words may sound grandiose or idealistic. But they are simply concerned with how you choose to live your life and interact with others. What difference would it make in your life if you engaged the world with a conscious commitment to end sorrow or pain wherever you meet it? What difference would it make to wake in the morning and greet your family, the stranger beside you on the bus, the troublesome colleague, with the intention to listen to them wholeheartedly and be present for them? Compassion doesn't always call for grand or heroic gestures. It asks you to find in your heart the simple but profound willingness to be present, with a commitment to end sorrow and contribute to the well-being and ease of all beings. A word of kindness, a loving touch, a patient presence, a willingness to step beyond your fears and reactions, are all gestures of compassion that can transform a moment of fear or pain. Aligning yourself with the path of understanding and compassion, you are learning to listen to the cries of the world.

The universe is full of beings, those you know and those who will forever be strangers. The world is made up of those you care for, those you are indifferent to, and those you fear or dislike. With those you love and care for, your compassion is often unhesitating; you reach out to console, support, and encourage without reservation. With those who are strangers, your response may vary. You may feel an indifference that you are ashamed of or a vague sympathy that is quickly forgotten in the busyness of your life. With those whom you dislike, your compassion for their suffering can be subtly mixed with an embarrassed satisfaction over their suffering.

Compassion is an invitation to cross the divide that separates "us" from "them." At times these almost imperceptible barriers are lifted. You see lines of pain in the faces of refugees or the homeless woman on the street, and your heart trembles. You listen again to the anguish of the person you resent and find that your history of struggle with him is released, as the hardness of your heart begins to soften. Suddenly you are present in a new way—free of prejudice and fear. It is as if your heart has expanded, revealing all of life in one organism.

The idea that you bear the responsibility for rescuing all beings from sorrow is an impossible ideal and perhaps is even arrogant. Compassion is a response of the present. How do you receive the person who is right before you? When you look at the myriad beings of the world, you also meet your own prejudices: There are those you are delighted to connect with and serve and those you resist, maybe thinking they deserve their pain. When you meet the hapless victim of a road accident or a child dying of cancer, your heart over-flows with natural, spontaneous compassion. When you meet the person dying of cirrhosis of the liver induced by alcoholism or the person imprisoned for violence, your heart may close, and you may find yourself deaf to their cries.

When you are faced with your own prejudices, you begin to un-derstand that learning to nurture a heart without boundaries is truly a journey that asks for profound understanding, receptivity, and courage. What would your life be like if you were able to turn toward this world without discrimination or prejudice and embrace it with the care and tenderness you would naturally extend to the person you most love? Compassion invites you to receive every instance and event of sorrow as if it has etched upon it the message "understand me, hear me."

The bodhisattva vow acknowledges and accepts that greed, anger, and delusion are endless. You do not have to be perfect to be compassionate. Compassion includes the willingness to embrace in a loving and accepting way all those moments of resistance and judgment. Compassion is concerned not only with how you receive others but how you receive your own mind and heart. At times you are afraid, agitated, or cruel. These are moments of suffering. Anger, fear, and judgment are not in themselves obstacles to compassion, but they become obstacles when they are left unquestioned. In themselves, they are invitations to compassion. Can you listen to yourself in the moments when you feel most enraged, afraid, or re-sentful? Finding compassion for yourself in these moments is the forerunner of being able to extend compassion without conditions to others, whose rage, fear, and confusion are no different than your own. Because you can understand the pain of those experiences in your own heart and are willing to stay present and be intimate with the pain, you can find the steadfastness and courage to be present for another person entangled in the same pain.

You may be tempted to postpone compassion, feeling that you have to first complete a self-improvement project. You have to fix your anger, your selfishness, your greed, and then perhaps you can open your heart and listen to the cries of the world. But self-improvement can be an endless project; it is an expression of a judgmental belief system in which you deny compassion to yourself. You feel ashamed of your negativity, fear, and the avalanche of pettiness and criticism, and believe you have somehow to erase them from your heart. Heroically, you try to banish your anger, only to find it replaced by jealousy. You may strive to overcome that and then feel proud of yourself. Pride becomes the new focus of your endeavors to perfect yourself, and then you are horrified to find it replaced by greed. At some point, it may dawn upon you that the entire project is motivated by nonacceptance and idealized notions of perfection.

A student instructed to meditate upon compassion came to his teacher in despair. "This is too hard," he complained. "I sit and try to extend compassion to the countless beings in the world, and all the time I find myself criticizing how my neighbor wears her robes, how much noise my roommate makes, how much my knees hurt, and how bad the food is. How can I ever get beyond this?" The teacher listened patiently to the long litany of complaints, then sat and pondered for a time. Hoping for words of reassurance or a shortcut to transcendence, the student waited expectantly. Finally the teacher opened her eyes and said, "These difficulties are going to be with you for the rest of your life."

Although this may not be a literal truth, it's worthwhile to question how you would respond if you knew that anger, fear, resistance, and anxiety might be lifelong companions. You could continue to deny them, condemn them, or try to purge them from your heart. Is it possible to embrace all that you are most prone to condemn or fear with receptive kindness? Can you accept the moments of anger and fear as guests, be willing to receive them with kindness without feeling obliged to serve them a five-course meal? No one likes being angry or afraid, but they are not your enemies. They are painful feelings that invite investigation, understanding, and tenderness. You can learn to accept these feelings with equanimity and allow them to arise and pass without blindly identifying with them or acting upon them. It is often in the hardest moments of our lives that we find the deepest compassion. To postpone compassion is to postpone your capacity to engage with your life in the fullest and wisest way.

The bodhisattva promises that "although enlightenment is beyond attainment, I vow to embody it fully." *Embody* is a key word. Compassion is more profound than simply entertaining altruistic thoughts or idealizing some future attainment. The great teachers and mystics of the past and present have deeply inspired us because they have embodied in their words and actions the wisdom and compassion we yearn for. We admire them not just for some remarkable spiritual experience that occurred under a bodhi tree, in a desert, or on a mountaintop, but because their lives have been visible manifestations of selflessness and freedom. They inspire us not through their aloofness but through their engagement and example: the Buddha who reached out to bathe the body of a diseased monk that no one would touch, the Christ who welcomed the outcast that everyone disdained. For compassion to make a difference, it must be embodied.

Compassion is multifaceted. Over the centuries Avalokitesvara, or Kuan Yin, has been portrayed in a variety of different forms. At times she is depicted as a feminine presence, her face serene, her arms outstretched, and her eyes open, embodying a warm, receptive presence. She is often portrayed seated on a lotus flower, symbolizing the opening and flowering of the heart and mind. In one hand she holds a book of teachings, symbolizing her nondualistic understanding, and in her other hand she holds a vase, signifying the pouring out of boundless love and compassion. In China, she is sometimes portrayed holding a willow branch, symbolizing her capacity to bend in the face of the fiercest storms and winds of life without being broken. The weeping willow represents her compassionate care for the pain of the world. At times Avalokitesvara is painted with a thousand arms and hands, and in the center of each hand is an eye depicting her constant awareness of anguish and her all-embracing responsiveness. Kuan Yin is also portrayed as an armed warrior, laden with a multitude of weapons. She carries a crossbow, a thunderbolt, a spear, and a shield. She embodies the fierce, uncompromising face of compassion. She is a protector and a guardian who is committed to uprooting the causes of sorrow.

Compassion is not just a feeling; it is a response to pain that is deeply rooted in wisdom. It is a commitment to alleviating suffering and the cause of suffering in all its forms. The human story is both personal and universal. Our personal experiences of pain and joy, grief and despair, may be unique to each of us in the forms they take; yet our capacity to feel grief, fear, loneliness, and rage, as well as delight, intimacy, joy, and ease, are our common bonds as human beings. They are the language of the heart that crosses the borders of "I" and "you." In the midst of despair or pain, you may be convinced that no one has ever felt this way before. Yet there is no pain you can experience that has not been experienced before by another in a different time or place. Our emotional world is universal.

Much of life is dedicated to minimizing pain and maximizing happiness. We have become more and more sophisticated in our technology—we can live in space and map the human genome. Yet we have not been successful in our quest to end sorrow. Our age-old problems of prejudice, cruelty, and division persist, simply taking new forms over the centuries. For fear, separation, and sorrow to end, you must understand their cause. You can search the world for causes, but in the end you must look within yourself. Mistrust, alienation, and rage are not life sentences. They arise in your engagement with the world, and they can be transformed in your engagement with the world. The classroom of the bodhisattva is life. True compassion is not forged at a distance from pain but in its fires.

Shantideva, a great Indian mystic, taught, "Whatever you are doing, ask yourself, *What is this state of my mind?* With constant mindfulness and alertness, accomplish good. This is the practice of the bodhisattva." Compassion is born of wisdom, through genuine insight into the nature of reality, through an appreciation of impermanence and all its implications, and through a willingness to be aware of the suffering and its cause. Wisdom and compassion are like two wings of a bird: both are necessary for the bird to soar; both are necessary for our hearts to open and heal.

Compassion holds within it resilience and equanimity. Patience, receptivity, awareness, and honesty are all part of its paradigm. Forgiveness and courage and a willingness to be intimate with life give compassion its power. The willingness to surrender self-centeredness and self-righteousness form part of the character of compassion. Your willingness to explore these qualities enables you to find courage in adversity and meaning in the moments of great barrenness. Compassion can rescue you from despair and blame and allow you to live with dignity and integrity. Ultimately it can bring to an end the most painful separation between self and other.

Compassion is sometimes defined as "the heart that trembles in response to pain," or as the capacity to "feel with." When you can truly listen to the cries of the world, you can begin to understand what Milarepa, a great Tibetan master, meant when he said, "Just as I instinctively reach out to heal and care for a wound in my leg as part of my own body, why should I not reach out instinctively to hear and care for any wound wherever it exists, as part of this body?"

GUIDED MEDITATION: COMPASSION WITHOUT BOUNDARIES

Settle into a calm and centered posture. Breathe gently and sense the life of your body, mind, and heart in this moment. Sense your own yearning for peace, safety, and well-being. Feel, too, the way you defend against sorrow and pain.

Invite into your attention someone you care for, sensing the sorrows in their life, and their longing for happiness, peace, and well-being. Notice how your heart can open to embrace those you care for, feeling their sorrow and responding with a natural compassion. Offer to yourself, to the one you love, the articulated intentions of compassion.

May I find healing and peace.
May you find healing and peace.

Let your attention rest gently in these phrases for a time, and then allow the range of your attention and compassion to expand. Sense the countless beings in this world who in this moment have their own measure of anguish, their own longings for peace and healing. Imagine yourself seated in the center of a mandala, surrounded by the innumerable beings who at this moment are hungry, bereft, afraid, or in pain. Imagine yourself breathing in that immeasurable pain, the sorrow and the ignorance that causes sorrow. With each breath, sense yourself breathing out unconditional compassion.

May all beings find healing.
May all beings find peace.
May all beings be held in compassion.

Allow yourself to sense the countless beings in the world who are ill or dying, who are grieving, who are lonely and estranged. Embrace in your attention those who are imprisoned and those who imprison, those who are caught in the terrors of war and violence and those who war and inflict violence. Without reservation enfold all beings in a heart of compassion.

May all beings be free from sorrow.
May all beings be free from suffering.
May all beings be free.

Let your heart fill with the compassion possible for all of us, the compassion that listens deeply to the cries of the world.

Death Don't Have No Mercy ⟫

A Memoir of My Mother's Death

Mariana Caplan

Here is something rare in this world: an honest account of a difficult death. It took courage for Mariana Caplan to tell this story; it takes courage for us to read it, for the terrors and loss of humanity that many people experience at death are not usually spoken of in our society. In a way, Buddhism looks at all of life as just preparation for the decisive moment of death. In this story, we see why this is so important.

> Well Death will go in any family in this land
> Well Death will go in every family in this land
> Well he'll come to your house and he won't stay long
> Well you'll look in the bed and one of your family will be gone
> Death will go in any family in this land.
> —*from "Death Don't Have No Mercy," by* REV. GARY DAVIS

Not many of us have seen another person receive a death sentence. Fewer still have been present to watch their own mother be given the final verdict.

I had returned just days before from Asia. Ironically, the intention of the trip was to sit at the famous cremation grounds of Varanasi in India and in Pashpatinath in Nepal, where funeral pyres have burned for thousands of years. I was trying to face death as intimately as possible, to take the next step in a lifetime struggle to come to terms with my ultimate fate. A Jew by birth, I had been practicing for a decade under the guidance of Lee Lozowick in the Western Baul tradition, a rare synthesis that combines Vajrayana Buddhism with the devotional ecstasy of Vaisnava Hinduism, adapted to the needs of the contemporary Western practitioner.

I engaged my experiment well, bearing witness to the death and decomposition of the body. I had contemplated death nearly every day of my life since the age of four, and such close exposure was somehow comforting—until it was my own mother who was about to disappear forever from my life.

My mother had not been feeling well while I was in India, and I knew I must visit her.

The day after I arrived we went to the hospital: my mother, my father, and I, a combination that hadn't occurred in at least a decade. The doctor came in with my mother's test results. He told her that while they had hoped her cancer had stemmed from the ovaries, in fact it was sourced in the pancreas.

In that moment, I saw something dreadful flash across my mother's face, something that even a woman who had mastered the art of concealing pain could not hide. I did not know what or where the pancreas was, or that cancer stemming from that part of the body represented almost certain death, but the look told all. I was watching my mother sentenced to death, which would come much sooner for her than for those sentenced to death by any court. It was a death she did not want and was not prepared for, and it was coming far too quickly to bring with it any reasonable chance of acceptance.

"What is the average life expectancy for pancreatic cancer?" she stuttered, her training in pseudo-strength regrouping itself with amazing rapidity.

"We think in terms of months rather than years," the doctor replied.

There were moments when I couldn't help feeling it was unfair that I would be motherless by the age of thirty-one. By the time you lost a parent you were supposed to have a family of your own—a husband to support you through it and the demands of children to fill the empty space. You were supposed to have matured into adulthood. You were supposed to be better prepared somehow. Your parents were supposed to have felt they had lived a full life, had drunk deeply from experience. Death was supposed to be a natural and expected consequence of a life fully lived.

Intellectually, I knew there were many who had it worse than I did—who had lost one or both parents at a young age to accidents or early cancer. My mother herself had lost a mother, a sister, and a brother by the time she was twenty-seven. My circumstance was hardly unique, and yet it was not the norm. People my age who had lost a parent were the exception. Everyone else seemed to have a mother.

Day by day, the inventory of loss surprised me with its accumulating detail. My mother would not be at my wedding when I finally married, the fantasy we had shared since I was six. There would be no mother to call and tell that I was pregnant. No grandma. No too-many-gifts for the baby. No one I could go to later to say, "Now I understand what you went through with me. I am so sorry."

Yet she had kept a sacred vow she had made to me many years earlier. Because of it I trusted I would have the strength to carry me through. She had promised me she would not die until I was old enough to be able to understand, to be okay with it. Twenty-seven years earlier, when I had first found out about death, when I had been told that I and everyone I loved would eventually die, I sobbed through endless nights, first for my own death, then for my mother's, and then for everyone else's. It was then she had promised me she would not die before I was ready.

I did not feel, as my brother did, that we had been wronged in some way. I could not allow myself the indulgence of thinking, If there is a God, how could he do this? I knew the Lord of Death was the same as the Lord of Birth. Still, there is something indescribably personal and intimate when the most common thing that ever happens in the universe happens to you.

I didn't know that hell had so many doors, so many rooms, so many details, so many different people in it. My brother arrived at the hospital shortly after the doctor had pronounced the verdict—my cherished big brother, my childhood hero, who loved his mother so—and there in the sterile white hall outside the elevator I told him his mother would die and we held each other and cried, without consolation. Later we tracked down my estranged brother in Cambodia, and still later watched my mother, half-dazed, bravely pick up the telephone and call her younger brother and sister-in-law and her closest girlfriends. We watched her see her young grandchildren for the first time after receiving such news, watched her trying to comprehend that she was not going to see these young people who were the light of her life grow up. There is no story more universal than this one, nor one more unique and singular.

Just when I thought it could not get worse, an uninvited guest arrived: the demon of denial. The first round of phone calls had been completed, the first shock waves passed, and my mother was puttering around the house. She had recouped some of her energy and we were acting as though nothing had happened. We were living in a fictional world where ideas of how we were supposed to feel replaced real feelings, and a logical understanding about the inevitability of death replaced the human sorrow of impending parting. We were all playing a make-believe game called "Let's Pretend Mom Isn't Dying."

People who study death from a spiritual and psychological perspective know that to respect another's dignity we must allow them to die the way they choose to, and not how we believe they should. While this philosophy is easy to adopt theoretically, the righteous meditator and psychotherapist in me wanted to insist, "But this is your final chance to lift the dark veils of denial. To finally face all that is repressed and say 'yes' to everything within you. To forgive yourself and everyone you imagine has wronged you. To use the last great opportunity while alive to understand life itself." But I knew I must remain silent.

Finally, as I prepared to return to my own home in the Bay Area, I sat down to spend the last few minutes with her, not knowing if these would be the last. Instead of sitting down with me, my mother took out her comb, fixed her hair, and used her small bit of remaining energy to put away some things in the kitchen. I could not blame her for choosing distracting activity to numb the pain and sorrow of yet another good-bye. How many times can you bear it? It is agonizing to do even once. For how do you say a final good-bye to your mother? The many times you rejected her, pushing her away to gain your independence, you knew she was still there keeping the hearth warm. But now you have to say good-bye forever. Each time I left to return to California I was sure it was the last time I would see her alive. Each time I left I bore witness to the degree of pain it is possible for the human heart to feel.

On trips to see her as the months progressed, I watched my mother lose one aspect of herself after another. All spiritual tradition tells us that we are not our bodies and that suffering is caused by an illusory misidentification with the body. Yet, in the face of death, such teachings are likely to yield only a vague intellectual consolation at best.

Within seven months, my mother lost one freedom after another: first, the freedom to drive, then to participate in creative action to affect the world, then to go out at all. She soon lost the ability to walk, and shortly after, the gift of hunger disappeared. I remember the two of us standing in front of the bathroom mirror as she commented, with a mix of irony and humor, that after thirty years of dieting she had finally achieved her desired weight.

I watched her measure each bit of remaining energy and determine its best use, relinquishing the attachment first to old friends, then to relatives, then to the dog, and finally even to the grandchildren, until only husband, children, and her own body remained. I lay by her side and watched these gifts being taken from my mother day by day, sometimes hour by hour, asking myself, where was God's mercy? I knew it must be there, only I could not fathom its logic.

Sometime before she died she was lying on the couch one afternoon while I kneeled on the floor beside her, holding her hand. I cannot say exactly when it was, because measuring time is not important when you are hanging out with death so intimately. The only reason to keep track of time at all is to ensure that enough morphine is provided. Weather doesn't matter. Missed meetings don't matter. Parties and new furniture and computer problems— all the things we normally obsess over—don't matter. All that matters is the love that exists between people, the capacity to bear the physical and emotional weight of death, and the nature of one's spiritual practice.

On this particular day we were talking about death in one of our rare moments of shared relaxation and acceptance. Suddenly a visual morphing took place and I saw what it must have been like for her, when she was even younger than I was, to sit just like this, in the house only a few miles away where she was raised, holding her mother's hand while she was dying. How quickly those years must have passed, and it would be but a blink of an eye before I would be lying on a similar couch somewhere, and my still unborn child would be sitting there with me, bearing the most difficult life lessons as well.

I shared my thought with her, and she said, "Mariana, there are so few things in life that really matter." She was talking of the ordinary causes of our worry and stress—a gray hair, a broken-down vehicle, a wrinkle, a steep mortgage, a lost job, a misunderstanding. It is not that such things don't need to be *lived,* and lived fully and completely. But instead of allowing them to pass with undramatic acceptance and recognizing the opportunities they offer us, we become their captive, foregoing precious moments to live fully the life we are given.

I received a call from my aunt saying that I should come soon. I caught the next plane east, wondering if this was indeed the time. When I arrived, I expected that she would be there, very weak but still conscious, and that I would try to embrace further the combination of agony and profound communion that had come to characterize the experience of being with her. Yet there was nothing that could have prepared me for what I felt that evening.

I walked into her room and knelt near her bed to say hello. Her body was there, but her limbs had begun to curl and whiten, no longer able to function. The suffering of the body had gone past the point of no return and had taken the identity of "mother" with it. *She* was still there, but she was no longer wife, mother, grandmother, sister, caretaker, philanthropist, Jew, gardener, homemaker, nature-lover. All were gone. Left was a still-breathing body with consciousness and a dwindling life force. Some distant remnants of personality remained buried beneath the torrents of pain continually assaulting her body. Her soul, her essence, her suffering body were there. But my mother was not. I was an orphan, experiencing my first moments on earth as a motherless child.

My heart broke. I could feel it physically, and I was stunned by the degree of breakage that can happen to the human heart. It was not "awful," because there was no value judgment to be placed upon it. It was far too true to be right or wrong. It simply was.

I think that most of what we call heartbreak is really a heart bruise, or perhaps a sprain or rupture. It is a heart contracted in fear or sorrow, or a heart pressured by the expansion of suffering. Only rarely does the heart actually break, and when it happens, you know exactly what it is.

There is a kind of pain for which there is no consolation. Ironically, it does not mean that all in life is lost. Far from it. A true acceptance of inconsolable pain means that we no longer need live our lives constructing false personalities and finding conscious and unconscious ways to protect our hearts from being broken. To allow ourselves to live heartbroken is to be freed from having to shield ourselves from life. We are totally vulnerable, offered to the mercy of life to do with us what it will. We are released *into* life.

The next six nights, the final ones of my mother's life, I alternated sleeping next to her, my back pressed against the steel bars of the hospital bed with my arms holding her, and lying on the floor to stretch my back and distance myself for a few moments from the suffering I felt lying beside her. Often I would awake from a few minutes of sleep to the sound of her choking, and grab the plastic container to catch the green and brown bile she was vomiting. If I didn't get there quickly enough, I would clean her up. Sometimes I would awaken to her moans and take her into my arms as though she were my sweet, dying child, talking to her softly long into the night. "It will pass. All things do. I am here. I am here. You are not suffering alone. It may not feel like it, but love is at the base of everything. You are loved. I love you. You are loved."

I did not know one could grow that quickly. Through sheer necessity, resources of strength I had not known kept revealing themselves to me. In such circumstances one suddenly understands the valiant acts of bravery performed in the face of tragedies and disasters as a force that comes through a human being as a consequence of love for another. It is not noble. It is nothing to be proud about. It is not personal at all. It is simply a necessity. Such awareness takes the remaining pieces of the broken heart and grinds them into sand.

I hear a lot of stories about peaceful deaths, leaving one to believe that most people die completed, at great peace. I've heard people say that so-and-so died without pain, at ease, that there was a kind of ethereal quality in the room, that there was a small smile on their face, suggesting great serenity and a graceful passing. Maybe those are the only types of deaths people really talk about.

The other kind, which are probably most, are both terribly difficult to digest and taboo to discuss. You don't go out for dinner with someone and hear about how someone's anger or attachment or fear was blown up to an unimaginable degree at the time of his or her death, and that the person left struggling all the way. People don't talk about such things, but I think they should, because it might help us to avoid the kind of death my mother experienced. Her inability to let go in life caught up with her as she was dying. The very cells of her body were programmed to hang on, to control, to resist, even when it was time to finally let go.

The day before she died, there was a sudden uprising within her. She had not moved or spoken for days, and suddenly her arms and upper chest rose up from the bed. She began to flail and moan, using all of her remaining strength to battle demons that surely exist, though not in a reality most of us live in. Her face registered a look of someone being beaten and slain, fighting for her life. Hesitating to enter a battlefield I could not see, I nevertheless approached her, put my hand on her shoulder, and began to comfort her as best I could.

My father, who was nearby, spoke to me firmly and told me to let her be. As I had always been rebellious, I had rarely listened to him, but this time he was right. In that moment he was a true father to me and husband to his wife. I backed off and let her fight her own battle. Finally, after an exhausting struggle, she lay down again to rest. Her defeat seemed certain and we expected her death within moments.

But she did not die. The body went on, and something eerie and deeply disturbing ensued. It was as if the wrathful entity of Resistance, the embodiment of control, stubbornness, fight itself—the Great NO—inhabited her body. It was as if the soul of my mother departed, leaving behind a dark entity occupying an empty, heaving shell of a body. When her grandchildren came in to visit her that afternoon, they ran with terror from the room, as did their mother. My brother, her own son, could hardly tolerate being in her presence.

I kept vigil, determined to love her and stay by her side to the last. I began to wonder if I was demonstrating love or simply attachment. I wondered if her bond with her daughter, my continued comforting of her, was keeping her alive past the lawful moment. I made a decision that was one of the most difficult I have made in my life. I spoke firmly to her heaving body, and to any spirit that remained, saying that I indeed loved my mother but that I could no longer support her enduring that much suffering. I told *it*, for it no longer felt like her, that I would sit there and offer presence and space but that I would distance myself emotionally and support it only to know that it must leave. It was the kind of gesture one can make authentically only in desperation. And so I sat there for the next day, holding vigil but now from the other bed, tending to my father's wish that I write her obituary so that something nice would appear in the paper.

How we know what we know in such moments is incomprehensible. We are plunged into another world, foreign yet intimately familiar, and operate under rules known only by our souls.

The day my mother died the regular nurse was off duty, and a replacement came instead. The notable feature of this woman was that, although by practical standards she was simply a good Christian and a middle-aged mother, she had a particular reputation: those who were stuck, unable to let go into death, would often make the transition upon her visit. She did not do anything to make this happen, or if she did it was intuitive and secretive. It just happened. She was an angel of death.

She came in and took my mother's pulse and vitals. The body was heaving, beginning to reek of death, though still alive. She said that my mother would die that day, probably within several hours. Then, as we sat by the bed and talked, she glanced over at my mother's body and said, "I was wrong. She is likely to die within two hours." Then, a few minutes later, "She will die within an hour." Then, "She will die within the next twenty minutes." And finally— the whole conversation taking place in less than thirty minutes: "She will die within the next few minutes. Whoever wants to be here should come."

I resumed my familiar spot, lying between her body and the bars of the hospital bed. My brother and sister-in-law came in and began the usual litany: "You were the best mother. I don't want you to die. I love you, Mom." Their words were loving and understandable, but I feared they were not what she needed. Communicating to her silently but as clearly as I could, hoping to override the voice of their sentimentality, I told her, "Let go. Let go. Let go into Love. Surrender into God. Don't worry about us. Leave us wholly and release yourself completely into the Light. Please, release yourself completely." It was the best way I knew to love my mother.

Suddenly, it all stopped. She had been suffering and clinging for what seemed an eternity. Then suddenly, she was gone.

There was no plan for that moment. There was no map to guide us. It was over. She was gone. We were all there and she was not and there was an emptiness so stark and wide that it seemed the whole world could fit into it. It went beyond the mind's imagining. How inconceivable a God that could create a heart capable of bearing such vast emptiness. The only mercy of those moments was the near-smile on her face after the breath left. The expression was that of a human being free from all tensions of incarnation, all pains of body and mind released.

I saw from the way my mother died that perhaps the best preparation one can make to avoid such a death is to practice surrendering in life. This is much of the purpose of spiritual practice: to learn—consciously, mentally, emotionally, physically—to let go. This learning can take place through service of all kinds: through mothering a child and learning to place another's needs and preferences above your own; through being a truly loving partner who makes conscious sacrifices for the well-being of the other; through the sacrifice of spiritual discipline in which one learns to persist in the face of preferences and resistance; to be no longer enslaved to the powerful forces of greed, lethargy, and craving.

There are thousands of moments each day in which we are offered the opportunity to practice surrendering to what is: to the traffic keeping us from an appointment, to another's suffering, to an unpleasant thought, to the many things that do not go the way we would like them to. All of these moments provide an opportunity to engage life in the moment, surrendering to it as it is, as well as preparing for death and the call for final surrender.

The moment of death will come all too soon. Whether it is a month or ten years or forty years from now, suddenly I will be the one who is on the deathbed. I will be making the choice to die unconsciously and hope for the best, or to look squarely into the unknown and jump, without waiting to be pushed.

I will not want to die, of this I am certain, but if I am fortunate enough to be fully conscious in that moment, may I die with dignity and elegance. May I bid farewell to the people around me in love and blessing, call trustingly upon my God for support, and then, as the precise moment draws near, go to the place where I am not separate from the universe, and let go.

If I am taken by sudden trauma, may I have finally learned to react with something more conscious than, "Oh, *shiiiiit*," or the childhood imprint of, "*Mommmy!!!*," bringing instead some name of God to my lips, perhaps even briefly chuckling that I have returned to being a Jew in my final moments, then rapidly adjusting myself to the mood of radical acceptance.

If pain and illness have overcome me so my attention is dispersed, may I find a moment of complete acceptance, fully allowing God's ravishment of my body. If my condition at that time is senility or sleep, or if the process of disease has demolished my conscious identity, may I have acquired a lifetime of habits based on intention and merit so that surrender, rather than grasping, will guide my passage. May the unconscious and dark forces within have been owned and received so that no hidden demons arise at that moment.

And if I must die young, may I die boldly, in an exemplary manner, having lived so fully that my life is complete already; having lived free from all compromise, knowing what it is to forgive and to accept. May I know no regret. May I die saying YES.

No Time to Lose))

Pema Chödrön

*Anger, greed, jealousy, lust—how often do these powerful emotions sweep
over us, seemingly against our will, and cause unnecessary suffering? How
we free ourselves from the energy of these conflicting emotions is one of life's
most important questions, and a specialty of the Mahayana school of Buddhism. Here the American nun Pema Chödrön brings her own wisdom to
bear on the classic Mahayana text* The Way of the Bodhisattva *to explain
how we can free ourselves from these emotional afflictions.*

Rousing the bodhi heart means connecting with our longing for
enlightenment, with the clear desire to alleviate the escalating suffering we see in the world today. Most people do not give much thought
to enlightenment. But most of us do long for a better world situation, and we long to be free of neurotic habits and mental anguish.
This is the ideal state of mind for awakening bodhichitta, the aspiration to achieve enlightenment for the sake of all sentient beings. We
know we want to be part of making things better, and that we need
to get saner to do this effectively. It's the perfect place to start.

If we can commit to pursuing this goal, we're on the same page
as Shantideva. Like us, he had to work with a wild mind, overpower-
ing emotions, and entrenched habitual patterns. Like us, he was able
to use his life, just as it was, to work intelligently with his reactivity.
The yearning to do this is "aspiration bodhichitta." Although we may

not always be able to stop ourselves from bringing pain to others, our intention to sort out our confusion and be of service remains unwavering.

In chapters 1–3 of *The Way of the Bodhisattva* (*Bodhicarya-vatara*), Shantideva shares his aspiration to make waking up and benefiting others his top priority. In the following three chapters, he provides methods for insuring that this bodhichitta passion doesn't decline.

This is a very important topic. When we're young, we have a natural curiosity about the world around us. There's a natural spark that energizes us and motivates us to learn, as well as a fear of becoming like some of the older people we see: stuck in their ways, with closed minds and no spirit of adventure.

It's true that as some people get older, they begin spending more time in pursuit of comfort and security. But Shantideva is passionately determined to keep his youthful curiosity alive. He aspires to continually stretch his heart beyond its current preconceptions and biases. Instead of staying stuck in his cocoon, he wants to grow in flexibility and enthusiasm.

The bodhisattva path is not about being a "good" person or accepting the status quo. It requires courage and a willingness to keep growing.

In chapter 4 of *The Way of the Bodhisattva,* Shantideva addresses two topics essential to keeping one's passion alive. The first is attentiveness; the second is working skillfully with emotions. The title of this chapter in Tibetan is *pag-yü,* which has been translated many different ways. Here it is translated as "awareness"; elsewhere it is called "conscientiousness," "heedfulness," and "carefulness." I feel the most descriptive translation is "attentiveness": paying attention with intelligent awareness of what's happening. A traditional analogy is walking along the edge of a deep crevasse: we're attentive and keenly aware of the consequences of carelessness.

Attentiveness is a significant component of self-reflection. By paying attention when we feel the tug of *shenpa,* we get smarter about not getting hooked. *Shenpa* is the Tibetan word for attachment. Dzigar Kongtrül describes it as the "charge" behind emotions: the charge behind "I like and don't like," the charge behind self-importance itself. Shenpa is the feeling of getting "hooked," a nonverbal tightening or shutting down. Suppose you are talking to someone and suddenly you see her jaw clench; she stiffens or her eyes glaze over. What you're seeing is shenpa: the outer manifestation of an inner tug, the subtlest form of aversion or attraction. We can see this in each other; more importantly we can feel this charge in ourselves.

In chapter 4, Shantideva gives five examples of when to apply attentiveness: when bodhichitta arises; before we make a commitment; after we've made a commitment; when relating with the cause and effect of karma, or consequences of our actions; and finally, when we are seduced by our kleshas.

The Sanskrit word *klesha* refers to a strong emotion that reliably leads to suffering. It's sometimes translated as "neurosis" and, in this text, as "afflictions" and "defiled emotions." In essence, kleshas are dynamic, ineffable energy, yet it's energy that easily enslaves us and causes us to act and speak in unintelligent ways.

Kleshas arise with the subtle tension inherent in dualistic perception. If we don't catch this tension, it sets off a chain reaction of "for" or "against." These reactions quickly escalate, resulting in full-blown aggression, craving, ignorance, jealousy, envy, and pride—in other words, full-blown misery for ourselves and others. Kleshas survive on ignorance—ignorance of their insubstantial nature and the way we reinforce them—and they are fueled by thoughts. That their power can be diffused by attentiveness is the main theme of chapter 4.

4.26
For it's as if by chance that I have gained
This state so hard to find, wherein to help myself.
And now, when freedom—power of choice—is mine,
If once again I'm led away to hell,

4.27
I am as if benumbed by sorcery,
My mind reduced to total impotence
With no perception of the madness overwhelming me.
O what is it that has me in its grip?

From moment to moment, we can choose how we relate to our emotions. This power of choice gives us freedom, and it would be crazy not to take advantage of it.

On the other hand, when habitual reactions are strong and long-standing, it's difficult to choose intelligently. We don't intentionally choose pain; we just do what's familiar, which isn't always the best idea. I think we can all relate with *feeling benumbed by sorcery, reduced to total impotence,* or overwhelmed by *madness.* But what actually has us in its grip? The answer is our kleshas: *limbless and devoid of faculties*—with, in essence, no substance or solidity at all!

4.28
Anger, lust—these enemies of mine—
Are limbless and devoid of faculties.
They have no bravery, no cleverness;
How then have they reduced me to such slavery?

This is the sixty-four-thousand-dollar question. How can this powerful but completely ungraspable, ineffable energy do us so much harm? In the following verses Shantideva begins to answer this question by presenting the five faults of the kleshas, the five problematic aspects of our confused emotions.

The first fault, presented in verse 28, is that we become enslaved by the kleshas. This insight alone would undercut their power, if we were attentive to it. But as Shantideva says, it's as if we're under a spell.

Emotional reactivity starts as a slight tightening. There's the familiar tug of shenpa and before we know it, we're pulled along. In just a few seconds, we go from being slightly miffed to completely out of control.

Nevertheless, we have the inherent wisdom and ability to halt this chain reaction early on. To the degree that we're attentive, we can nip the addictive urge while it's still manageable. Just as we're about to step into the trap, we can at least pause and take some deep breaths before proceeding.

4.29
I it is who welcome them within my heart,
Allowing them to harm me at their pleasure!
I who suffer all without resentment—
Thus my abject patience, all displaced!

The second fault of the kleshas is that we welcome them. They're familiar. They give us something to hold on to, and they set off a predictable chain reaction that we find irresistible. This insight can be especially helpful.

When we realize that we *like* our kleshas, we begin to understand why they have such power over us. Hatred, for example, can make us feel strong and in charge. Rage makes us feel even more powerful and invulnerable. Craving and wanting can feel soothing, romantic, and nostalgic: we weep over lost loves or unfulfilled dreams. It's painfully and deliciously bittersweet. Therefore, we don't even consider interrupting the flow. Ignorance is oddly comforting: we don't have to do anything; we just lay back and don't relate to what's happening around us.

Each of us has our own personal way of welcoming and encouraging the kleshas. Being attentive to this is the first and crucial step. We can't be naïve. If we like our kleshas, we will never be motivated to interrupt their seductiveness; we'll always be too complacent and accommodating.

A good analogy for the kleshas is a drug pusher. When we want drugs, the pusher is our friend. We welcome him because our addiction is so strong. But when we want to get clean, we associate the pusher with misery, and he becomes someone to avoid. Shantideva's advice is to treat our crippling emotions like drug pushers. If we don't want to stay addicted for life, we have to see that our negative emotions weaken us and cause us harm.

It is just as difficult to detox from emotions as it is to recover from heavy drugs or alcohol. However, when we see that this addiction is clearly ruining our life, we become highly motivated. Even if we find ourselves saying, "I don't want to give up my kleshas," at least we're being honest, and this stubborn declaration might begin to haunt us.

But I'll tell you this about klesha addiction: without the intelligence to see that it harms us and the clear intention to turn it around, that familiar urge will be very hard to interrupt before it's going strong.

Do not, however, underestimate the healing power of self-reflection. For example, when you're about to say a mean word or indulge in self-righteousness or criticism, just reflect on the spot: "If I strengthen this habit, will it bring suffering or relief?"

Of course, you need to be completely honest with yourself and not blindly buy into what the Buddha and Shantideva have to say. Maybe your habits give you pleasure as well as pain; maybe you'll conclude that they really don't cause you to suffer, even though the teachings say they should. Based on your own personal experience and wisdom, you have to answer these questions for yourself.

Verses 30 and 31 say more about the futility of habitual responses to kleshas, and the danger of welcoming that which causes suffering.

4.30
If all the gods and demigods besides
Together came against me as my foes,
Their mighty strength—all this would not avail
To fling me in the fires of deepest hell.

4.31
And yet, the mighty fiend of my afflictions,
Flings me in an instant headlong down

To where the mighty lord of mountains
Would be burned, its very ashes all consumed.

Here he reflects that getting emotionally worked up has consequences so painful and intense they could reduce the mightiest of
mountains to dust. But, again, the Buddhist teachings encourage us
to reflect on our own experience to see if what's being taught rings
true.

In verse 32, we have the third fault of the kleshas: if we're not attentive, the kleshas will continue harming us for a very long time.

4.32
No other enemy indeed
Has lived so long as my defiled emotions—
O my enemy, afflictive passion,
Endless and beginningless companion!

Long after those we despise have moved away or died, the hatred
habit remains with us. The more we run our habitual patterns, the
stronger they become—and, of course, the stronger they get, the
more we run them. As this chain reaction becomes harder to interrupt, our experience of imprisonment becomes more intense until
we feel hopelessly trapped with a monstrous companion. No outer
foe will ever plague us as much as our own kleshas.

Verse 33 presents the fourth fault: give the kleshas an inch and
they'll take a mile.

4.33
All other foes that I appease and wait upon
Will show me favors, give me every aid,
But should I serve my dark defiled emotions,
They will only harm me, draw me down to grief.

Shantideva warns us not to be naïve about the pusher; we have
to know his strategies and seductive ways. Likewise, we simply can't

afford to be ignorant about the power of emotions. We can neither welcome nor indulge them in hopes they'll bring us happiness or security.

When the teachings tell us to "make friends with our emotions," they mean to become more attentive and get to know them better. Being ignorant about emotions only makes matters worse; feeling guilty or ashamed of them does the same. Struggling against them is equally nonproductive. The only way to dissolve their power is with our wholehearted, intelligent attention.

Only then is it possible to stay steady, connect with the underlying energy, and discover their insubstantial nature. We can't be stupid about this process. There's no way to abide with our dynamic, ungraspable emotions if we keep fueling them with thoughts. It's like trying to put out a fire with kerosene.

4.34
Therefore, if these long-lived, ancient enemies of mine,
The wellspring only of increasing woe,
Can find their lodging safe within my heart,
What joy or peace in this world can be found?

In verse 34, Shantideva presents the fifth and final problematic aspect of the kleshas: as long as we are enslaved by them, there will never be world peace. We will have no peace of mind personally, and the suffering of beings everywhere will continue unabated. War will continue; and violence, neglect, addiction, and greed will continue endlessly. By steadying ourselves *before* we're taken over by our emotions, we create the causes of peace and joy for us all.

4.35
And if the jail guards of the prisons of samsara,
The butchers and tormentors of infernal realms,
All lurk within me in the web of craving,
What joy can ever be my destiny?

Typically we blame others for our misery. But Shantideva says we create our own *infernal realms*: our personal hells are interdependent with our klesha-ridden minds. In his view, we must take responsibility for what happens to us. If we give safe lodging to neurosis, then how can we expect it to result in joy?

Just before the Buddha attained enlightenment, his kleshas arose in full force. He was tempted by anger, desire, and all the rest; but unlike most of us, he didn't take the bait. He is always pictured as wide awake, fully present—on the dot—relaxed and undistracted by the powerful energy of the kleshas.

In one of the Harry Potter books, the budding bodhisattva, Harry, is put under a curse that creates an extremely strong urge to give in to the kleshas and do harm. The power of Harry's intelligence and kindness, however, is even stronger. He doesn't believe the voices of the kleshas or get seduced by their promises of comfort, and so the curse doesn't work.

4.36
I will not leave the fight until, before my eyes,
These enemies of mine are all destroyed.
For if, aroused to fury by the merest slight,
Incapable of sleep until the scores are settled,

4.37
Foolish rivals, both to suffer when they die,
Will draw the battle lines and do their best to win,
And careless of the pain of cut and thrust,
Will stand their ground, refusing to give way,

4.38
No need to say that I will not lose heart,
Regardless of the hardships of the fray.
These natural foes today I'll strive to crush—
These enemies, the source of all my pain.

Because Shantideva was a prince in the warrior tradition, it's natural for him to use images of war. His words, however, are not meant to convey aggression. The courage of the samsaric warrior is used as an analogy for the compassionate courage of the bodhisattva. We need bravery to nonaggressively stand our ground against the kleshas. With the weapons of clear determination, intelligent awareness, and compassion, we can short-circuit their seductiveness and power.

Of course, we may experience discomfort in the process, the same discomfort and restlessness we go through with any withdrawal. According to tradition, giving in to the lure of kleshas is easy in the beginning, but makes our lives increasingly more difficult in the end. In contrast, withdrawing from habitual responses is difficult in the beginning, but our lives become increasingly more relaxed and free in the end.

When we're going through klesha withdrawal, it helps to know we're on the right track. Shantideva remarks that—just as *foolish rivals* endure physical pain, sleeplessness, and even death—he will go through the anguish of detox to cease being a slave to his kleshas. He will not lose heart and give up because of pain or fear.

4.39
The wounds inflicted by the enemy in futile wars
Are flaunted by the soldier as a trophy.
So in the high endeavor for so great a prize,
Why should hurt and injury dismay me?

In the wars fought because of greed or hatred, soldiers proudly display their wounds: their injuries are like trophies for bravery. We can also expect "wounds" when we interrupt the momentum of the kleshas. In such a worthy endeavor as liberation from samsara, we could take pride in the suffering we go through. Instead of complaining, let's regard these wounds as trophies.

4.40

When fishers, butchers, farmers, and the like,
Intending just to gain their livelihood,
Will suffer all the miseries of heat and cold,
How can I not bear the same to gain the happiness of beings?

People go through hell for their livelihood. Fishermen go out on icy waters in the bitter cold. Farmers lose everything when there's an untimely frost. Athletes endure incredible pain to win the prize. We're willing to go through almost anything if we think it will pay off. What if we were that willing to do what it takes to nurture the bodhi heart? With this kind of intention, we could achieve the greatest satisfaction for ourselves and others—far greater than the benefits of any other pursuit.

4.41

When I pledged myself to free from their affliction
Beings who abide in every region,
Stretching to the limits of the sky,
I myself was subject to the same afflictions.

4.42

Thus I did not have the measure of my strength—
To speak like this was clear insanity.
More reason, then, for never drawing back,
Abandoning the fight against defiled confusion.

This is what distinguishes a mature bodhisattva, such as Shantideva, from bodhisattvas-in-training. When he says that taking the bodhisattva vow was *clear insanity,* he's not expressing feelings of despondency or inadequacy. He's saying it as an incentive to get busy, to do whatever it takes to live his life as attentively and wakefully as possible. Instead of indulging in guilt and other variations on the theme of failure, he spurs himself on.

The next time you are feeling hopeless because you can't make a dent in your confusion, you can encourage yourself with Shantideva's words: *More reason, then, for never drawing back.*

Every courageous gesture we make, whether or not we think it's successful, definitely imprints our mind in a positive way. The slightest willingness to interrupt our old habits predisposes us to greater bravery, greater strength, and greater empathy for others. No matter how trapped we feel, we can always be of benefit. How? By interrupting our defeatist story lines and working intelligently and wisely with our kleshas.

4.43
This shall be my all-consuming passion;
Filled with rancor I will wage my war!
Though this emotion seems to be defiled,
It halts defilement and shall not be spurned.

In verse 43, *this emotion* is anger. Although it is usually seen as a problem, Shantideva takes a homeopathic approach and vows to use anger to cure anger. Rousing his passionate enthusiasm for the task, he proceeds with all-consuming warriorship and joy.

4.44
Better if I perish in the fire,
Better that my head be severed from my body
Than ever I should serve or reverence
My mortal foes, defiled emotions.

As the years go by, I understand this kind of passionate determination and confidence more and more. The choice is mine. I can spend my life strengthening my kleshas or I can weaken them. I can continue to be their slave; or, realizing they're not solid, I can simply accept them as my own powerful yet ineffable energy. It's increasingly clear which choice leads to further pain and which one leads to relaxation and delight.

4.45
Common enemies, when driven from the state,
Retreat and base themselves in other lands,
And muster all their strength the better to return.
But our afflictions are without such stratagems.

4.46
Defiled emotions, scattered by the eye of wisdom!
Where will you now run, when driven from my mind?
Whence would you return to do me harm?
But oh—my mind is feeble. I am indolent!

Now Shantideva presents the bright side. He is joyful that he can free himself from the kleshas and expresses this joy from verse 45 to the end of the chapter.

Happiness comes with knowing that once they're uprooted by *the eye of wisdom,* the kleshas can never return. Their power evaporates once we see their empty, ephemeral nature. Dzigar Kongtrül recalls how terrified the youngest monks in his monastery would be by the annual snow lion dance. When they got older and realized the snow lion wasn't real, that it was only a costume, they automatically lost their fear. This is an apt analogy for the essential emptiness of the kleshas.

4.47
And yet defilements are not in the object,
Nor yet within the faculties, nor somewhere in between.
And if not elsewhere, where is their abode
Whence they might wreak their havoc on the world?
They are simple mirages, and so—take heart!
Banish all your fear and strive to know their nature.
Why suffer needlessly the pains of hell?

Despite all this war imagery, Shantideva is not really encouraging us to do battle with the kleshas. He is asking us to examine them carefully and discover their illusory nature.

The next time you start to get angry, ask yourself, "Where does this klesha abide? Does it abide in the person I'm angry with? Does it abide in my sense perceptions? Or somewhere in between? What is the nature of this anger? And who is it that's angry?"

Look closely, too, at how you fuel the kleshas with your thoughts. Just look at any thought and ask, "Where did this thought come from? Where is it right now?" And then, "Where did it go?" If you can find anything solid to hold on to when you look at the arising, dwelling, and passing of a thought, I'd like to be the first to know.

We build up fantasy worlds in our minds, causing the kleshas to escalate. Then, like awakening from a dream, we discover this fantasy has no substance and the kleshas have no basis.

My friend's father has Alzheimer's disease. Previously he was a very angry man. But since he lost his memory, he's changed. Because he can't remember what he was angry about, he can't fuel his bitterness. When he becomes irritated, he just can't make it stick. Without his story lines, the causes for anger dissolve.

Of course we don't always feel up to working so attentively with our kleshas. As Shantideva says, our minds sometimes seem feeble and lazy. But take heart: we don't have to gear up for a big struggle. The enemy is a mirage!

4.48
This is how I should reflect and labor,
Taking up the precepts just set forth.
What invalid in need of medicine
Ignored his doctor's words and gained his health?

Just as a sick person won't get well without following her doctor's advice, we won't be helped by these teachings unless we put them into practice. This is not academic study; we could study the *Bodhicaryavatara* daily, and still keep strengthening our kleshas. These teachings are a way of life. To awaken bodhichitta, nurture it, and have it flourish, take Shantideva's words very personally and use them whenever you find yourself getting hooked and carried away.

The Three Lords of Materialism ◎❨

Carolyn Rose Gimian

*Sometimes the spiritual path seems so straightforward—a lot of Buddhist
writing can give that impression—but that's because we're not paying
enough attention to ego's cunning. The genuine spiritual path, from ego's
point of view, is the worst possible news, and ego is capable of subverting
or co-opting any part of the path in order to reestablish its ground. Here
Carolyn Gimian gives us an insightful analysis of ego's strategy and, in
doing so, helps us define what is genuine spirituality and what is not.*

The Kalachakra tantra talks about a time when the three *lalos,* the
barbarian kings, will rule the earth. In the 1970s, Buddhist author
Chögyam Trungpa referred to the three lalos as "the Three Lords of
Materialism." That translation has been adopted as the standard,
perhaps because it so aptly describes the attitude that rules the modern world. Indeed, materialism is king.

The Three Lords are the Lord of Form, who rules the world of
physical materialism; the Lord of Speech, who rules the realm of psychological materialism; and the Lord of Mind, who is the ruler of the
world of spiritual materialism.

All Three Lords serve their emperor, ego, who is always busy in
the background keeping his nonexistent empire fortified with the

ammunition supplied by the Lords. According to the Buddhist understanding, the ego is a collection of rather random heaps of thoughts, feelings, perceptions, and basic strategies for survival that we bundle into a nonexistent whole and label "me." The Three Lords act in the service of this basic egomania, our deluded attempt to keep this sense of self intact.

On a simple level, these aspects of materialism deal with the challenges of everyday life: fulfilling one's needs for food and shelter for the body, food for thought, and spiritual sustenance. The problem arises when we begin to pervert these parts of our lives, adopting them as the saving grace or using them to protect us from our basic insecurities.

Why are you unhappy? What is it that you need in life? When you begin to think that the pink pair of shoes you saw last week at the mall is going to really rock your boat and rescue you from depression, that is the moment when the Lord of Form, or physical materialism, begins to hold sway. Think that all your problems will be solved by winning the lottery, writing a best seller, or being the winning contestant on *Survivor*? Welcome to the game show of the Lord of Form.

Just about any religion or spiritual movement will tell you that physical materialism is not the ultimate solution. It is an extremely powerful force, especially in the world today, but it is easier to deconstruct than the other two Lords—although not necessarily easy to escape from. Psychological materialism, on the other hand, is much more subtle, and religion is split on whether or not psychology, philosophy, and scientific systems of belief are enemies or friends.

The Lord of Speech rules the realm of our thoughts, our conceptual understanding of ourselves and the world. Why is speech connected with psychological materialism? Because we construct ourselves with words; we present ourselves to the world with speech, whether written or spoken. Your business card tells people who you are, as does your rèsumè. When you meet somebody, you introduce yourself with your name, and then usually you tell the other person a little bit about yourself. That's your story.

Behind the story, we are saying "This is me. This is who I am." Most of the time, most of us want to protect this basic sense of self at all costs. The Three Lords understand this perfectly and that's how they make their living, so to speak. If the Lord of Form hasn't convinced you that plain old physical materialism will satisfy you and keep you safe, then the Lord of Speech takes over the sales pitch.

In the Buddhist teachings, intellectual sharpness and understanding are highly prized. *Prajna,* or discriminating awareness, is thought of as almost a goddess of wisdom. However, using systems of thought to enhance our sense of self and to ward off confusion and insecurity creates a prison for the intellect, and in the end, we stop seeing clearly. We are no longer investigating the world with open eyes; we are just working harder and harder to describe our fantasy world and to solidify it until we think it's the real thing.

Science has served over the centuries as the handmaiden for the Lord of Speech, yet it has also served as a source of knowledge and investigation that tears down or deconstructs the illusory world of psychological materialism. Witness Copernicus and Galileo. They were huge threats to the egocentric universe, such a deadly threat that in Galileo's case he had to be branded an enemy of religion, debunked, and put under house arrest. Today, as far as I know, even the most extreme literal-minded religious fanatics accept that the earth revolves around the sun. In those days, it was heresy, a repudiation of who people thought they were and what they thought the meaning of the universe was. We thought God made the world and the whole universe for us, just for us. He made the sun and the moon for us. It all revolved around us.

Charles Darwin is still controversial. Of course, it's been less than two hundred years since he looked at the evidence of human evolution and suggested that we were related to other animals and that we were a somewhat random occurrence in the universe, governed not by divine providence but by a principle called "survival of the fittest." We might now accept that the earth revolves around the sun, but on this earth, God created us as his chosen ones.

Or did he? That is still being debated in our schools, our

churches, our courts, and most importantly, in our own minds. So-phisticated, educated people might scoff at creationists, but on a fundamental level, we all want to feel that we're special, and that not just we but "I" have a special place in the universe.

We certainly see ourselves as the center of our individual uni-verse. We seem to be wired that way: our modes of perceiving and interacting in the world bring everything back to what we experi-ence as "central headquarters," or our ego. And the Lord of Speech is waiting right there to tell us that this view of ourselves is a good thing, a great thing in fact. The Lord of Speech tells us that we should ward off any fundamental threats to our sense of self-importance by keeping our story lines intact and adopting those views of the world that support us, me, I.

Freud was another scientific researcher who threatened our sense of self, by suggesting that the conscious "I" was not nearly as securely in control as we would like to think. He pioneered the use of the term *ego* to refer to the self, though not necessarily in the same way the term has been adopted by Buddhism in the West.

For Freud, a healthy ego had the ability to adapt to reality and interact with the outside world. But he also talked about something called the id, that out-of-control little beastie that unleashes our in-stinctual desires onto the world. As well, Freud's suggestion that even infants are affected by sexual impulses and deep, dark emotions was an unsettling challenge to our persona, the nice but mythical person with whom we would like to identify ourselves. Today psy-chology has become much more tame and acceptable, and we often use therapy to help us feel more secure and to cure our malaise. Is this the predominance of sanity or the work of the Lord of Speech? Perhaps it is a little of both.

Religious and spiritual beliefs, when they are used to manufacture a sense of security and meaning, are the stronghold of the Lord of Mind. Sickness, old age, and death are unpleasant, painful facts of life, hard truths we find extremely difficult to deal with or under-stand. Why do people suffer? Why do they die? We have been asking these questions since we could frame a question at all. Everyone would like to feel that both their life and their death have meaning. The problem is, we don't find meaning in the living of life itself, so we want reassurance. We want to know that our memory will survive, or our soul will go on, or that there is some greater meaning to our suffering.

Spiritual materialism, the specialty of the Lord of Mind, is the tendency of the ego to appropriate a religious or spiritual path to strengthen, rather than dismantle, our sense of self-importance. Chögyam Trungpa, who popularized this term, often used it to point to the self-congratulatory use of Eastern religions and New Age philosophies, especially in the sixties and seventies in North America. It can, however, refer to the tendency within any religious movement to use spirituality to reinforce rather than to reveal.

We often avoid authentic spiritual engagement that involves humbling ourselves or giving in. A pernicious form of spiritual materialism, orchestrated by the Lord of Mind, is to imitate or ape spiritual experiences, rather than to actually engage them. We get high, we get absorbed in nothingness or the godhead, we have a cathartic religious experience, but all on our own terms. God loves us, the universe loves us, we love ourselves.

Genuine spirituality offers various paths to investigate what we might call the real mysteries of life. It offers the opportunity both to look more deeply into life and to open out further into the world. It offers exploration, it offers communication, it offers investigation. It offers us genuine questions. Spiritual materialism, on the other hand, says: You don't have to question. Do this and you'll be fine. Believe this and you'll be fine. When you die, you'll be fine.

The Lord of Mind keeps his fortress intact by banishing a sense of humor. Someone has even made a serious psychological discipline or spiritual path out of laughter. Laugh every day. Go ahead. Start now. Keep it up for five minutes. Keep going. Keep laughing. Now you feel better, don't you? You don't? You must not have laughed enough. Let's go back to the technique and start laughing again.

The Lord of Mind makes religion into a deadly serious business. If there are jokes, they are little in-jokes that don't threaten our worldview but shore it up. In addition to co-opting conventional religions, the Lord of Mind is happy to make meditation, yoga, astral projection, chanting, and channeling into deadly serious matters. A Buddhist minister and his sangha or a swami and his *sannyasins* can be every bit as pious and self-righteous as a Christian priest and his congregation.

Sometimes the Lords work together. For example, in pre-Nazi Germany, the Lord of Form was helped out by the Lord of Speech, it would appear. The difficult economic times made it hard for the Lord of Form to hold sway. So the Lord of Speech seems to have gotten in league with Adolf Hitler to construct a system of thought, National Socialism, that allowed many Germans to blame their economic problems on somebody else, a religious minority.

When we can externalize the threats to our self-existence, we feel justified, we feel strong, and we feel ready to kick some butt. This approach tells you who your enemy is, which also makes you feel good, because it assures you that *you* are not the problem. Karl Marx also employed this approach, although he fingered different bad guys: capitalism and the ruling class. He too used psychological materialism to shore up the realm of physical materialism. Interesting marriage that.

That kind of "us and them" approach is very powerful but very dangerous, because it becomes a rationale for hurting other people, and sometimes for using hideous means to intimidate, torture, or kill them—and all in the name of the good. In this "unholy" alliance, the Lord of Form, the Lord of Speech, and the Lord of Mind all work together to obscure the real threats to our security and to give us simple answers to our sense of fear and malaise. Holy wars and ethnic cleansings are often the extreme results when the Three Lords work together to play the blame game.

Any provocative or new way of thinking is viewed as a threat to be neutralized by the Three Lords of Materialism. Genuine spiritual inquiry can, and properly should be, threatening. Although Buddhism is an ancient religion, it is a relatively new discovery in the West, especially as a practice lineage, so that makes it potentially fresh and revolutionary in this culture. The Three Lords would like to dismantle Buddhism, but if that's not possible, they will do their best to appropriate it.

These days, the Lord of Form would like to make Buddhism chic. Have you seen the head of Lord Buddha in a gift store as a candle? You can actually burn the Buddha in your home, as an artistic or aesthetic statement, thanks to the Lord of Form. Zen—the Lords got all over Zen in the world of gourmet cuisine and interior decoration. It's even a way of thinking or talking: "Oh, that's so Zen."

This is somehow a little different than saying, "Oh, that's so Baptist." In any culture, the Three Lords figure out what you can trivialize and what you can't. In the West, in general, you can't trivialize the Judeo-Christian tradition. In the Middle East, you do not lightly show disrespect for Allah.

Several years ago, I saw an ad in the paper for the opening of a "Buddha Bar." The advertisement showed a large sprawling Buddha in a bathrobe, holding a martini, with part of his big belly exposed. I didn't see any letters to the editor objecting to this image, nor were there angry Buddhists picketing at the opening of the bar. I don't think you would get away with a "Jesus Bar" advertised by a leering Christ holding a chalice of wine.

Such caricatures often trivialize a culture, a minority, a way of thinking, or a genuine tradition that is not mainstream. Our stereotypes of the Beat Generation, for example, make us laugh at "Daddy-O," rather than howling at the universe as Beat poet Allen Ginsberg would have had us do.

When you describe the Three Lords and their territory in any detail, it begins to feel as though there is nothing outside of their domain. That's exactly what they would like you to believe. You may say, "Why bother to try to get beyond all this? Isn't this just what we generally call 'life'? What's the problem?" Fair enough.

Or perhaps you are be waiting for me to tell you how to get out of this predicament. I'm sorry, but I don't know. The point is that every person has to work on this for him- or herself. Any "-ism" I try to sell you to solve your problems can just become another static system of belief, another vehicle for the Three Lords of Materialism.

Here's a hint, however, and perhaps a twist: the solution is not necessarily to give up tradition. It could be, but traditions are the keepers of wisdom as well as confusion. There is that kind of co-emergent quality to life altogether. Problem/promise, neurosis/sanity, awake/asleep: they are inextricably bound together. Uncertainty, paradox, conundrum, irony: these confound the Three Lords, because they would like us to be certain about who we are.

Uncertainty: the Three Lords of Materialism don't know what to do in that space. *We* don't know what to do in that space, which is why we usually opt for some form of certainty, some solution, at that point. What good comes from uncertainty?

All the good in the world. The Lords can't outsmart that empty feeling that comes back, no matter how much you achieve. You may keep going for eons, maybe lifetimes, but eventually, even if you get everything you want, it's not enough. You can get all the power and material things, you can get all the therapy, you can get all the religion, you can get all the bliss, and eventually it will not be enough. When somebody has reached that conclusion, they might become desperate and kill themselves, which is missing the point, or they might begin to think about something beyond themselves.

Thus, if you decide you want to help others, that is something the Three Lords of Materialism really don't like. However, if you only sort of want to help others, that might be okay with them. A certain amount of volunteer work is fine, if it looks good on your résumé and you can check off the "help others" box in your brain. This may sound terribly cynical, but truth be told, a lot of helping others is about helping me feel better about myself.

However, even if you are doing good to make yourself feel good, if you keep going with the helping part and you get far enough down the rabbit hole, you may eventually lose the reference point of yourself. For example, Stephen Lewis is the premier activist in the West working on the AIDS crisis in Africa: he's definitely not in it for himself. Roméo Dallaire, the Canadian general who headed up the U.N. Peacekeeping Force to Rwanda: all he got was nightmares. Schindler saving the Jews in his factory in Nazi Germany: he ruined himself. Gandhi and Martin Luther King: it wasn't a "me" thing. You don't have to start with perfect motivation. Young volunteers who are just checking off a box on their résumé might get sidetracked if they go far enough, look far enough. One of them might become the next Stephen Lewis.

The Buddhist tradition, which exposed the Three Lords of Materialism for what they are, presents other clues for how one might transcend materialism and put the kibosh on the Three Lords. The alternative presented in the Buddhist teachings is called taking refuge.

In this case, it is taking refuge *from,* rather than taking refuge *in.* The swirling world of samsaric confusion is immensely powerful; it covers every single millimeter and millisecond of our experience. It papers over our mind with thoughts, feelings, emotions, perceptions, beliefs, and convictions. We take refuge in our wardrobe, we take refuge in our sports car, we take refuge in our B.A., M.A., Ph.D. We take refuge in our psychoanalyst. We take refuge in Astanga yoga, we take refuge in our families, we take refuge in our jobs, we take refuge in our gods, we take refuge, we take refuge, we take refuge.

The Buddha is an example of someone who walked out on this deception. He walked away from the palace. He realized that it wasn't actually that good to be the king (apologies to Mel Brooks). He walked away from every system of thought and every ascetic setup that was offered to him as an alternative. The closer he got to actually waking up, the heavier was the assault from the Three Lords—which by the way is an important part of their M.O. If you start to get out of this predicament, they will really come at you. The night the Buddha became enlightened, they sent beautiful maidens, every Playboy Bunny in the realm, to seduce him. They sent armies, they sent weapons. They threatened him. They did whatever they could to drag him back into the whole sordid mess.

What did he do? Nothing. That was his ace in the hole. The Three Lords don't know what to do with nothing. What can you make out of nothing? Who owns it? Nobody. And nobody is what they don't want you to become. Please. Be somebody. Make something of yourself. Buddha said, No thanks. That's what made him the Buddha. And if you take refuge in the Buddha, you are taking that as your example of how to live, how you might actually live your life. Does it sound attractive? Probably not. But it might be.

You can still live at home, keep your job, raise a family, even go to church—but it's not about you. That's the only thing. It's not about me either. And that is really what freaks us out. We know at some level that nobody gives a fig about us. When somebody is patting you on the back and telling you how great you were, or are, or will be, most of the time they are doing that so that you will tell them how great they are. The society of mutual backslapping has a big room in the lodge of the Three Lords.

There is such a thing as genuine friendship, appreciation, and communication. In Buddhism, that is what is meant by the sangha: the people who are also, together, on the path of "It's really not about me." It's not that we give up "me" all at once, but if we admit to ourselves and then admit to others that we know that this "all about me" is a big myth, if even for an instant we admit that, then it's never the same again.

It's like after you sleep with somebody. It's never the same. That's why the secret revelations on the sitcoms about how your best friend slept with your husband before you were married and never told you—that's why that story is both so funny and so unsettling. It is never the same. And that's the sangha. When you are being a flaming jerk and your friend, who knows this, gives you "the look," it deflates you just a little bit. Because you both know. That's the beginning of sangha. Take refuge in the sangha. Tell the truth. Just a little.

Then what? What are you going to do? Freud was trying to find answers in psychoanalysis, but he ended up with discontent. Einstein was trying to solve the mysteries of the universe and instead he found genuine mystery. That approach is called the path—taking refuge in the dharma, the teachings. *Dharma* just means "things as they are." Take refuge in that. Fundamentally, dharma is not dogma; it's about being willing to look, being willing to see. Like Galileo did. Like Darwin did. Like we all do when we are awestruck by beauty or terror in a moment.

It's so penetrating because you have let down your guard. It's terrible, wonderful. It's real. That is the point of meditation, which is the basis of the path of dharma: it reveals things clearly to you, over and over again in the most ordinary, insubstantial little ways.

The path of meditation is one way to get out of our mess. Start practicing with any motivation you want. Go ahead, meditate to make yourself feel better, and you might find a much bigger world than you bargained for.

There are other ways in other traditions. The Three Lords of Materialism hope that you won't find any of them, and if you get close, they have some good tricks up their sleeves. In fact, they are making me a big offer, a really good offer, to shut up. And I'm certainly on a first-name basis with the Three Lords. You better believe it. I'm going to yoga next week, I already own those great pink shoes, and the Lords are making me a terrific deal on a condominium and a seminar called "The Secret Teachings of Not about You" in Costa Rica next winter. And it's going to be good. I really want to get out of Nova Scotia in February. I'm ready to sign on the dotted line.

Wash Your Bowls

Norman Fischer

One antidote to ego's tricks is earthiness. Just chop wood and carry water, say the Zen masters, and don't make a philosophy out of it either. Poet and Zen teacher Norman Fischer discusses how Zen's emphasis on practical, earthy reality cuts through intellect and speculation, and eventually takes the practitioner to a deeper and richer experience of life.

There's an old Zen story that I like very much. A monk comes to the monastery of the acclaimed Master Zhaozho. Diligent and serious, he asks for instruction, hoping for some esoteric teaching, some deep Buddhist wisdom, or, at the very least, a colorful response that will spur him on in his practice. Instead, the master asks him, "Have you had your breakfast yet?" The monk says that he has. "Then wash your bowls," the master replies, the only instruction he is willing to offer.

Although this story might seem merely to illustrate the gruff, odd, and cryptic style of the Zen master, it actually makes a fundamental point. Zhaozho wants to bring the monk down to the immediate present of his training. "Don't look for some profound Zen instructions here. That's too heady and abstract. Open your eyes!" he seems to be indicating. "Just be present with the actual stuff of your ordinary everyday life—in this case, bowls." A commentary to the story, as it appears in one of the koan collections, says, "When food comes, you open your mouth; when sleep comes, you close your eyes. As you wash your face, you find your nose; when you take off your shoes, you feel your feet." Another commentary simply says, "It is so clear, it is hard to see."

I have always appreciated the Zen emphasis on the material, practical aspects of our lives. Like the monk in the story, I came to San Francisco Zen Center years ago with huge metaphysical concerns. A student of literature, philosophy, and religion, and a product of the sixties drug and anti–Vietnam War culture, I was full of questions about what was real, what was right, what was enlightenment, what was consciousness. The world that I had inherited from my parents, in which so much was taken for granted, seemed no longer tenable. Everything was up for grabs; reality, apparently, needed to be reconstructed. I came to Zen Center propelled by this spirit, and I was willing to go to almost any length to meditate, read texts, practice austerities, listen to lectures—anything to answer my all-consuming questions.

But my questions weren't answered at all. They seemed to have very little to do with the Zen enterprise as it was presented to me. Instead of study and discussion (the only modes of truth discovery I knew at the time), I was taught how to mop the floor, wash the dishes, and tend the garden. Actually it was very good training for me. It was exactly what I needed. And out of the grounding that this training gave me, my metaphysical concerns began to be slowly and soulfully settled. As it turned out, the answers I was looking for were not propositional. Nor were they to be found in spiritual experiences, enlightenment flashes, or meditative states—although there were enough of these over the years to keep me going. Little by little, through tending to the daily life of the temple in the context of regular, disciplined meditation practice and just enough Buddhist instruction, I began to live my answers instead of talk them, to breathe and feel them bodily instead of intellectually.

Sometimes the Buddhist instruction I received had to do with the religious teachings of the tradition. I did hear a certain amount about impermanence, about emptiness, about nirvana. But more often I heard about being present, simply being present with body and mind fully engaged. Once, in the middle of a long silent retreat, I remember hearing my teacher begin speaking during a meal in a grave tone, as if he were about to explain the secrets of the universe. "When you eat the three-bowl meal during retreat," he intoned, "you should eat out of the first bowl first, and then eat some food from the second bowl, and then the third bowl, and then go back to the first bowl. This is the best way to eat."

This kind of instruction, this style of training, is quite in line with the classical Zen approach. Master Zhaozho was not unique. Over and over again throughout Zen literature you read of students approaching their masters with many complicated matters, only to be brought back down to earth directly. "What is Buddha?" a student asks. "The cypress tree in the courtyard!" the master replies. "What is the Way?" "A seven-pound shirt!" Like the teachers of old who saw that their students' existential concerns could best be met here on earth rather than high up in the clouds, my teachers grounded me and helped me keep my balance. "It's right here—in front of your nose," they told me over and over again.

The word *Zen* means "meditation," and meditation is certainly the most well-known of all Zen practices. But the meditation practice this tradition emphasizes is not exactly spiritual contemplation. In the Soto Zen that I practice, meditation is called *shikantaza*, which means "just sitting." Soto Zen teachers continually stress the actual mechanics of sitting as sitting. When you receive meditation instruction, you are not given lofty objectives, mantras, or deep koans to meditate on. Instead the instructor will talk to you about many details of physical posture: the alignment of your ears and shoulders, the correct position of your hands and arms, the placement of hips and knees, and how to pay attention to your breathing. The instruction will be so physical, so concrete and specific, that you might well wonder when the "Zen" part begins. But this is the Zen part: the meditation practice is in fact quite physical. To pay attention intensely to the body in all its details, to be present with the body in its physical immediacy—this is the practice, and the depth of the practice derives from this.

In Soto Zen monasticism the emphasis on the physical as the fountainhead of the spiritual extends through and past the body to all aspects of monastic life. "Careful attention to detail," is the motto of the school. As Zhaozho instructs, monks are to be quite present with and careful of their bowls, their robes, their shoes. The temple work is considered not a necessary and unfortunate series of chores but rather an opportunity to realize the deepest truths of the tradition. Zen monastics take on the daily job of cleaning the temple inside and out, rushing up and down to wet-wipe the wood of the pillars and floors, raking leaves, cutting wood, drawing water. All these immediate physical tasks are seen as essential spiritual practices. The monks are continually taught that none of these physical maintenance jobs differ in any way from sutra chanting, text contemplation, or meditation itself. All is physical, all is immediate, all is the stuff of enlightenment. Meaning comes not so much from what you understand as simply through the way you do whatever it is you are doing.

Following a key text by Japanese Soto founder Dogen Kigen, called "Instructions to the Head Cook," Soto Zen temples, both in America and Japan, are especially devoted to kitchen work. Monks carefully wash, chop, and combine ingredients, clean pots and pans, mop floors, serve meals with dignity and beauty. Workers in Zen kitchens are instructed to approach their tasks, however menial or repetitive, with full religious attention, giving themselves fully to what they are doing. In Zen centers, "kitchen practice" is a revered undertaking with detailed procedures for the mindful care of food and tools. In our center, for instance, there is a "knife practice": knives are always washed immediately after use rather than being placed in a sink for washing later on (someone might be cut). There is also a "counter-cleaning practice" (wiping down with vinegar at the end of each work period), a "cutting-board practice" (different boards carefully stacked in different locations for fruit, onions, and other foods), and a "chopping practice" (specific ways of holding the knife and the food to be cut for various styles of chop). All of these teach the practitioner that the manner in which something is accomplished, its proper "dharma," as well as the way in which the cleaning up is done, is just as much a part of the work practice (if not much more!) as the result.

Careful attention to detail is not confined to kitchen work. The daily schedule usually calls for a period of mindful silent cleaning immediately following meditation. Even the maintenance shop has a Buddhist altar in it. Tools are to be handled with respect and put away in their proper places, not after work is done but as an integral part of the work. Monks and laypeople ordained in the tradition sew their own Buddhist robes and are enjoined to care for them as sacred vestments. Bowls used for eating in the meditation hall are to be handled "as if they were Buddha's own head." Being present with and respectful of all material things, as if each and every one of them were a sacred object, is a primary practice and a primary value. The head monk in a monastic training period not only gives lectures and meets privately with students; he or she is also in charge of taking out the garbage and cleaning toilets. These traditional assignments are seen as holy tasks to be undertaken with full respect and honor (remembering an old koan: "What is Buddha?" "A shitstick!"). For students in training, the sight of the head monk diligently carrying garbage pails or wielding a toilet brush with full attention is as much a part of his or her teaching as the words uttered in the dharma hall.

In training period, too, Zhaozho's words about bowls are taken quite literally in the practice of *oryoki* (formal Zen eating practice). Monastics take all of their meals with full formality in the meditation hall, eating out of a set of three bowls, which are wrapped ceremonially in a set of cloths, often hand sewn by the practitioner. The choreography of managing the cloths, laying out the chopsticks and spoons, receiving the formally served food, chanting, eating, and, yes, washing out the bowls with the hot water offered with bows and tender care is truly prodigious. It takes years to master and feel comfortable with the practice, but when you do, you find the movements enjoyable and beautiful. What at one point seemed fussy, complicated, and arbitrary, now having fully entered into the fingers and palms of the hands seems simply lovely in its quiet grace. Like playing the piano, which requires much clumsy exercise before fluency is achieved, the physical acuity of simply eating a meal is transformed through oryoki into a profound religious act. Such a practice of quiet physical carefulness—to the point where it becomes deep almost beyond speaking of it—has been extended from Zen into Japanese culture. Here the acts of making and drinking a cup of tea, arranging flowers, or writing a simple phrase with a brush on a piece of paper have become high forms of religious art.

Far from offering a path to transcend the material world, then, the process of Zen practice deepens and opens the material world, revealing its inner richness. This is accomplished not by making the physical world symbolic or filling it up with explanations or complications but simply by entering the physical world wholeheartedly, on its own terms. When you do that, you see that the material world is not just the material world, something flat and dumb, as we might have thought. The way we have always, unimaginatively, understood the material world to be is not in fact what it is. As the Zen masters show us, the material world is not superficial or mundane. What is superficial and mundane is our habitual view of the material world, which we have so long insisted on reducing to a single dimension. Dissatisfied with that, we look elsewhere for some relief, some depth. Zen master Yanguan knew this and tried to illustrate it for his attendant. "Bring me my rhinoceros fan," he said one day. "The fan is broken," the attendant said. "Then bring me the rhinoceros," Yanguan said.

To see the material world as it really is is to recognize its nondifference from the highest spiritual reality. For where is spiritual reality if it isn't right here in the middle of our lives in the material realm, bleeding through space and time at every point? Zen training is the effort to learn to enter the material world at such a depth and to appreciate it. As the story of Zhaozho indicates, the way to see the material world as it really is in its fullness is to be present with it and to take care of it. Thus, "Wash your bowls!"

All this is to say that Zen is quite a materialistic tradition. Far from proposing a spiritual alternative to materialistic life, Zen affirms the materialistic realm as nondifferent from the spiritual. In other words, Zen spirituality is not achieved through avoiding, bypassing, or transcending the material realm: it is achieved by entering the material realm in a mindful and thoroughgoing way.

Once many years ago, not long after I was ordained as a Zen priest, I visited my cousin in Miami. An oral surgeon, good at what he does and consequently rather wealthy, my cousin is quite enamored with cars. When he takes a fancy to a particular kind of car (once it was a Mercedes-Benz sports convertible, later a Ford Bronco), he buys several versions of it, so that he typically has a small fleet of cars, all the same model, in different colors and with slightly different features. On this particular visit, he was quite taken with the Chevrolet Corvette. Quite tentatively he asked me whether I'd like to have a ride in one, and I said sure. He rolled the convertible top down, and we went out onto the highway, speeding along at a good clip and stirring a wonderful warm south Florida breeze as we went. I was impressed with the automobile's smooth handling and considerable power, and I enjoyed the ride thoroughly.

On our return I expressed my enthusiasm for the car. My cousin was surprised at my reaction. Clearly he'd expected that as a religious person I'd have disapproved of his conspicuous consumption. Maybe I did. But apart from any ideas I may have had about that, I could appreciate the actual experience of the automobile and enjoy it. He asked me how that was. "In experiencing the material world," I explained to him, with all the didactic authority of a newly ordained priest, "there are always two elements in play, the material object—in this case a car, the highway, the scenery going by—and the sense organs and mind that apprehend that object. You need both object and organ to have an experience of the material world. We all have bodies, we all eat food. So we are all materialists. So-called materialists emphasize the object; so-called nonmaterialists, or religious people, emphasize the sense organs and the mind. But we all always need both. The fact is, though, if the mind and the sense organs are acute enough, even a fairly humble object can bring a great deal of satisfaction. Think of how much money I save by practicing Zen! I can get a lot of good out of just one ride; I don't have to buy the car!" He saw my point. Just as he spent long hours working on teeth and jaws, and more hours studying the cars he wanted to purchase, I spent long hours on my meditation cushion cultivating my mind and perceptions, each of us working from his own angle on the question of being alive in this material world.

Honing the sense organs and mind (which includes the heart and spirit) does take cultivation. It takes mindfulness, the skill of quieting the mind so it can be present with what actually is, rather than with received, knee-jerk ideas about what is. The truth is, what we call "materialism" isn't really materialistic—it is idealistic. In other words, it is not the objects that we are after in our consuming—it is what those objects mean to us and to the people in our world. If you don't think this is true, just consider advertising. While advertising may once have had a mostly informative purpose, now its function is to create an aura of emotion and ideology around an object, so as to make it seem much more desirable than it actually is. A friend pointed this out to me in a magazine ad for a van. In the photo the van was parked on a gorgeous beach, with its doors wide open on both sides. On one side of the van was a man reclining. On the other side was a beautiful woman in a bathing suit, lying on the sand with her feet in the sea. A luminous, almost ethereal, shaft of sunlight shone down from the sky, right through the open doors of the van and onto the woman's sensuous face. The photo, digitally touched up with rich colors and smooth surfaces, suggested something delightful, which had nothing whatsoever to do with the actual van it was depicting.

This is a far cry from "wash your bowls," which emphasizes taking a very humble object and making it magnificent—not by applying images of desire but by simply and repeatedly taking care of it mindfully. Once, the twentieth-century Japanese Zen master Naka-gawa Soen Roshi gave a retreat in America. The retreat took place in a rented school building, so there wasn't much kitchenware available for serving meals. The daily schedule included a tea service, and since there were no teacups, paper cups had to be used. On the first day of the retreat, after the initial serving of tea, the retreatants began to wad their cups to throw them away, but the Roshi stopped them. "No!" he scolded. "We need to use these same cups each day, so you have to save them." For seven days the retreatants used the same paper cups for tea. When the retreat was over, Soen Roshi said, "Okay, now we can throw away the paper cups." But the students wouldn't hear of it. "Throw them away?! These are our cups that we have used mindfully every day. How could we possibly throw them away? They are precious to us!"

My friends are always astonished when I tell them how much I enjoy shopping malls, especially at Christmastime when they are full of shoppers. I enjoy the feeling of joining together with other people who are out looking for gifts for their loved ones, anticipating a fes-tive meal with them, happy to be spending lots of money in a cele-bration of life. I am, of course, aware of all the waste and misery that also accompanies the holiday season, but mostly that is not what I focus on. Yes, the parking lot is too crowded, and yes, the amount of merchandise in the stores is overwhelming. But I can't help it, I still enjoy myself.

The contemporary American shopping mall may seem like a re-cent blight on social life, but the truth is shopping malls are as old as human civilization. I have visited Jerusalem several times and walked through the narrow streets of the Old City. They are now, as they have been for millennia, crowded with shops overflowing with merchandise, jammed in cheek by jowl with each other, shopkeepers shouting at passers-by to get their attention. I have also spent many happy hours at the great Indian market in Oaxaca, Mexico, where you see women selling tamales, butchers displaying sides of beef, and all manner of clothing, jewelry, liquor, and food, including the Oaxacan specialty, peppered grasshoppers. Although I don't buy much at any of these places, I enjoy the spectacle. I especially enjoy the feeling of being with the people, shoppers and shopkeepers alike—all of us brought together in one teeming location by the simple human need for material goods that we hope will bring pleasure, comfort, and sustenance into our lives.

In the end, commerce is communication, a way of being together, transacting, each of us helping the other to fulfill our human needs. Thirteenth-century Japanese Zen master Dogen says in his essay "Bodhisattva's Four Methods of Guidance": "To launch a boat or build a bridge is an act of giving. . . . Making a living and producing things can be nothing other than giving." I know that it is possible for us to engage in commerce as an act of participation and compassion—to buy and sell in that spirit. Through the process of spiritual practice, we can cultivate a view of material things that appreciates them for what they are in themselves and recognizes in them an opportunity for meeting each other on the ground of our shared human needs.

When you do business with someone, you are cementing a relationship with that person. You could see the relationship as adversarial (who will get the best of whom?), but you could just as easily see it as mutual, each of you providing as fairly and as pleasantly as possible what the other needs. It is within the power of any of us to cultivate an attitude of mutuality in our economic transactions. In doing so, we come to see our customer, our supplier, our dealer, our banker, as friends, people who, like us, want to be happy, want to take care of their families and earn a living. To look at commercial life like this and to conduct ourselves as if it were so takes sensitivity and mindful awareness. This we need to develop over time, working with our thoughts and responses just as we work with our breath on the cushion. Part of that work is to be honest and realistic about our own greed, our own fear, our own confusion. But if we can do this with enough clarity and patience, then it may be possible for us to conduct our economic lives with some peacefulness and enjoyment.

For instance, we could pay attention to our thoughts and feelings as we engage in the acts of purchasing or selling to examine honestly our attitudes about money. To what extent is our feeling about money connected to our sense of self-worth—our sense of being powerful and important, or weak and unimportant? Clearly money, in and of itself, has very little to do with these feelings. Whatever feelings of high or low self-esteem we may have, they probably exist independently of money. We have only projected these feelings onto money and are very likely conducting our financial lives in a distorted or at the least an unconscious way. Perhaps our ingrained, habitual, and unexamined attitudes about money are just the playing out of childhood conditioning. Having grown up deprived, we may be worried that there won't be enough; or, having grown up with plenty, we may feel guilty that there is too much or be constantly expecting more. Reflecting on this—not so much by thinking about it in the abstract as by observing in detail what we do, say, and feel as we deal with money—we can find a way to clarify how money actually functions in our private world. If its function is not reasonable or healthy for us, we can find, based on our honest investigations, the relief that always comes when something unconscious and dysfunctional comes to conscious awareness. Eventually we might be able to view money more clearly as a means of exchange between people, a convenient device for the distribution of the material things necessary for living. We might come to see money less as a source of worry, pride, or guilt and more as a way for us to share life together.

Contemporary commerce is characterized by its immense complexity. There is very little about it that is local. Goods we buy and sell involve unknown and unseen participants from all over the globe, many of whom may be exploited or exploiting others in the process of fulfilling our needs. To conduct our economic lives mindfully requires us not only to be mindful of our attitudes, the goods we buy, and our relationships to the people who supply us these goods but also to be as informed as we can be about the possible exploitation involved in our purchases, and to use our purchasing power to reinforce goodness and weaken greed and exploitation. When we know that a company or product is harmful to its workers, competitors, or the environment, we simply don't buy that product. When we know that a company or product is making a conscious effort to offer something useful in as harmless a way as possible, we go out of our way to buy it. When this is our consideration, price or convenience becomes less important than relationship. We want to give our business to people we can really support, and whose efforts we are interested in encouraging.

I suppose the effort to keep informed about companies we do business with (whose policies change constantly, and who seem these days to be bought and sold with alarming and tremendous frequency) could become crazy-making in the midst of the complicated lives we are all leading. Still, knowing that it is impossible to do it perfectly, we can nevertheless do it as perfectly as possible, trusting our intention more than our information. Information in the present age is powerful, but it goes out of date almost as soon as it's gathered. Intention, on the other hand, can remain firm and can help keep us on a wholesome course. While it is shortsighted to be uninformed, trusting to intention alone, intention's power to transform the world should never be underestimated.

It seems to me that the world is in need of a new economic theory to replace the one that is now in effect—unrestrained free-market capitalism. This system operates on the faith that an "unseen hand," as Adam Smith called it, will see to it that things don't go out of bounds. That free-market capitalism is, in this sense, fundamentally based on religious or mystical foundations has been more or less lost on us. There is, as we all know, plenty of greed, injustice, and gross manipulation in our economic system. Yet the world's capitalistic movers and shakers apparently believe in the mystical rightness of "the market," that somehow the market (which often seems to take on the proportions of a deity) will in the end serve us all as well as anything else could, and is less subject to corruption and disaster than other, more rational systems. In fact, the unseen hand has been relatively reliable. Although our world economy is in fairly terrible shape (especially when you consider its ecological costs), it is also miraculous that it is in as good a shape as it is (considering its complexity and the fact that it is ruled by people who are not as well-meaning as one would like). Many people starve, but more people are being fed every day. And little by little some of the more enlightened nations are joining together to cooperate for the collective good not only of each other but of the planet.

I don't know if Adam Smith ever proposed a definition of the "unseen hand," but here's mine: it is the sum total of human goodness, of our love for ourselves and each other, and of our hopes for a future that will be more humane than the present or the past. Perhaps we can trust the unseen hand to inspire us to more mindful consumption and production as time goes on, and to discover, eventually, some new organizing principles for our economic life. Until then—and long after!—we have our spiritual practice to guide our daily conduct as we go forth into the world, earning and spending as we must.

Dr. King's Refrigerator

A short story by Charles R. Johnson

Not all spiritual revelations take place in caves, on mountaintops, or after forty days in the desert; they can hit us in completely ordinary situations. Could one of the great spiritual figures of the twentieth century have discovered the truth of interdependence while rummaging through the refrigerator looking for a late-night snack? Why not?

> Beings exist from food.
> —*Bhagavad-Gita*, Book 3, Chapter 14

In September, the year of Our Lord 1954, a gifted young minister from Atlanta named Martin Luther King, Jr., accepted his first pastorate at the Dexter Avenue Baptist Church in Montgomery, Alabama. He was twenty-five years old, and in the language of the Academy, he took his first job when he was ABD at Boston University's School of Theology—All But Dissertation—which is a common and necessary practice for scholars who have completed their course work and have families to feed. If you are offered a job when still in graduate school, you snatch it, and, if all goes well, you finish the thesis that first year of your employment when you are in the thick of things, trying mightily to prove—in Martin's case—to the staid, high-toned laity at Dexter that you really are worth the $4,800 salary they are paying you. He had, by the way, the highest-paying job of any minister in the city of Montgomery, and the expectations for his daily performance—as pastor, husband, community leader, and son of Daddy King—were equally high.

But what few people tell the eager ABD is how completing the doctorate from a distance means wall-to-wall work. There were always meetings with the local NAACP, ministers' organizations, and church committees; or, failing that, the budget and treasury to balance; or, failing that, the sick to visit in their homes, the ordination of deacons to preside over, and a new sermon to write *every* week. During that first year away from Boston, he delivered forty-six sermons to his congregation, and twenty sermons and lectures at other colleges and churches in the South. And, dutifully, he got up every morning at five-thirty to spend three hours composing the dissertation in his parsonage, a white frame house with a railed-in front porch and two oak trees in the yard, after which he devoted another three hours to it late at night, in addition to spending sixteen hours each week on his Sunday sermons.

On the Wednesday night of December first, exactly one year before Rosa Parks refused to give up her bus seat, and after a long day of meetings and writing memos and letters, he sat entrenched behind a rolltop desk in his cluttered den at five minutes past midnight, smoking cigarettes and drinking black coffee, wearing an old fisherman's knit sweater, his desk barricaded in by books and piles of paperwork. Naturally, his in-progress dissertation, "A Comparison of the Conceptions of God in the Thinking of Paul Tillich and Henry Nelson Wieman," was itching at the edge of his mind, but what he really needed this night was a theme for his sermon on Sunday. Usually, by Tuesday Martin had at least a sketch, by Wednesday he had his research and citations—which ranged freely over five thousand years of Eastern and Western philosophy—compiled on note cards, and by Friday he was writing his text on a pad of lined yellow paper. Put bluntly, he was two days behind schedule.

A few rooms away, his wife was sleeping under a blue corduroy bedspread. For an instant he thought of giving up work for the night and climbing into sheets warmed by her body, curling up beside this beautiful and very understanding woman, a graduate of the New England Conservatory of Music, who had sacrificed her career back East in order to follow him into the Deep South. He remembered their wedding night on June eighteenth a year ago in Perry County, Alabama, and how the insanity of segregation meant he and his new bride could not stay in a hotel operated by whites. Instead, they spent their wedding night at a black funeral home and had no honeymoon at all. Yes, he probably *should* join her in their bedroom. He wondered if she resented how his academic and theological duties took him away from her and their home (many an ABD's marriage ended before the dissertation was done)—work like that infernal unwritten sermon, which hung over his head like the sword of Damocles.

Weary, feeling guilty, he pushed back from his desk, stretched out his stiff spine, and decided to get a midnight snack.

Now he knew he shouldn't do that, of course. He often told friends that food was his greatest weakness. His ideal weight in college was 150 pounds, and he was aware that, at 5 feet, 7 inches tall, he should not eat between meals. His bantam weight ballooned easily. Moreover, he'd read somewhere that the average American will in his (or her) lifetime eat sixty thousand pounds of food. To Martin's ethical way of thinking, consuming that much tonnage was downright obscene, given the fact that there was so much famine and poverty throughout the rest of the world. He made himself a promise—a small prayer—to eat just a little, only enough tonight to replenish his tissues.

He made his way cautiously through the dark, seven-room house, his footsteps echoing on the hardwood floors as if he was in a swimming pool, scuffing from the smoke-filled den to the living room, where he circled around the baby grand piano his wife practiced on for church recitals, then past her choices in decoration— two African masks on one wall and West Indian gourds on the mantel above the fireplace—to the kitchen. There, he clicked on the overhead light, then drew open the door to the refrigerator.

Scratching his stomach, he gazed—and gazed—at four well-stocked shelves of food. He saw a Florida grapefruit and a California orange. On one of the middle shelves he saw corn and squash, both native to North America, and introduced by Indians to Europe in the fifteenth century through Columbus. To the right of that, his eyes tracked bright yellow slices of pineapple from Hawaii, truffles from England, and a half-eaten Mexican tortilla. Martin took a step back, cocking his head to one side, less hungry now than curious about what his wife had found at a public market, and stacked inside their refrigerator without telling him.

He began to empty the refrigerator and heavily packed food cabinets, placing everything on the table and kitchen counter and, when those were filled, on the flower-printed linoleum floor, taking things out slowly at first, his eyes squinted, scrutinizing each item like an old woman on a fixed budget at the bargain table in a grocery store. Then he worked quickly, bewitched, chuckling to himself as he tore apart his wife's tidy, well-scrubbed, Christian kitchen. He removed all the beryline olives from a thick glass jar and held each one up to the light, as if perhaps he'd never really *seen* an olive before, or seen one so clearly. Of one thing he was sure: No two olives were the same. Within fifteen minutes Martin stood surrounded by a galaxy of food.

From one corner of the kitchen floor to the other, there were popular American items such as pumpkin pie and hot dogs, but also heavy, sour-sweet dishes like German sauerkraut and schnitzel right beside Tibetan rice, one of the staples of the Far East, all sorts of spices, and the macaroni, spaghetti, and ravioli favored by Italians. There were bricks of cheese and wine from French vineyards, coffee from Brazil, and from China and India black and green teas that probably had been carried from fields to faraway markets on the heads of women, or the backs of donkeys, horses, and mules. All of human culture, history, and civilization lay unscrolled at his feet, and he had only to step into his kitchen to discover it. No one people or tribe, living in one place on this planet, could produce the endless riches for the palate that he'd just pulled from his refrigerator. He looked around the disheveled room, and he saw in each succulent fruit, each slice of bread, and each grain of rice a fragile, inescapable network of mutuality in which all earthly creatures were codependent, integrated, and tied in a single garment of destiny. He recalled Exodus 25:30, and realized that all this before him was showbread. From the floor Martin picked up a Golden Delicious apple, took a bite from it, and instantly prehended the haze of heat from summers past, the roots of the tree from which the fruit had been taken, the cycles of sun and rain and seasons, the earth, and even those who tended the orchard. Then he slowly put the apple down, feeling not so much hunger now as a profound indebtedness and thanksgiving—to everyone and everything in Creation. For was not *he* too the product of infinite causes and the full, miraculous orchestration of Being stretching back to the beginning of time?

At that moment his wife came into the disaster area that was their kitchen, half asleep, wearing blue slippers and an old housecoat over her nightgown. When she saw what her philosopher husband had done, she said, *Oh!* And promptly disappeared from the room. A moment later she was back, having composed herself and put on her glasses, but her voice was barely above a whisper:

"Are you all right?"

"Of course, I am! I've never felt better!" he said. "The whole universe is inside our refrigerator!"

She blinked.

"Really? You don't mean that, do you? Honey, have you been drinking? I've told you time and again that that orange juice and vodka you like so much isn't good for you, and if anyone at church smells it on your breath—"

"If you must know, I was hard at work on my dissertation an hour ago. I didn't drink a drop of *anything*—except coffee."

"Well, that explains—" she said.

"No, you don't understand! I was trying to write my speech for Sunday, but—but—I couldn't think of anything, and I got hungry . . ."

She stared at the food heaped on the floor. "*This* hungry?"

"Well, no." His mouth wobbled, and now he was no longer thinking about the metaphysics of food but, instead, of how the mess he'd made must look through her eyes. And, more important, how *he* must look through her eyes. "I think I've got my sermon, or at least something I might use later. It's so obvious to me now!" He could tell by the tilt of her head and the twitching of her nose that she didn't think any of this was obvious at all. "When we get up in the morning, we go into the bathroom where we reach for a sponge provided for us by a Pacific Islander. We reach for soap created by a Frenchman. The towel is provided by a Turk. Before we leave for our jobs, we are beholden to more than half the world."

"Yes, dear." She sighed. "I can see that, but what about my kitchen? You *know* I'm hosting the Ladies Prayer Circle today at eight o'clock. That's seven hours from now. Please tell me you're going to clean up everything before you go to bed."

"But I have a sermon to write! What I'm saying—*trying* to say— is that whatever affects one directly, affects *all* indirectly!"

"Oh, yes, I'm sure all this is going to have a remarkable effect on the Ladies Prayer Circle—"

"Sweetheart . . ." He held up a grapefruit and a head of lettuce, "I had a *revelation* tonight. Do you know how rare that is? Those things don't come easy. Just ask Meister Eckhart or Martin Luther—you know Luther experienced enlightenment on the toilet, don't you? Ministers only get maybe one or two revelations in a lifetime. But *you* made it possible for me to have a vision when I opened the re- frigerator." All at once, he had a discomfiting thought. "How much *did* you spend for groceries last week?"

"I bought extra things for the Ladies Prayer Circle," she said. "Don't ask how much and I won't ask why you've turned the kitchen inside out." Gracefully, like an angel, or the perfect wife in the Book of Proverbs, she stepped toward him over cans and containers, plates of leftovers and bowls of chili. She placed her hand on his cheek, like a mother might do with her gifted and exasperating child, a prodigy who had just torched his bedroom in a scientific experiment. Then she wrapped her arms around him, slipped her hands under his sweater, and gave him a good, long kiss—by the time they were fin- ished, her glasses were fogged. Stepping back, she touched the tip of his nose with her finger, and turned to leave. "Don't stay up too late," she said. "Put everything back before it spoils. And come to bed—I'll be waiting."

Martin watched her leave and said, "Yes, dear," still holding a very spiritually understood grapefruit in one hand and an ontologically clarified head of lettuce in the other. He started putting everything back on the shelves, deciding as he did so that while his sermon could wait until morning, his new wife definitely should not.

Coming to Our Senses

Jon Kabat-Zinn

We usually think of meditation as something separate from our lives, some-
thing special we do sitting on a cushion in a quiet place. Of course, that's
where it starts, but that's not where it ends. Otherwise, what's the point?
The goal of the spiritual path is to live every moment of our lives with
mindfulness—with care, attentiveness, and wholeness. Jon Kabat-Zinn has
brought hundreds of thousands of people to meditation practice through his
Mindfulness-Based Stress Reduction program and his best-selling books. He
believes that living mindfully is the answer not only to our own suffering
but also to the problems that threaten humanity's very future. But it all
starts on that cushion in a quiet place.

> It may be when we no longer know what to do,
> we have come to our real work,
> and that when we no longer know which way to go,
> we have begun our real journey.
> —WENDELL BERRY

I don't know about you, but for myself, it feels like we are at a critical juncture of life on this planet. It could go any number of different ways. It seems that the world is on fire and so are our hearts,
inflamed with fear and uncertainty, lacking all conviction, and often
filled with passionate but unwise intensity. How we manage to see

ourselves and the world at this juncture will make a huge difference in the way things unfold. What emerges for us as individuals and as a society in future moments will be shaped in large measure by whether and how we make use of our innate and incomparable capacity for awareness in this moment. It will be shaped by what we choose to do to heal the underlying distress, dissatisfaction, and outright dis-ease of our lives and of our times, even as we nourish and protect all that is good and beautiful and healthy in ourselves and in the world.

The challenge is one of coming to our senses, both individually and as a species. I think it is fair to say that there is considerable movement in that direction worldwide, with little noticed and even less understood rivulets and streams of human creativity and goodness and caring feeding into growing rivers of openhearted wakefulness and compassion and wisdom. Where the adventure is taking us as a species, and in our individual private lives, even from one day to the next, is unknown. The destination of this collective journey we are caught up in is neither fixed nor predetermined, which is to say there is no destination, only the journey itself. What we are facing now and how we hold and understand this moment shapes what might emerge in the next moment, and the next, and shapes it in ways that are undetermined and, when all is said and done, undeterminable, mysterious.

But one thing is certain: This is a journey that we are all on, everybody on the planet, whether we like it or not; whether we know it or not; whether it is unfolding according to plan or not. Life is what it is about, and the challenge of living it as if it really mattered. Being human, we always have a choice in this regard. We can either be passively carried along by forces and habits that remain stubbornly unexamined and that imprison us in distorting dreams and potential nightmares, or we can engage in our lives by waking up to them and participating fully in their unfolding, whether we "like" what is happening in any moment or not. Only when we wake up do our lives become real and have even a chance of being liberated from our individual and collective delusions, diseases, and suffering.

Years ago, a meditation teacher opened an interview with me on a ten-day, almost entirely silent retreat by asking, "How is the world treating you?" I mumbled some response or other to the effect that things were going OK. Then he asked me, "And how are you treating the world?"

I was quite taken aback. It was the last question I was expecting. It was clear that he didn't mean it in a general way. He wasn't making pleasant conversation. He meant right there, on the retreat, that day, in what may have seemed to me at the time like little, even trivial ways. I thought I was more or less leaving "the world" in going to this retreat, but his comment drove home to me that there is no leaving the world, and that how I was relating to it in any and every moment, even in this artificially simplified environment, was important, in fact critical to my ultimate purpose in being there. I realized in that moment that I had a lot to learn about why I was even there in the first place, what meditation was really all about, and underlying it all, what I was really doing with my life.

Over the years, I gradually came to see the obvious, that the two questions were actually different sides of the same coin. For we are in intimate relationship with the world in all our moments. The give-and-take of that rationality is continually shaping our lives. It also shapes and defines the very world in which we live and in which our experiences unfold. Much of the time, we see these two aspects of life, how the world is treating me and how I am treating the world, as independent. Have you noticed how easily we can get caught up in thinking of ourselves as players on an inert stage, as if the world were only "out there" and not also "in here"? Have you noticed that we often act as if there were a significant separation between out there and in here, when our experience tells us that it is the thinnest of membranes, really no separation at all? Even if we sense the intimate relationship between outer and inner, still, we can be fairly insensitive to the ways our lives actually impinge upon and shape the world and the ways in which the world shapes our lives in a symbiotic dance of reciprocity and interdependence on every level, from intimacy with our own bodies and minds and what they are going through, to how we are relating to our family members; from our buying habits to what we think of the news we watch or don't watch on TV, to how we act or don't act within the larger world of the body politic.

That insensitivity is particularly onerous, even destructive, when we attempt, as we so often do, to force things to be a certain way, "my way," without regard for the potential violence, even on the tiniest but still significant scale, that such a break in the rhythm of things carries with it. Sooner or later, such forcing denies the reciprocity, the beauty of the give-and-take, and the complexity of the dance itself; we wind up stepping, wittingly or unwittingly, on a lot of toes. Such insensitivity, such out-of-touchness, isolates us from our own possibilities. In refusing to acknowledge how things actually are in any moment, perhaps because we don't want them to be that way, and in attempting to compel a situation or a relationship to be the way we want it to be out of fear that otherwise we may not get our needs met, we are forgetting that most of the time we hardly know what our own way really is; we only think we do. And we forget that this dance is one of extraordinary complexity as well as simplicity, and that new and interesting things happen when we do not collapse in the presence of our fears, and instead stop imposing and start living our truth, well beyond our limited ability to assert tight control over anything for very long.

As individuals and as a species, we can no longer afford to ignore this fundamental characteristic of our reciprocity and interconnectedness, nor can we ignore how interesting new possibilities emerge out of our yearnings and our intentions when we are, each in our own way, actually true to them, however mysterious or opaque they may at times feel to us. Through our sciences, through our philosophies, our histories, and our spiritual traditions, we have come to see that our health and well-being as individuals, our happiness, and actually even the continuity of the germ line, that life stream that we are only a momentary bubble in, that way in which we are the life-givers and world-builders for our future generations, depend on how we choose to live our own lives while we have them to live.

At the same time, as a culture, we have to come to see that the very Earth on which we live, to say nothing of the well-being of its creatures and its cultures, depends in huge measure on those same choices, writ large through our collective behavior as social beings.

To take just one example, global temperatures can be accurately charted back at least 400,000 years and can be shown to fluctuate between extremes of hot and cold. We are in a relatively warm period, not any warmer than any of the other warm eras Earth has experienced. However, I was staggered to learn recently, in a meeting between the Dalai Lama and a group of scientists, that in the past forty-four years, atmospheric CO_2 levels have shot up by 18 percent, to a level that is higher than it has been in the past 160,000 years, as measured by carbon dioxide in snow cores in Antarctica. And the level is continuing to rise at an ever-increasing rate.

This dramatic and alarming recent increase in atmospheric CO_2 is entirely due to the activity of human beings. If unchecked, the Intergovernmental Panel on Climate Change predicts that levels of atmospheric CO_2 will double by 2100 and as a result, the average global temperature may rise dramatically. One consequence seems to be that there is already open water at the North Pole, ice is melting at both poles, and glaciers worldwide are disappearing. The potential consequences in terms of triggering chaotic fluctuations destabilizing the climate worldwide are sobering, if not terrifying. While intrinsically unpredictable, they include a possible dramatic rise in sea level in a relatively short period of time, and the consequent flooding of all coastal habitations and cities worldwide. Imagine Manhattan if the ocean rises fifty feet.

We could say that this is one symptom, and only one of many, of a kind of autoimmune disease of the earth, in that one aspect of human activity is seriously undermining the overall dynamic balance of the body of the earth as a whole. Do we know? Do we care? Is it somebody else's problem? "Their" problem, whoever "they" are . . . scientists, governments, politicians, utility companies, the auto industry? Is it possible, if we are really all part of one body, to collectively come to our senses on this issue and restore some kind of dynamic balance? Can we do that for any of the other ways in which our activity as a species threatens our very lives and the lives of generations to come, and in fact, the lives of many other species as well?

To my mind, it is past time for us to pay attention to what we already know or sense, not just in the outer world of our relationships with others and with our surroundings, but in the interior world of our own thoughts and feelings, aspirations and fears, hopes and dreams. All of us, no matter who we are or where we live, have certain things in common. For the most part, we share the desire to live our lives in peace, to pursue our private yearnings and creative impulses, to contribute in meaningful ways to a larger purpose, to fit in and belong and be valued for who we are, to flourish as individuals and as families, and as societies of purpose and of mutual regard, to live in individual dynamic balance, which is health, and in collective dynamic balance, what used to be called the "commonweal," which honors our differences and optimizes our mutual creativity and the possibility for a future free from wanton harm and from that which threatens what is most vital to our well-being and our very being.

Such a collective dynamic balance, in my view, would feel a lot like heaven, or at least like being comfortably at home. It is what peace feels like, when we really have peace and know peace, inwardly and outwardly. It is like being at home in the deepest of ways. Isn't that somehow what we are all claiming we really want?

Ironically, such balance is already at our fingertips at all times, in little ways that are not so little and have nothing to do with wishful thinking, rigid or authoritarian control, or utopias. Such balance is already here when we tune in to our bodies and minds and to those forces that move us forward through the day and through the years, namely our motivation and our vision of what is worth living for and what needs undertaking. It is here in the small acts of kindness that happen between strangers and in families and even, in times of war, between supposed enemies. It is here every time we recycle our bottles and newspapers, or think to conserve water, or act with others to care for our neighborhood or protect our dwindling wilderness areas and other species with whom we share this planet.

If we are suffering from an autoimmune disease of our very planet, and if the cause of that autoimmune disease stems from the activity and the mind states of human beings, then we might do well to consider what we might learn from the leading edge of modern medicine about the most effective approaches to such conditions. It turns out that in the past thirty years, medicine has come to know, from a remarkable blossoming of research and clinical practices in the field variously known as the mind/body medicine, behavioral medicine, psychosomatic medicine, and integrative medicine, that the mysterious, dynamic balance we call "health" involves both the body and the mind (to use our awkward and artificial way of speaking that bizarrely splits them from one another), and can be enhanced by specific qualities of attention that can be sustaining, restorative, and healing. It turns out that we all have, lying deep within us, in our hearts and in our very bones, a capacity for a dynamic, vital, sustaining inner peacefulness and well-being, and for a huge, innate, multifaceted intelligence that goes way beyond the merely conceptual. When we mobilize and refine that capacity and put it to use, we are much healthier physically, emotionally, and spiritually. And much happier. Even our thinking becomes clearer, and we are less plagued by storms of the mind.

This capacity for paying attention and for intelligent action can be cultivated, nurtured, and refined beyond our wildest dreams if we have the motivation to do so. Sadly, as individuals, that motivation often comes only when we have already experienced a life-threatening disease or a severe shock to the system that may leave us in tremendous pain in both soma and psyche. It may only come, as it does for so many of our patients in the Stress Reduction Clinic, once we are rudely awakened to the fact that no matter how remarkable our technological medicine, it has gross limitations that make complete cures a rarity, treatment often merely a rear-guard action to maintain the status quo, if there is any effective treatment at all, and even diagnosis of what is wrong an inexact and too often woefully inadequate science.

Without exaggeration, it is fair to say that these new fields within medicine are showing that it is possible for individuals to mobilize deep innate resources we all seem to share by virtue of being human, resources for learning, for growing, for healing, and for transformation that are available to us across the entire life span. These capacities are folded into our genes, our brains, our bodies, our minds, and into our relationships with each other and with the world. We gain access to them starting from wherever we are, which is always here, and in the only moment we ever have, which is always now. We all have the potential for healing and transformation no matter what the situation we find ourselves in, of long duration or recently appearing, whether we see it as "good," "bad," or "ugly," hopeless or hopeful, whether we see the causes as internal or external. These inner resources are our birthright. They are available to us across our entire life span because they are not in any way separate from us. It is in our very nature as a species to learn and grow and heal and move toward greater wisdom in our ways of seeing and in our actions, and toward greater compassion for ourselves and others.

But still, these capacities need to be uncovered, developed, and put to use. Doing so is the challenge of our life's time, that is, a chance to make the most of the moments that we have. As a rule, our moments are easily missed or filled up with stuff, wanted and unwanted. But it is equally easy to realize that, in the unfolding of our lives, we actually have nothing but moments in which to live, and it is a gift to actually be present for them, and that interesting things start to happen when we are.

This challenge of a life's time, to choose to cultivate these capacities for learning, growing, healing, and transformation right in the midst of our moments, is also the adventure of a lifetime. It begins a journey toward realizing who we really are and living our lives as if they really mattered. And they do—more than we think. More than we can possibly think, and not merely for our own enjoyment or accomplishment, although our own joy and feelings of well-being and accomplishment are bound to blossom, all the same.

This journey toward greater health and sanity is catalyzed by mobilizing and developing resources we all already have. And the most important one is our capacity for paying attention, in particular to those aspects of our lives that we have not been according very much attention to, that we might say we have been ignoring, seemingly forever.

Paying attention refines awareness, that feature of our being that, along with language, distinguishes the potential of our species for learning and for transformation, both individual and collective. We grow and change and learn and become aware through the direct apprehension of things through our five senses, coupled with our powers of mind, which Buddhists see as a sense in its own right. We are capable of perceiving that any one aspect of experience exists within an infinite web of interrelationships, some of which are critically important to our immediate or long-term well-being. True, we might not see many of these relationships right away. They may be more or less hidden dimensions within the fabric of our lives, yet to be discovered. Even so, these hidden dimensions, or what we might call *new degrees of freedom,* are potentially available to us, and will gradually reveal themselves to us as we continue to cultivate and dwell in our capacity for conscious awareness by attending intentionally with both awe and tenderness to the staggeringly complex yet fundamentally ordered universe, world, terrain, family, mind, and body within which we locate and orient ourselves, all of which, at every level, is continually fluxing and changing, whether we know it or not, whether we like it or not, and thereby providing us with countless unexpected challenges and opportunities to grow, and to see clearly, and to move toward greater wisdom in our actions, and toward quelling the tortured suffering of our tumultuous minds, habitually so far from home, so far from quiet and rest.

This journey toward health and sanity is nothing less than an invitation to wake up to the fullness of our lives while we actually have them to live, rather than only, if ever, on our deathbeds, which Henry David Thoreau warned against so eloquently in *Walden* when he wrote:

I went to the woods because I wished to live deliberately, to confront only the essential facts of life and see if I could not learn what it had to teach and not, when I came to die, discover that I had not lived.

Dying without actually fully living, without waking up to our lives while we have the chance, is an ongoing and significant risk for all of us, given the automaticity of our habits and the relentless pace at which events unfold in this era, far greater than in his, and the mindlessness that tends to pervade our relationships to what may be most important for us but, at the same time, less apparent in our lives.

But as Thoreau himself counseled, it is possible for us to learn to ground ourselves in our inborn capacity for wise and openhearted attention. He pointed out that it is both possible and highly desirable to first taste and then inhabit a vast and spacious awareness of both heart and mind. When properly cultivated, such awareness can discern, embrace, transcend, and free us from the veils and limitations of our routinized relationships, and from the frequently turbulent and destructive mind states and emotions that accompany them. Such habits are invariably conditioned by the past, not only through our genetic inheritance, but through our experiences of trauma, fear, lack of trust and safety, feelings of unworthiness from not having been seen and honored for who we are, or from longstanding resentment for past slights, injustices, or outright and overwhelming harm. Nevertheless, they are habits that narrow our view, distort our understanding, and, if unattended, prevent our growing and our healing.

To come to our senses, both literally and metaphorically, on the big scale as a species and on the smaller scale as a single human being, we first need to return to the body, the locus within which the biological senses and what we call the mind arise. The body is a place we mostly ignore; we may barely inhabit it at all, never mind attending to it and honoring it. Our own body is, strangely, a landscape that is simultaneously both familiar and remarkably unfamiliar to us. It is a domain we might at times fear, or even loathe, depending on our past and what we have faced or fear we might. At other times it may be something we are wholly seduced by, obsessed with the body's size, its shape, its weight, or look, at risk of falling into unconscious but seemingly endless self-preoccupation and narcissism.

At the level of the individual person, we know from many studies in the field of mind/body medicine in the past thirty years that it is possible to come to some degree of peace within the body and mind and so find greater health, well-being, happiness, and clarity, even in the midst of great challenges and difficulties. Many thousands of people have already embarked on this journey and have reported and continue to report remarkable benefits for themselves and for others with whom they share their lives and work. We have come to see that paying attention in such a way, and thereby tapping into those hidden dimensions and new degrees of freedom, is not a path for the select few. Anybody can embark on such a path and find great benefit and comfort in it.

Coming to our senses is the work of no time at all, only of being present and awake here and now. It is also, paradoxically, a lifetime's engagement. You could say we take it on "for life," in every sense of that phrase.

The first step on the adventure involved in coming to our senses on any and every level is the cultivation of a particular kind of awareness known as *mindfulness*. Mindfulness is the final common pathway of what makes us human, our capacity for awareness and for self-knowing. Mindfulness is cultivated by paying attention, and, as we shall see, this paying attention is developed and refined through a practice known as *mindfulness meditation,* which has been spreading rapidly around the world and into the mainstream of Western culture in the past thirty years, thanks in part to an increasing number of scientific and medical studies of its various effects. But if, in even hearing the word *meditation,* you are all of a sudden feeling that it sounds either weird, strange, Pollyannaish, or just not for you because of the ideas and images you have of what meditation is or involves, consider that—whatever your ideas about meditation, and however they were shaped—meditation, and in particular mindfulness meditation, is not what you think.

There is nothing weird or out of the ordinary about meditating or meditation. It is just about paying attention to your life as if it really mattered. And it might help to keep in mind that, while it is really nothing out of the ordinary, nothing particularly special, mindfulness is at the same time extraordinarily special and utterly transformative in ways that are impossible to imagine, although that won't stop us from trying.

When cultivated and refined, mindfulness can function effectively on every level, from the individual to the corporate, the societal, the political, and the global. But it does require that we be motivated to realize who we actually are and to live our lives as if they really mattered, not just for ourselves, but for the world. This adventure of a lifetime unfolds from this first step. When we walk this path, we find that we are hardly alone in our efforts, nor are we alone or unique even in our difficulties. For in taking up the practice of mindfulness, you are participating in what amounts to a global community of intentionality and exploration, one that ultimately includes all of us.

Such healing of the greater world is the work of many generations. It has already begun in many places as we realize the enormity of the risks we face by not paying attention to the moribund condition of the patient, which is the world; by not paying attention to the history of the patient, which is life on this planet and, in particular, human life, since its activities are now shaping the destiny of all beings on Earth for lifetimes to come; by not paying attention to the autoimmune diagnosis that is staring us in the face but which we are finding difficult to accept; and by not paying attention to the potential for treatment that involves a widespread embracing of what is deepest and best in our own nature as living and therefore sensing beings, while there is still time to do so.

Healing our world will involve learning, however tentatively, to put our multiple intelligences to work in the service of life, liberty, and the pursuit of real happiness, for ourselves, and for generations of beings to come. Not just for Americans and Westerners either, but for all inhabitants of this planet, whatever continent or island we reside on. And not just for human beings, but for all beings in the natural, more-than-human world, what Buddhists often refer to as *sentient beings.*

For sentience, when all is said and done, is the key to coming to our senses and waking up to the possible. Without awareness, without learning how to use, refine, and inhabit our consciousness, our genetic capacity for clear seeing and selfless action, both within ourselves as individuals and within our institutions—including businesses, the House and the Senate, the White House, seats of government, and larger gatherings of nations such as the United Nations and the European Union—we are dooming ourselves to the autoimmune disease of our own unawareness, from which stem endless rounds of illusion, delusion, greed, fear, cruelty, self-deception, and ultimately, wanton destruction and death.

It is time to choose life, and to reflect on what such a choice is asking of us. This choice is a nitty-gritty, moment-to-moment one, not some colossal or intimidating abstraction. It is very close to the substance and substrate of our lives unfolding in whatever ways they do, inwardly in our thoughts and feelings, and outwardly in our words and deeds moment by moment by moment.

The world needs all of its flowers, just as they are, and even though they bloom for only the briefest of moments, which we call a lifetime. It is our job to find out one by one and collectively what kind of flowers we are, and to share our unique beauty with the world in the precious time that we have, and to leave the children and grandchildren a legacy of wisdom and compassion embodied in the way we live, in our institutions, and in our honoring of our interconnectedness, at home and around the world. Why not risk standing firmly for sanity in our lives and in our world, the inner and the outer a reflection of each other and of our genius as a species?

The creative and imaginative efforts and actions of every one of us count, and nothing less than the health of the world hangs in the balance. We could say that the world is literally and metaphorically dying for us as a species to come to our senses, and now is the time. Now is the time for us to wake up to the fullness of our beauty, to get on with and amplify the work of healing ourselves, our societies, and the planet, building on everything worthy that has come before and that is flowering now. No intention is too small and no effort insignificant. Every step along the way counts. Every single one of us counts.

Just Sitting ⟫

Tenshin Reb Anderson

Why is sitting and doing nothing the most difficult, mysterious, joyful, painful, profound, and life-changing thing we can do? Because it is the radical opposite of everything in samsara. By creating, accepting, and rejecting nothing, by resting simply in life as it is, we contradict all the beliefs, urges, and habits that ego has accumulated over countless lifetimes. That's why doing nothing—which is to say, being fully who we are—is so difficult and radical. The practice of shikantaza, *or "just sitting," is the specialty of the Soto school of Zen, and one of its most interesting American teachers is Tenshin Reb Anderson, a dharma successor of Shunryu Suzuki Roshi. Here are his thoughts on why "just sitting" is so difficult.*

For the past two hundred years in Japanese Soto Zen, the understanding of most teachers has been that *shikantaza*, literally translated as "just sitting," was Dogen Zenji's essential practice. In accord with this mainstream understanding, Shunryu Suzuki Roshi established shikantaza as our essential practice at the San Francisco Zen Center. A great deal of his teaching was intended to help us understand what it means to practice just sitting in its true sense. He also told us that his main job as a Zen priest was to encourage people to practice just sitting.

He would often say that our practice is just to sit, and then he would say that it might sound easy, but that actually it is rather difficult to understand what it means to just sit. In order to help us understand what this just sitting really is, he went on to say that it is just to be ourselves. Finally, he made it clear, at least to me, that we cannot just be ourselves by ourselves alone. We can only just be ourselves, and thus realize the just-sitting practice of the buddha ancestors, by practicing in the same manner as the entire universe and all beings. Perhaps other Soto Zen teachers have taught just sitting in this way, but I have not heard it so clearly from anyone but Suzuki Roshi. I deeply appreciate the way he stressed this point.

Suzuki Roshi taught that, in order to actualize our way of just sitting by being ourselves, we must express ourselves fully. So, paradoxically, realizing the selflessness of just sitting depends on full self-expression. Full self-expression, in turn, can only be realized by meeting and practicing together with all living beings in the entire universe. Therefore, he taught that to realize the full function of the practice of just sitting, we must go and meet face-to-face with our teacher. Such meetings offer the opportunity to settle completely into the truth of just sitting. Only when we meet intimately with another person can we fully be ourselves. As the *Lotus Sutra* says, "Only a buddha together with a buddha can thoroughly master the buddha-dharma."

My understanding of Suzuki Roshi's teaching of just sitting is that it encompasses a dynamic interdependence between two dimensions: an intrapsychic aspect and an interbeing, or interpersonal, aspect. According to this view, I see Shakyamuni practicing upright, just sitting under the bodhi tree, and attaining the way as only part of the story of just sitting. Only when he met his students and they attained the way together was the full function of the selfless practice of just sitting realized.

So, in our practice of just sitting, we cannot actually fully be ourselves unless we go to see the teacher, and the teacher cannot fully be himself unless he comes to meet us. Suzuki Roshi was a teacher who taught that sometimes we have to disagree and argue with our teacher and that sometimes we have to surrender to our teacher. Similarly, the teacher must sometimes disagree with us and must sometimes surrender to us. This interbeing aspect of just sitting generously encompasses all agreement and disagreement.

To be fully themselves in this formal student-teacher relationship, both must assert themselves completely and recognize each other fully. You will sometimes disagree with your teacher, and at the same time you must surrender to your teacher. Your teacher, of course, must bring herself to meet you, and must surrender to you. The only way that you can fully be yourself is if your teacher, and ultimately all beings, come to meet you.

When Suzuki Roshi was alive, meeting with him was a very high priority in my life. I made a big effort to bring myself to meet him, but, often, as soon as I made this strong effort to assert myself in his presence, I became aware of my anxiety and vulnerability and wanted to get away. However, when I didn't present myself strongly, if I was with him halfheartedly, I didn't feel the need to escape. It was only when I presented myself wholeheartedly to him that I felt vulnerable.

When Suzuki Roshi ordained me as a priest, he gave me the name *Tenshin Zenki.* On that day he told me that *tenshin* means "Reb is Reb." Then he said, "People may have a problem with that, but there is no other way." Today, the way I understand his teaching is that when Reb is fully Reb, when you are fully you, we are completely vulnerable. To what are we completely vulnerable? When we are fully ourselves, we are vulnerable to the entire universe. The second part of my name, *zenki,* may be translated as "the whole works." In just being fully ourselves, *tenshin,* we open ourselves to the working of the entire universe, *zenki.* This name describes how the entire universe works thoroughly through each person in the practice of just sitting.

Over the years, I gradually came to understand what a wonderful gift he gave me in that name. *Tenshin Zenki* is actually a gloss for *shikantaza.* So now I see that just sitting is not something that I can do by myself. It is not something that Suzuki Roshi could do by himself either. It is something that we do together. We practice it together when we bring ourselves completely to our meeting and completely assert ourselves while completely recognizing each other.

When I discussed with a friend the various views of just sitting, he recalled that famous story of the blind men feeling the elephant. One person says the elephant is a wall, another person says the elephant is a huge leaf; one says it is a rope and another says it is a tree trunk. I thought to myself, "But in this case, there really isn't such a thing as an elephant."

There is not actually something out there that is just sitting. It is just that we enter the reality of this wonderful practice by giving ourselves entirely to a situation where "the other" comes and meets us entirely. But since the other meets us entirely, just sitting can't be a thing. What we do is not just sitting. Just sitting is the dynamic interdependence of what we give and what comes to meet us. That is not a thing. Nobody knows what that is. Even all the buddhas together cannot fully measure it. However, we can throw ourselves into it.

Although I say "throw ourselves into it," even this is not a unilateral activity. We still need to have a significant other with whom we meet face-to-face. Therefore, it is not so easy to throw ourselves into such a practice, because we may feel anxious or afraid of the unknown possibilities of such concerted activity. Nevertheless, we still have to jump wholeheartedly into the unknown reality of just sitting.

There is a story about the great master Yaoshan just sitting. His teacher, Shitou, who was practicing together with him, asked, "What are you doing?" Yaoshan replied, "I'm not doing anything at all." Shitou said, "Then you are just idly sitting." Yaoshan replied, "If I were idly sitting, I would be doing something." Finally Shitou said, "You say that you are not doing anything at all. What is it that you are not doing?" Yaoshan said, "Even the ten thousand sages don't know."

Zazen is sitting upright in the present moment, right here, in the midst of Buddha's mind. There is a text about zazen by Dogen Zenji called *Zazen Shin*. There are two ways of understanding this title. *Zazen* means—well, no one knows what it means—zazen is zazen. *Shin* means "needle," particularly the bamboo needles that were used in the old days for acupuncture. The first way to understand this title is that zazen is a needle that we stick into our lives; it's the needle with which we care for life. If we put this zazen needle in the right place, it will tenderize our lives. We will become sensitive to the totality of our lives, tender to all beings, so responsive that we realize how deeply connected we all are. This tenderness transforms us and others. This is what happens when we understand zazen as an acupuncture treatment for our lives. The other way to understand *zazen shin* is as a medicine for zazen itself. It's a needle to treat our attempts to practice zazen. It's a medicine to treat our misunderstanding of the practice of zazen.

When we first begin, most of us practice zazen just as we do other things. We practice zazen to get something out of it, to improve some situation. We practice zazen as though there were something we could do by ourselves. We understand the self as something that can do things—do Buddhist practice, do zazen—and this misunderstanding is deeply ingrained in us. This is normal; we all do this.

Dogen Zenji wrote, "When you first approach the way, you remove yourself from its neighborhood." When you first approach Buddhist practice, you go away from it just by the very fact that you are approaching it, rather than realizing it on the spot. We can't help this. We're looking to improve things. It's the way we see everything; it's unavoidable. Once we start practicing, we need treatment; we need a little medicine for our misunderstanding of what practice is. So may I insert a needle into your zazen practice?

Zazen is just like our lives, and our lives are like riding in a boat. You can't ride in a boat by yourself. As Dogen Zenji says, you raise the sail, you sit up straight, you put your tongue on the roof of your mouth, you cross your legs, and you row with the oars. And although you row, the boat gives you a ride. Without the boat, no one could ride, but your riding makes the boat what it is. This realm of mutual creation with all sentient beings—where we make one another what we are—is the realm of zazen. Zazen is the way we care for our lives together.

We can care for our lives by ourselves, and that's the way we're accustomed to living. We have all done a pretty good job of it. You got this far because you did a good job of taking care of yourself by yourself. But this is not zazen. Now that you've taken care of yourself so well, you have a chance to enter the great mind of Buddha, to learn how to take care of yourself along with all sentient beings. This is "cultivating an empty field." Cultivating the empty field is the same as cultivating the sky. Do you know how to plow the clouds? This cloud farming is done with all sentient beings. It's also called zazen.

Someone once approached Suzuki Roshi and asked, "Why haven't you enlightened me yet?" Suzuki Roshi answered politely, "I'm making my best effort." He might have told the student to make more effort herself, but he didn't say that. He said, "I'm making my best effort." Zazen is the way I care for my life with all beings. I can't do it by myself. Can you have faith in a way that you can't do by yourself? Most people can trust only a way that they do by themselves. But living a life that you can do by yourself is unadulterated misery. Completely trusting a way that you can't do by yourself, a way that you do with all sentient beings, is immediate liberation.

Some people say that Zen is hard to understand. It is hard to understand, but not because it's obscure. It's hard to understand because it's like the sky. Look at the blue sky. It's nice to look at, but it's hard to understand. It's so big and it goes on forever. How are you going to get it? It's hard to understand all sentient beings, too, but it's not difficult to sit upright and be aware of them.

One day, a monk asked the great teacher Matsu, "What is Buddha's mind?"

Matsu said, "Mind itself is Buddha."

Later someone told Matsu, "I hear you said, 'Mind itself is Buddha.'"

"I say that to children, so they will stop crying."

"What do you say after they stop crying?"

"I say, 'No mind, no Buddha.'"

The practice of "no mind, no Buddha" is based on great faith. This is trusting what is actually happening. This is trusting "what." Put aside your doubts and trust it. Trust *what.* Don't trust *it,* a thing that you can think of. Trust what you can't think of. Trust the vastness of space. Trust every single living being. Trust cause and effect: vast, inconceivably complex and wondrous cause and effect. This faith has unlimited possibilities. Think about not moving. Think about giving up all action. And remember, giving up all action does not mean stopping action. That would be another action. "Giving up" means giving up the attempt to do things by yourself, and embracing the way of doing things with everyone.

Trust Buddha's mind. Trusting Buddha's mind means trusting all sentient beings. This is fearless love. You can give it all up, and then you can love every single thing.

Dogen said, "Mind itself is Buddha. Practice is difficult; explanation is not difficult." People like a practice where you can explain how to do it. It feeds the deluded karmic mind. First you do this, and then you do that, and then you do this; people like this. But what is easy to explain is difficult to practice, because the explanations move us further away from the practice itself, and we need all kinds of antidotes to get us back on track. "No mind, no Buddha" is not difficult to practice, but it is difficult to explain. Sitting still is not difficult to practice, because it's just like the sky, but it's as difficult to understand as the sky.

Practicing goodness is like riding in a boat. When you make a bag lunch and give it to someone who is hungry or take a present to someone who is sick, if you think you are doing this by yourself, you're missing the point. You can't ride in a boat by yourself. You need the boat; the boat gives you a ride. If you make a lunch for someone, the food gives you a ride; the food makes it possible for you to make the lunch. All sentient beings give you the food. All sentient beings make the lunch through your hands and your eyes and your body. Without you, the lunch couldn't be made. Without them, the lunch couldn't be made. Now let me ask you: If the practice of all the buddhas and ancestors is being realized right now, who is it being realized by?

If you answer "All beings," you're right. Yes—all beings! All beings are sharing the way at this moment. Never graspable, yet totally available. There is no other thing outside of this. My question is, do we trust it?

Looking at myself, the only thing I can find that holds me back from completely trusting the practice in which all sentient beings are now engaged is lack of courage: lack of courage to affirm all life, which is the same as the lack of courage to affirm death. Without being able to affirm death, I cannot affirm life. This is the courage that comes with insight, so I could say that what holds me back is a lack of insight.

When I'm with some sentient beings, I lack the courage to meet them. I'm afraid of what he or she may do, and what I may do in response. So I hold back, and by holding back, I don't affirm life. Holding back, I'm unable to care for the other person completely.

But I can make a vow, which for me is the same as practicing zazen. The vow will not be to meet each person completely by my own willpower. I will not make that vow. I will vow to trust that all sentient beings meet in my life, as my life. I will witness the arrival of all things as my life. That's my vow.

What will be your vow? Do you want to commit yourself to the way of Buddha, the way that all sentient beings practice together? Or do you wish to continue an ancient karmic pattern of living by your own willpower? Consider my question and tell me the answer. Again and again, tell me the answer, so I can understand the heart of your zazen, the heart of your love, the heart of your wisdom.

I recently saw a good example of the practice of just sitting in the form of Olympic women's figure skating. These young women—actually girls, fourteen to sixteen years old—fully expressed themselves. They asserted themselves with extraordinary energy, strength, precision, and grace. What was so touching to me was that at the very moment of their fullest self-assertion they simultaneously surrendered to the entire universe. At the moment of most powerful self-expression—when they were flying through the air, performing amazing feats of turning through time and space—at that very moment they were completely vulnerable to the whole world. They were vulnerable to falling on the ice, they were vulnerable to nineteen judges' minute and severe scrutiny, they were vulnerable to their parents and their coaches. A billion people were watching them. Right in the midst of their transcendent wholeheartedness, they were completely vulnerable and open to the support and love of the entire world. It is this concerted and cooperative activity of all beings that the practice of just sitting celebrates and realizes.

After the competition, these young champions were interviewed. They were shown tapes of their performances, and they were asked what they were thinking at the moment of their total, impeccable self-expression and complete openness to the universe. As I remember, they weren't able to say; they didn't know what it was they were "not doing." As Yaoshan said, "Even the ten thousand sages don't know what just sitting is."

After the Flood

Erik Hansen

The Buddhist writer Erik Hansen was one of those forced to flee their homes after Hurricane Katrina breeched the levees of New Orleans. Although bloodcurdling stories of violence and crime circulated in the immediate aftermath of the hurricane (most of them untrue and tinged with racism), Hansen found that these terrible events actually brought out the best in people.

As usual a cigarette is dangling from our friend Smokey's lips as she pulls up in front of our house with a load of spare plywood. "Be Nice or Leave," it says on the rear window of her weathered old pickup truck, and "New Orleans, proud to crawl home."

It's early Sunday morning, August 28, and clouds are moving quickly across the sky. Overnight, Hurricane Katrina powered up to a Category 5, and our neighborhood is alive with last-minute preparations. Smokey helps unload the plywood, gives me an evacuation map and a kiss, then hurries home to pick up her hip boots; she knows there's going to be water. Lots and lots of water. Then she drives to Tulane Hospital, where she will spend the next four days preparing meals around the clock for dozens of doctors, nurses, patients, policemen, and firemen.

As Katrina draws near, on our block and throughout the city, neighbors are helping neighbors. Brothers Mark and Mike take time from their own preparations to help Din and Carolyn cover up their windows. Din and Carolyn drove through the night to pick up their cats; now they're too tired to evacuate, so Todd and Dann, our neighbors on the south, offer them shelter, cats and all. It's wonderful to observe so many acts of kindness in the teeth of an impending disaster.

My focus is on our beloved twelve-year-old dog, Daisy, who cannot move. She had spinal surgery five days ago and was recuperating at the vet's when we retrieved her late last night. We couldn't bear the thought of going through this, whatever is to come, without her near. Forty-eight hours from now we'll realize this was the smartest decision we've ever made.

My wife, Shannon, and I run around the house, frantically doing what should have been done yesterday, fueled by a kind of nervous, giddy exhilaration. It's as if the fabric of our lives is being ripped to confront us with the great unknown that always lurks underneath. I feel like I'm seeing the fragile contingency of life; how, at any minute, it can turn on a dime. But I'm not really. Not yet.

Even though Daisy is still heavily sedated, showing whites where her brown eyes should be, our disjointed preparations are making her anxious. She won't stop yelping. It's awful; her voice is strange and hoarse. It's not until I carry her down the stairs and slide her into the backseat of our car that she finally settles down. We say our goodbyes to our wonderful friends on the street. No tears. We all think we'll be seeing each other in a day or two.

One block from our house, at the corner of Esplanade and Rampart, we pass a black family waiting for the bus to take them to the Superdome. Mom, dad, grandma, and two kids carrying blankets, several bags of food, and an ice chest. The bus pulls up and our destinies diverge.

We join the slowest-moving line of traffic you've ever seen on the I-10 headed east, toward Mississippi and places north. Everyone behaves remarkably well, but still, we're going so slowly that some people who started out with full tanks of gas are running out and stopping on the side. Under normal conditions I might get mad or impatient—the westbound lanes are empty, the Mississippi governor has sealed his state's border, there's no sign of planning anywhere—but every time I look in the backseat and see Daisy's head resting in Shannon's lap, sleeping contentedly at last, I'm overwhelmed with gratitude. It might seem strange, but for the fourteen hours it takes to get to Birmingham, Alabama, I could not be happier.

Day two finds us taking refuge in Smokey's sister Martha's small apartment. What with the dog not walking and our cat climbing on the furniture, it's kind of like the circus has come to town. What's more, Martha and Dave have taken in a whole host of their Louisiana and Mississippi relatives.

Nevertheless, for a few hours, everybody's happy. We're watching CNN, and it looks like New Orleans has dodged another bullet. But then, in the evening, Smokey calls. The policemen coming back to her hospital are badly shaken, she says; the levees are breaking; they're pulling bodies from the water in St. Bernard Parish. Tuesday morning confirms it. The nightmare is real and just beginning.

No word from our friends who stayed in the city. The lines are all down, and the government is absent. We try to comfort Jean, Smokey's partner, who is worried sick.

I keep thinking about the black family waiting for the bus. They're stuck in hell while we're safe with friends. I hear them in my head: "You left us. You drove right by in your white bubble. What is wrong with you?" But we only had room for one, I think, sick with remorse and anger. I don't want this to be about race. Let it be about poor planning or mismanagement or class; it's just too sickening that our city and our country could let this happen because of race. What is wrong with us?

I keep thinking about those empty westbound lanes and the fleet of school buses submerged under water: with proper planning they could've saved people, could've run shuttles out the I-10 West all day. I'm furious at our leaders, city, state, and national. But I don't just blame Bush. I blame our country. His policies—tax cuts for the rich, the war in Iraq—express the preference of a majority of Americans, and they had a direct impact on the condition of our levees. But it's not just that. A paroxysm of caring and support is sweeping the nation, but what about the suffering in Iraq? Horrific bombings get fifteen seconds on the nightly news, then we go blithely about our business, ignoring the country that we pitched into hell. What about the hundreds of millions of hungry, desperate people who subsist on under a dollar a day? Why is our caring so selective, so media-driven? What is wrong with us?

On day five we head north to Brooklyn, at the generous invitation of Maureen, my stepson's mother-in-law.

Everybody in our little New Orleans circle has been accounted for: Smokey is reunited with Jean; the others are spreading out across the country. Only Bob stayed behind to keep an eye on the houses, which received a minimum of flooding.

Driving through beautiful Tennessee, it hits me: Oh, I'm not just okay. I'm happy. Shouldn't I be depressed or worried? Our house could still be looted or burned down. What about survivor's guilt? The images on television have been too sad and awful for words. The answer comes back: to feel bad would be to ignore the evidence of my senses—a lovely day, rolling green hills, Shannon safe by my side. For sixteen years of meditation I've trained my mind to dwell in the present, and this is the consequence. I'm here and everything is okay.

"I keep thinking about Ed," I say to Shannon, referring to our late Zen teacher, Dr. Edward Wortz. "Me, too," she says. In fact, we're thinking the same thought, and have been since the beginning of this crisis. Given these circumstances, we know exactly what Ed would say: "Don't add to the suffering mass."

The "suffering mass" could be thought of as the aggregate of suffering of all beings on our planet, an unimaginable quantity of suffering. It's a perspective that most of us, fortunately, will never experience. But it is real. And it's from this perspective that an enlightened person like Ed would say: we have a responsibility to both ourselves and others to avoid needless suffering.

But what about New Orleans? What about compassion? Well, I know I'm not the last word on the subject, but this I'm sure of: compassion is not watching CNN and feeling bad. It's getting out your checkbook, or being considerate on the road, or helping a teacher at your kid's school. It's never painful. It's not guilt. If there's a feeling/emotion in compassion, it's the sweetness of doing something kind for another being. How could that ever feel bad?

The example Ed often cited was Mother Teresa, who, even while surrounded by unspeakable misery, seemed to maintain her equanimity and humor. Imagine if she'd felt obliged to mirror the suffering of every person she touched: dear God, she'd have been a quivering mass of jelly in the corner, no good to anybody.

So much emphasis is placed in Buddhism on "cultivating compassion" that it can seem like an esoteric practice, reserved for lofty beings or advanced stages of our development. It's not. In fact it's been right here all along, like the Tin Man's heart, in the smallest and simplest acts of our daily lives: a smile, a hug, an expression of sympathy or interest. Of course it's in the bigger acts, too—helping friends board up their windows, looking for survivors on rooftops, taking refugees into your home.

We're living in Brooklyn now. I'd love to report a heroic act of my own since this began, but none so far. Over the last two weeks, instead, Shannon and I have been the recipients of many other people's kindness—friends, family, and strangers. I've learned a lot from them about compassion. It's in the act; it feels good; and it will mean more to the other person than you'll ever know.

A Life Cut to Pieces

Diana Atkinson

A great Zen teacher went to visit an American friend who had suffered a terrible car accident. He looked down at him in his hospital bed, shook his head, and said, "Lucky, lucky man." Buddhists don't welcome or invite such suffering, but they do recognize the tremendous opportunity for spiritual growth it represents. Diana Atkinson is a writer of great talent who has suffered repeated hospitalization and surgery since she was a child. Her Buddhist practice has given a spiritual context to her loss of privacy, security, and bodily integrity.

> What major surgery produces is a certain quality of loss, a loss with its own nuances, its own character.
> —LARRY McMURTRY, *in his 1999 memoir "Walter Benjamin at the Dairy Queen: Reflections at Sixty and Beyond"*

You must be naked. You must remove all jewelry, all traces of scent, makeup, polish on fingernails, toenails. Body hair is shaved, as swimmers shave, as though to streamline beneath the waters of consciousness. The body is shaved to prepare it for meat-cutting: bloody invasion with scalpel, disemboweling in the confusing name of "care," which takes place within the parentheses of consciousness but which is not an aside—is, in fact, a central event, only obscured from the subject's life-narrative by the fact that he or she is unconscious, and therefore, absent.

Many times I have had to divest for this deepest of dives: major surgery. Preparing to pass through the eye of the needle, I picture myself walking out of my house, never to return. As I walk the solitary desert toward the great, shining needle, clothes and jewelry fall away. Descending as for a ritual bath in the Red Sea.

They kill, then unkill me, and I emerge changed. Less and less able to hold on to material possessions. Less and less interested in holding on. I collect smells, the least tangible presence. They come in very small bottles. I can fit them all in my carry-on, which fits in the locker corresponding to my bed in the bowel ward at Mount Sinai Hospital, Toronto. (There are two posters by the nursing station: one depicting Crohn's disease and the other ulcerative colitis. Every patient belongs to one of the two tribes. Sooner or later, we each end up in front of "our" poster saying, "See? Here's what gut I'm missing," as we explain the editing of our organs to a companion.) Tucked in among my clothes, the tiny vials disappear, like immigrants adapting to the customs of the new country.

I cannot seem to take root. All my furniture folds: desk, massage table, the card table at which I've eaten. When I move into a new place, I don't paint, nor do I drive nails into the walls. I glance around regularly, mentally computing what I'd net if I held a yard sale. I'm prepared, at some subconscious level, to throw things into a rucksack for a night flight, the way my Jewish ancestors fled the Egyptians across the plains.

Years ago, when I was a stripper in British Columbia, the shows were less important to me than the fact that—every six days—I could leave. *Had* to leave. Find the bus depot or the airstrip; occasionally, the Canadian Pacific Railroad. No one knew my real name, so it was all off the record, in privacy-protecting parentheses.

At four years old, I was diagnosed with acute chronic ulcerative colitis, an autoimmune disease in which the body inexplicably registers the lining of the colon as enemy. The immune system mistakenly attacks it, trying to digest it. Its cause is unknown, but a genetic link to Ashkenazic Jews seems evident. Certainly, stress aggravates it.

The next eight years I was in the hospital more than in school. In that series of hospital rooms, which felt impermanent as any motel, I learned the haiku of objects. A vase of tulips, a stack of books stood out among the generic, hospital-issue, split-back gown, plastic comb, toothbrush, box of tissues. My mother brought me these tulips; my father, these books. All else was standard issue. Over the years, attempts to subvert the rule of the institution fail. A diary disappears. A teddy bear gets lost in the hospital laundry. I learned: best not risk what you can't afford to lose. (Later, I realize: *this is why I haven't had children.*)

Your parents sign your body rights away. Conspiring among themselves, adults determine the fate of your body, its treatment and handling. Large strangers orchestrate its exposure and invasion by needle, enema, nasal-gastric tube, scalpel. You learn: you can fall asleep intact and wake up three days later vandalized. Heavily edited in the organ department. Strangers broke in during the night and re-arranged the furniture.

At twelve, after eight years of incarceration, you are sent forth with a long, blood-encrusted incision scar and an external ileostomy that leaks shit all over your small, stunned abdomen. *We helped you,* is the message from the institution. *Have a nice life.* You learn: best not get too attached. Anything—anything!—can be taken from you at any time.

It's clear to me, almost three decades later, that you can take the person out of the institution but you can't take the sense of being a mouse in a clockwork out of the once institutionalized person. For example, I want stuff now—dresses, dishes, pretty little lamps—and I am glad to see myself have enough appetite for the world, enough of a sense of belonging here, that I want to decorate a room, adorn my scarred but still lovely body. The way I feel about material desire is similar to the way I feel about physical modesty: I was never allowed to have it. It was removed as an option before it had a chance to form.

Once I wailed to a man I liked, "But I have serious baggage."
He smiled. "Baggage can be unpacked."

As I heal from my latest surgery, pleasure—in pretty earrings, in colorful seed packets and speculative paint chips ("Shall I paint my desk area lavender?"), in lace trim on camisoles and my fat, hand-thrown pottery tea mug—pleasure is how I feel my life force returning. I love the datura a friend bought me for my garden. I made it a special, round bed, surrounded with chips of crystal, and tiny aster seedlings that should bloom forth when the summer ends and the datura and her beauty have fled. But for now, she glows in white-trumpeted glory from the center of her round bed, even at night.

Growing up in a teaching hospital, not only was I allowed very few personal possessions, but I was not modesty-draped by the teams of male med students, interns, gastroenterologists, and surgeons who examined me. You might say I grew up on exhibit. I was literally raised a public figure. Later, when I published a novel linking my experiences as a stripper with my earlier experiences being stripped for doctors, I found myself in a strangely familiar situation. Like waking from a dream—into another dream. As journalists filed past, probing me about my novel and its roots in my body, my life, I felt violated, uncertain of my rights to privacy. I wondered, *What are normal boundaries?* I'd begun to realize I'd never learned them.

"Reenactment," therapists call this business of waking up periodically along the course of one's life, to find oneself smack in the middle of a drama that, though removed in time and possibly distance from some early traumatic situation, nonetheless manages to recast its characters and reproduce its basic elements with uncanny clarity. In her novel *Enchantment*, Daphne Merkin writes:

> If your heart is broken early enough, do you begin to mistake pain for love? Do all attachments become inextricably linked with submission? Or do you, perhaps, learn to turn your back on the very idea of attachment—fraught with now-or-neverness, each casual leavetaking suspected of being the last? There are professionals who can be hired, at

great cost, to disprove the infallibility of this sort of damage; they talk about *nurturing* and *ego strength* and *reparenting*. It would be nice to think they were correct in their optimism or, at the least, devoted to the act of reparation. Like the psychiatrist who sums up James Stewart's prognosis in *Vertigo*: "You're suffering from severe melancholia and a guilt complex," he says briskly but not without compassion. "It will take a year to cure." The audience when I saw the movie howled at this.

I was never allowed to leave the ward, much less the building. I was often restricted to my room, and sometimes, my bed. In that era before clowns and child psychologists, visiting hours were short and strictly enforced. Nurses thought nothing of tying children to the bars of their beds. Of course I love to leave. I grew up gazing down the hall at the red exit sign.

In the McMurtry piece I quoted above, which I discovered in a wonderful anthology, *Unholy Ghost: Writers on Depression*, he talks about what he feels quadruple bypass surgery did to him:

> From being a living person with a distinct personality I began to feel more or less like an outline of that person— and then even the outline began to fade, erased by what had happened inside. I felt as if I was vanishing—or more accurately, had vanished . . . I became, to myself, more and more like a ghost, or a shadow. What I more and more felt, as the trauma deepened, was that while my body survived, the self that I had once been had lost its life . . . the sense of grief for the lost self was profound. I didn't feel like my old self at all, and had no idea where the old self had gone . . . I felt spectral—the personality that had been mine for fifty-five years was simply no longer there.

McMurtry goes on to say that he was unable to read for two to three years after the surgery, adding, "My inability to externalize seemed to be organ-based, as if the organs to which violence had been done were protesting so much that I couldn't attend to anything else." When I first read his words, I felt a pin slide from a bolt inside. Tears coursed down my face before I became aware of myself, first murdered at twelve, now a free civilian in my thirties with a book in my hand.

The external ileostomy at twelve was botched, so I received an internal ileostomy at fourteen. A great improvement on the disfiguring, hated, clear plastic bag of shit glued to my abdomen, it was a tidy little hole where the old outlet had been, on my lower right abdomen, drainable by inserting a tube that fits in my purse. Problem is, the internal, self-closing valve (made from my own tissue) has a tendency to break, and it did within the year. I had my third major surgery at fifteen. At seventeen, I won the national essay contest but dropped out of school anyway, since I couldn't get through the days without pounding my head against the green-painted cinderblock wall in the girls' restroom between classes. I was not an alcoholic, not a drug addict. I had very high marks. But despair ran in my blood; it sang in my head. *Kill yourself, kill yourself, you little shit.*

I had eighteen surgery-free years, during which I was a poster child for residual trauma. In my early twenties, people started standing up on *Oprah*. Hearing them testify felt like lightning illuminating the night, for a second. Still, incest wasn't what had happened to me. Septimus Smith, the World War I vet in Virginia Woolf's *Mrs. Dalloway*, was the nearest figure I could find who felt as I did—and he jumped out a window, since he couldn't stop scenes from the war from playing continually behind his eyes.

Modern abdominal surgery was first performed during the Civil War, in the 1860s. (It developed from gynecological experiments performed on black slaves. Unease about the average woman's relationship to the medical establishment, anyone?) McMurtry writes, "Such surgery, so noncommonsensical, so contradictory to the normal rules of survival, is truly Faustian. You get to live, perhaps as long as you want to, only not as yourself—never as yourself." And this is written by someone whose first surgery was at fifty-five. Who might I have been, good ... *God* ... *?!* It amazes me, actually, to think of all I've accomplished: homesteading in rural British Columbia, stripping (a triumph when you come from the subculture of serious illness—I am a heroine to girlfriends disfigured by ulcerative colitis or Crohn's disease), writing a novel, getting a B.A., becoming a massage therapist, becoming a good cook. Having friends. Managing, over and over, to swerve from the urge to commit suicide.

The surgery I had when I was fifteen lasted until 1998. I had it redone, only to have it fail within the year. I had it redone in 1999, and again in 2003, and that failed within the year, so I just had it again, three weeks ago as I write this. The alternative, an external ileostomy, is too hellish to contemplate, and so, like others with internal ileostomies, I will undergo as many revisions as it takes to get a stable version. Each time it's the same nine-inch incision, and I frankly don't know if I can do it again, so am prepared to (again) consider suicide if it breaks within the year. Don't you dare judge me.

If there's one thing I'm giving up on (I changed this to "letting go of," stared at the screen, then changed it back), it's the childish idealism that used to make me believe it was possible to be understood. I used to believe that through cultivating skillful precision with words, I could *make myself understood.* I don't think so now. I come from the subculture of longtime serious illness and multiple surgeries, and I make a distinction between the relatively unscathed, no matter how well-meaning, and those of us who've been through the war. When a nurse I've never met approaches me, I can tell immediately whether she's just read the guidebook or whether she's actually visited the country.

Most disturbing to me is the fear that, having been raised by countless changing shifts of all-but-faceless personnel, my expectations of, and subsequent capacity for, deep and lasting relationship is impaired. When a love relationship tanks, I have a tendency to move out of state. It's a compromise: I am profoundly uncomfortable in my body at such times, like when you can't find a cool spot in hot sheets, no matter where you turn. As a result, my address book is a mess, and friends write my name into theirs in pencil. The last several years, I've crisscrossed the country. Sometimes it feels like people swim up, move their lips, then they're gone. Like a video game.

To be fair to myself, though, all my moves have had reasons that still make sense to me. I lost my apartment in the surgery of 2003, for example, and turned up in southern California for a surreal few months, to stay with some friends who offered to take me in. Herein lies the grace of my precarious physical situation. I carry Pema Chödrön's advice, "Get used to the feeling of falling," on a scrap of paper in my mirrored compact. It's the fortune from the cookie of my life. When I am bereft, wandering the streets in a postsurgical altered state, kind strangers offer me their guest rooms. I walk their dogs, make soup, sweep the kitchen floor. Maybe we all have this strange charm, but only find it out when everything has been taken from us: car, credit cards, money, job, place to live, internal organs.

Sociologist Erving Goffman devoted a chapter ("On the Characteristics of Total Institutions") in his book *Asylums: Essays on the Social Situation of Mental Patients and Other Inmates* to the features common between long-term care hospitals and prisons. Prisoners, we all know, continually plot their escape. What is the difference between my experience as a child in hospital in those draconian days, and the experience of a man captured and tortured as a prisoner of war? Neither signs a consent form. Neither can refuse handling. Neither can leave. It comes down to intent. Supposedly, they were trying to "care" for me. What it felt like was, "We'll cure you if it kills you."

To this day, I'm not sure what I'm entitled to, whether I'm welcome in this world. Where does all this leave me, spiritually?

Jewish identity is at once a religion and a bloodline. Having shit blood for eight years with a disease not exclusive to, but disproportionately represented by, Jews, I feel Jewish all right. But, uh, not in a good way. (Probably didn't help that my father deserted the family and moved halfway around the globe to Israel the week of my first, disfiguring surgery, quoting the Talmud over his shoulder, as it were.)

I disliked God from the beginning, as it seemed He did not like me. And His Son, rising up from the dead, struck me as even creepier. Growing up as I did, with a morgue in the basement, a few floors below me, I already worried that the dead weren't really dead. The hospital air felt riddled with ghosts. Given the number of unanswered questions ("Why is this happening to me?" Not to mention, "Where does the soul go, under general anesthetic?"), Christian theology did not grab me, since it seemed to raise more questions than it answered.

I'd like to say Buddhism has been my rock and my comfort, but I don't know if that's really true. Still, you've gotta love any belief system in which sitting still and staring into the middle distance is considered perfect form. After all the drugs and all the falling, I barely recognize this I anymore, so it's a good thing that's okay with the Buddha!

David Malouf wrote, "You will be separate from yourself, and yet be alive." I feel dazed, and, at a remove, as if I am grieving. All my life I have been aware of a girl, and then a woman, who exists, if only on the plane of my imagination, living out the life I might have had If All This Hadn't Happened to Me. I'd have children by now, by my childhood sweetheart. A farmstead, where I'd can and pickle vegetables and make quilts. Yesterday, I bought a canning kettle at Wal-Mart. I will make dill beans and Indian-spiced eggplant pickle, a recipe from a book I've got, *Small-Batch Preserving*.

So much of my life has been a blend of moving a lot, and hospitalization for brief periods when my ileostomy becomes inflamed, and for longer periods when I have to have surgery. It's not a pretty life, nor a tidy one, even on paper. I notice that I feel ashamed a lot, as if I have somehow failed. I am ashamed to be an adult who is so, in one word, dazed.

A friend wrote to me recently about "the four limitless ones" (*brahmaviharas*) and the Buddhist idea of not being ashamed of your shame, etc. Only, I feel the need to joke, "Now I'm ashamed of being ashamed of my shame." In her book *Faith: Trusting Your Own*

Deepest Experience, Sharon Salzberg advises the meditator in pain to "take apart the chord," i.e., parse the elements, of the pain. So, I've identified a couple of the root causes for my shame: I am ashamed of the degree of longing I still carry. For physical touch, physical connection. I grew up a little lab animal, and I wanted to be petted. I am ashamed of not being an achiever like the women profiled in *O: The Oprah Magazine.* ("At 42, Helen Wheels is Chief Financial Officer of Important Bank, and has three strapping teenagers.") I don't see my story reflected in the media so that Larry McMurtry essay felt like little-Black-girl-sees-little-Black-doll-for-first-time.

Recently I've been attending church, despite my theological misgivings. It's a first for me. I don't understand much about Christianity, but I like the feel of the people around me, their open hearts as they sing the lovely hymns. Recently, a woman came up to me after the service. I saw that she was tremulous; I read an aura of shock—I guessed, impact trauma—in her carriage. Sure enough, when I told her I was a massage therapist who'd been accepted to do a master's in body psychotherapy at Naropa University, she told me of her car accident two years ago.

"I'm embarrassed," she murmured, "at the way I'm still affected by it. Almost in a fresh sense every day. Bodywork is helping me. I'm realizing, it's not 'just' my body. I am my body." Looking deeply into her hazel eyes, with their lashes like iris fronds rimming a pond, I said softly, "Ah, but the body does not register time in the same way the mind does." She looked so relieved. I felt I was speaking to her in her inner language of loss, of shock.

With the money I get from this piece of writing, I plan to buy peony bushes and tulip bulbs for my garden, even though this is a rental apartment and I don't know how long I'll stay. As I plant them, I know I will think, as I so often do these days, of *Queer Nation*'s slogan: "We're here. We're queer. Get used to it." I do not want to keep apologizing for my legitimately acquired wounds. And I'm glad, I'm really glad, I didn't kill myself back in January.

As I write these closing lines, I am now scheduled for another surgery next week. I'm on a liquid diet—four food groups: soup, juice, booze, and ice cream. My sister Rebecca drove me to two gelato factories, so I have three flavors in my freezer—grapefruit, passion fruit, and chocolate peanut butter. My friend Joyce brought bright yellow daisies, and I'm pleased at the thought that people will send flowers. Flowers are essential.

Murder as a Call to Love

Judith Toy

Forgiveness is an essential part of healing wounds. Often we think of forgiveness as benefiting those who have committed the wrong, but it is really the victim's wounds that are healed by forgiveness. Forgiveness is easy to preach, of course, but so difficult to do. Perhaps we can take inspiration from Judith Toy, whose difficult journey of forgiveness ended not just in healing but in love.

When I smoked cigarettes it was two packs, sometimes three, a day. My record for lit cigarettes simultaneously burning either in ashtrays or in my hand was four. Sometimes I chewed gum, too. Half cups of cold coffee were strewn about my office. I was skinny and nervous.

It was my habit to stay in constant motion. What bogeyman did I think would strike me if I stopped moving, watching television, listening to radio, eating, reading, writing, jogging, paying bills, talking on the phone? Maybe what was living inside of me following the murders of three of my family was anger, even rage. I had no lack of confusion, doubt, greed, self-contempt, jealousy, and ego.

If I stopped, I would have come face-to-face with my deeply inadequate self.

The murders of my sister-in-law, Louise, and my two teenage nephews, Dougie and Danny, brought me to my knees. It was October 15, 1990, and looking back, I see that for me and my family, it was the holocaust. Everything normal about our lives had been shattered; our shock and despair seemed too much to bear.

The DNA evidence proved that Louise, Dougie, and Danny's lives had been cut short by the boy across the street. Eric was a friend of Dougie and Danny, and had ranked in the top 2 percent of his high school graduating class. Three weeks prior to graduation, Eric had dropped out of school and began prowling the neighborhood at night. A year later, he stabbed and bludgeoned my family to death.

Eric's father was the only neighbor willing to be interviewed by the television reporters after the murders. He was like the movie character Rambo, telling reporters, "We're going to get whoever did this; we have guns and dogs!" This air of retribution was carried on by a mob of people after Eric was arrested in Florida and extradited to Pennsylvania. When Eric was brought back in restraints in the middle of the night, a waiting crowd screamed, "Kill him, kill him!"

Two months later, the trial ended with Eric's confession. From the murder through the trial and confession, my family and I had lost so much hope that we felt like we were going through life wading underwater.

Many months later I came face-to-face with a Soto Zen monk, Patricia Dai-En Bennage, who was to change my life in two important ways: by teaching me how to stop and enjoy my breathing, and by introducing me to the teachings of mindfulness by Thich Nhat Hanh. That was thirteen years ago.

The act of stopping took courage, because I came face-to-face with my deeply inadequate self. At first when I meditated, guilt and betrayal and rage floated to the surface. I learned that the only way out of my pain was to let it happen—to go through it. And on the other side of the pain, I was welcomed into paradise through noticing my breath.

Forgiveness a Breath Away

The breath became the gateway to my heart. Because I have learned to stop, sometimes I have felt my heart as an orb of a moonflower on the garden arbor, opening to the sky. I listen to my heartbeat. I let my heart open like a bud, like a leaf unfurling.

I did not plan to forgive the boy who murdered my family. But after five years of stopping, enjoying my breathing, and relaxing every day, I was able to look deeply and understand Eric. He was not a monster, but a boy who had temporarily become a beast when he murdered my family. When I forgave Eric, I felt such a surge of relief that I understood why Jesus said, "Before you enter the temple, forgive."

Through this insight, I knew Eric was suffering intensely for his actions. And I began to understand that the seeds of violence in our society and in his family partly caused the murders. Eric was serving three consecutive life sentences in prison, with no chance of parole. I began to place myself mentally in his prison cell and hold him gently in my arms. I will never know if this helped him. One day he took a laundry bag and hung himself to death in his cell. When I learned he was dead, I profoundly mourned his passing.

Gratefully, I turned to the refuge of the three jewels—the Buddha, the dharma, and the sangha. Realizing that everything changes and that I will sooner or later lose those I love, I began to appreciate deeply the preciousness of each moment. I began washing the dishes as if each one were the baby Buddha, and looking deeply into the eyes of my grandchildren. I allowed my grief to be absorbed by the earth during walking meditation, and felt the earth give back to me, cool grasses soothing the soles of my sometimes weary feet.

During seated meditation, when emotions arise, I try to notice and stay with them. As a pain or an itch arises, instead of moving or scratching for relief, I try not giving in to the urge, but just notice the pain or the itch. How refreshing, not to move or scratch! One hot July evening while sitting, I felt a mosquito sink its proboscis into my scalp and feed. Welcome, my friend! I guess you deserve to live, too, I thought. There was never any swelling or itch from that bite.

HEALING BOTH FAMILIES

My husband, Philip, and I take a bell to a medium security prison to share our practice with young inmates, some of whom had known Eric. The small bell with a beautiful sound is the centerpiece of our practice together. The noise of slamming metal doors and the prison public address system is the background even as we sit and walk in silence. Upon hearing the bell we breathe three times, returning to the moment. The men named themselves Fragrant Lotus Petal Sangha, a place of refuge.

I called and talked with Eric's mother. We cried together over the four needless deaths in our two families. She said that in the thirteen years since the murders, mine was the first phone call regarding her son. She and her husband have been so shunned that they have become invisible to their family and neighbors and friends. She thanked me and asked God to bless me for making the call.

The first holy truth of the Buddha is that life constantly offers up suffering. Life offered me my deeply inadequate self for transformation. I no longer smoke cigarettes and pace the floors, afraid to stop. In fact, now that I'm walking mindfully on the path of joy, everything in the actual world—the rising sun, the sound of sirens, a crying child, the squealing of brakes, a Mozart sonata, even a war—reminds me to breathe, to breathe in a universe that, while full of anguish, will always, always breathe with me.

Removing the Thorn ☽

Frank Olendzki

Buddhism makes a distinction between pain and suffering. As long as we have bodies, we will experience pain, but the Buddha said that we do not have to suffer. If we remove the thorn of desire, he said, we ease the sufferings of stress, disquiet, fear, and conflict that mark our lives. As Buddhist scholar Frank Olendski explains, this is the Buddha's key diagnosis of the human condition.

In a remarkable passage in the *Attadanda Sutta*, the Buddha speaks frankly about his fear and dismay about the state of society:

> Fear is born from arming oneself.
> Just see how many people fight!
> I'll tell you about the dreadful fear
> That caused me to shake all over.
> Seeing creatures flopping around,
> Like fishes in shallow water,
> So hostile to one another!
> —Seeing this, I became afraid.

This image—fishes flopping around in the shallows—seems as apt today as ever. As the world's resources diminish and the number of people in need of them increases, things may well get only more desperate. Even in the Buddha's time the situation seemed over-whelming. The Buddha acknowledges his despair, but he also de-scribes his breakthrough to a deeper understanding:

> Seeing people locked in conflict,
> I became completely distraught.
> But then I discerned here a thorn
> —Hard to see—lodged deep in the heart.
>
> It's only when pierced by this thorn
> That one runs in all directions.
> So if that thorn is taken out—
> One does not run, and settles down.
> (*Sutta Nipata* 935–39)

This pivotal insight shapes how conflict and peace are to be un-derstood in the Buddhist tradition. Human society is formed by the collective action of its individuals; it thus reflects the qualities of heart and mind of each person. Peace in people's hearts creates peace in the world; turmoil in people's hearts creates turmoil in the world. The harmful behavior people manifest in the world can be seen as having a single cause. That cause is desire.

Desire comes in two forms, attachment and aversion. The first makes us grab after the things we like and hold on to them; the sec-ond makes us avoid or resist or attack the things we don't like. At-tachment leads us to consume resources at any cost and take from others what has not been given to us; it drives us to exploit others for personal gain. It also underlies such personality traits as pride, arro-gance, conceit, selfishness, and the lust for power. Aversion compels us to turn away from what we find unpleasant, to shut out or dis-criminate against those we don't like, and to destroy what we fear or what we don't understand. It also causes such aberrant behaviors as violence, cruelty, bigotry, and other acts of hatefulness.

But these thorns in the heart can be removed. It is just the thorn, driving us mad with pain and fear, that makes us crazy enough to hurt and hate, that makes us lose touch with our innate goodness. Like a ferocious lion with a thorn in its paw, we are only in need of a healer to come pull out the thorn that afflicts us. The Buddha was such a healer. Having diagnosed the problem as desire—so embedded in the heart that it is often hard to see—his prescription was simply to apply awareness to the problem, and to do so in massive doses. Because the workings of desire are hidden in the unconscious functioning of the mind, we must bring greater consciousness to bear on the moment. We have only to learn to see things clearly, and a natural process of healing will occur.

To heal the individual wounds brought about by desire, the Buddha prescribed mindful meditation, the careful, moment-to-moment observation of everything arising and falling in the field of phenomenal experience. When we are able to see what is actually occurring within us, wisdom will gradually evolve. The principle is simple, but it takes practice. To heal the collective wounds of our planet, likewise brought about by desire in its various forms, it seems to me we might apply the same prescription. The way to bring collective mindfulness to bear on the collective field of experience is through witnessing and sharing what has been seen by others.

We can see many examples today of the beneficial things that can happen when an atrocity is caught on tape and shared widely with others, or when evidence of wrongdoing is brought to light and exposed before the court of world opinion. Just as the evil we are capable of as individuals lies lurking unexamined deep in our psyches, so also much of the cruelty and abuse that takes place in the world is hidden from view. And just as uncovering our personal demons can begin a process of healing, so also can the revealing of cruelties and injustices that have been kept secret have a transformative effect on global behavior.

According to the Buddha, the human world is protected by twin guardians, two forces in the mind that watch over and guide moral behavior. The first guardian of the world is *hiri*, a word that connotes conscience, moral intuition, and self-respect. It refers to that within the human psyche that knows the difference between right and wrong, between what is noble and ignoble, between what is worthy of respect and what is not. Each of us has within us an innate moral compass, and it is the view of the Buddhist tradition that religion is not the source of this but rather a form by which it is given expression. The second guardian of the world is *ottappa,* which comprises such notions as social conscience, a cultural or collective sense of morality, and respect for the opinions and the rights of others.

Buddhism teaches that anything we do that is wholesome will be done with the support and guidance of these two inner guardians. Conversely, everything we do that is unwholesome can only be done when these moral guides are disregarded. So if there is something morally reprehensible occurring in an individual or in a society, it means that we lack sufficient clarity of awareness of what we are doing. It means we are temporarily blinded by our greed, hatred, or delusion, or by some combination of the three, such that we refuse to attend openly to the deeds we are committing. When attention has been brought to bear on the matter—in sufficient amounts, with sufficient intensity, and with sufficient honesty—we will naturally shy away from doing harm to ourselves, to others, and to both.

Does this sound idealistic? I don't think it is. It is rooted in a very sophisticated understanding of human nature. So let's spend more time on that collective *zafu,* shining the light of awareness into the dark corners of the world. The possibility exists for radical universal transformation. We have merely to start the process, in our own mind, and the rest will naturally fall into place.

Ego Goes Global

David Loy

*One of Buddhism's geniuses has been to diagnose the causes of suffering
(as well as its remedy), but traditionally it has done that only at the level
of the individual. One of the great contributions of modern Buddhism is
to identify and analyze the suffering caused by social, political, and economic systems. David Loy is one of American Buddhism's most interesting
and original thinkers. Here he explains how the "three poisons" of greed,
ill will, and delusion operate through the collective, institutionalized
version of ego he calls "wego."*

Shakyamuni Buddha, the historical Buddha, lived in ancient India
at least 2,400 years ago. Buddhism is an Iron Age religion. So how
could it help us to understand and address modern issues such as the
war on terrorism, economic globalization, and biotechnology?

What the Buddha did know about was human suffering: how it
works, what causes it, and how to end it. But the word *suffering* is
not a good translation of the Pali term *dukkha*. The point is that
even those who are wealthy and healthy nonetheless experience a
basic dissatisfaction that continually festers. That we find life dissat-
isfactory, one damned problem after another, is not accidental or
coincidental. It is the very nature of the unawakened mind to be
bothered about something, because at the core of our being there is

a free-floating anxiety that has no particular object but can be plugged into any problematic situation.

In order to understand why that anxiety exists, we must relate dukkha to another crucial Buddhist term, *anatta,* or non-self. Our basic frustration is due most of all to the fact that our sense of being a separate self, set apart from the world we are in, is an illusion. Another way to express this is that the ego-self is ungrounded, and as a result we experience an uncomfortable emptiness or hole at the very core of our being. We feel this problem as a sense of lack, of inadequacy, of unreality, and in compensation we usually spend our lives trying to accomplish things that we think will make us more real.

But what does this have to do with social challenges? Doesn't it imply that social problems are just projections of our own dissatisfaction? Unfortunately, it's not so easy. As social beings, we tend to group our sense of lack, even as we strive to compensate by creating collective senses of self.

In fact, many of our social problems can be traced back to this deluded sense of collective self, what I call the "wego," or group ego. It can be defined as one's own race, class, gender, nation (the primary secular god of the modern world), religion, or some combination thereof. In each case, a collective identity is created by discriminating one's own group from another. As in the personal ego, the "inside" is opposed to the other "outside," and this makes conflict inevitable, not just because of competition with other groups, but because the socially constructed nature of group identity means that one's own group can never feel secure enough. For example, our GNP is not big enough, our nation is not powerful ("secure") enough, we are not technologically developed enough. And if these are instances of group-lack or group-dukkha, our GNP can never be big enough, our military can never be powerful enough, and we can never have enough technology. This means that trying to solve our economic, political, and ecological problems with more of the same is a deluded response.

Religion at its best encourages us to understand and subvert the destructive dualism between self and other, and between collective self and collective other. This kind of self-less universalism—or, better, nondiscrimination that does not place us over them—provides the basis for Buddhist social action. But in some ways our situation today is quite different from that of Shakyamuni Buddha's. Today we have not only more powerful scientific technologies, but also much more powerful institutions.

The problem with institutions is that they tend to take on a life of their own as new types of wego. Consider, for example, how a big corporation works. To survive in a competitive market, it must adapt to the constraints built into that market. Even if the CEO of a multinational company wants to be socially responsible, he or she is limited by the expectations of stockholders and Wall Street analysts; if profits are threatened by his sensitivity to social concerns, he is likely to lose his job. New forms of impersonal, collective self such as corporations are very good at preserving themselves and increasing their power, quite apart from the personal motivations of the individuals who serve them. This suggests that the response of a socially engaged Buddhism must become somewhat different too. We are challenged to find new ways to address the new forms of dukkha that institutions now create and reinforce.

There is another Buddhist principle that can help us explain this connection between dukkha and collective selves: the three roots of evil, also known as the three poisons. Instead of emphasizing the duality between good and evil, Buddhism distinguishes between wholesome and unwholesome (*kusala* and *akusalamula*) tendencies. The main sources of unwholesome behavior—the three roots of evil—are greed, ill will, and delusion. To end dukkha, these three need to be transformed into their positive counterparts: greed into generosity, ill will into loving-kindness, delusion into wisdom.

An important question for engaged Buddhism is, Do the three roots of evil also work impersonally and structurally in modern institutions?

Institutionalized greed. In our economic system corporations are never profitable enough and people never consume enough. It's a circular process in which we all participate, whether as workers, employers, consumers, investors, or pensioners, but we have little or no personal sense of moral responsibility for what happens. Awareness has been diffused so completely that it is lost in the impersonal anonymity of the corporate economic system.

Institutionalized ill will. In Buddhist terms, much of the world's suffering has been a result of our way of thinking about good and evil. The basic problem with a simplistic good-versus-evil way of understanding conflict is that, because it tends to preclude further thought, it keeps us from looking deeper. Once something has been identified as evil, there is no more need to explain it; it is time to focus on fighting against it. The best example of institutionalized ill will is, of course, collective aggression: the institutionalization of militarism. After World War II, the U.S. did not demilitarize, but decided to maintain a permanent war-economy to fight communism. The collapse of communism at the end of the 1980s created a problem for the military-industrial complex, but now a never-ending "war against terrorism" has taken its place.

Institutionalized delusion. The most fundamental delusion, both individually and collectively, is our sense of a self/other duality—that "I" am inside and the rest of the world is outside. Nationalism is a powerful institutional version of such a group wego. For that matter, so is the basic species duality between *Homo sapiens* and the rest of the biosphere, which is why we feel free to use and abuse nature technologically, with almost no regard for the consequences.

If we understand this third collective problem as institutionalized ignorance, it helps us to see that modern life in all developed nations is organized in a way that works to conceal the dukkha it causes. The system inflicts dukkha on all of us, but most of all on people whom we do not see and therefore do not need to think about. Thanks to clever advertising and peer pressure, my son can learn to crave Nike shoes and Gap shirts without ever wondering about how they are made. I can satisfy my coffee and chocolate cravings without any awareness of the social conditions of the farmers who grow those commodities. My son and I are encouraged to live in a self-enclosed cocoon of hedonistic consumption.

Realizing the nature of these institutional poisons is just as spiritual and just as important as any personal realization one might have as a result of Buddhist (or other spiritual) practice. In fact, any individual awakening we may have on our meditation cushions remains incomplete until it is supplemented by such a "social awakening." In both cases, what is needed is a greater awareness that goes beyond the limitations of ego- and wego-consciousness. Usually we think of expanded consciousness in individual terms, but today we must penetrate through the veils of social delusion to attain greater understanding of dualistic social, economic, and ecological realities.

Contemplating Emptiness ◎⟩⟩

The Dzogchen Ponlop Rinpoche

*It's easy to misunderstand the Buddhist doctrine of emptiness. It is a
subtle and layered understanding that goes far deeper than a simple
statement that "nothing exists." Traditionally, the exploration of emptiness
begins by contemplating and analyzing the nature of phenomena, including our own mind and body, and eventually this intellectual exercise will
lead to a direct and nonconceptual experience of genuine reality. An excel-
lent place to begin this journey is this series of contemplations by the
young Tibetan teacher Ponlop Rinpoche.*

The Buddha Shakyamuni first turned the Wheel of Dharma at Deer
Park in Varanasi, India, not long after his achievement of enlightenment. At that time, he introduced his students to the first stage of
understanding a profound notion that was to become a cornerstone
of all Buddhist view and meditation: emptiness.

According to this view, as individuals, we ultimately lack any
true, inherent, or independent existence of our own; our actual state
of existence is empty of anything that can be established as a "self."
Buddha continued to propound the teachings on emptiness and, at
Vulture Peak Mountain in Rajagriha, India, he taught this view even
more extensively. What his students heard at this time was that this

emptiness applied not only to the personal self but also to all phenomena of the relative world. Thus it was taught that the nature of our whole field of existence is this great emptiness—not a void, not a vacuum, not a mere absence, but something genuinely beyond the grasp and limitations of conventional mind.

All Buddhist schools today, from the Hinayana to the Vajrayana, hold in common the view of emptiness, and the practice tradition associated with this view is one of the distinguishing features of Buddhism. The meditation on emptiness encompasses two aspects: the emptiness of the self of person, and the emptiness of the self of phenomena. While meditations on emptiness can be found in other traditions as well, the meditation on the selflessness of person, in particular, is unique to Buddhism. That is our focus here.

EGO-CLINGING: THE ROOT OF SAMSARA

A spontaneous verse spoken by Khenpo Tsultrim Gyamtso Rinpoche explains why it is necessary to ascertain selflessness, or egolessness:

> Because fixation on a self is the root of samsara
> As well as the root of karma and mental afflictions,
> And since fixation on the self is the root of all suffering,
> Its opposite, selflessness, must be ascertained.

This verse says that the root of samsara is ego-clinging. How does fixation on a self engender samsara? As soon as the concept of "self" arises, the projection of "other" also arises. When we project and cling onto the self as "I" or "me," this fixation naturally creates the corresponding image of "others out there." This is how self-clinging is the cause of duality. It creates a separation between "self" and "other." Clinging to the self, we develop attachment, which then becomes a cherishing of the self. On that basis, we engage in all the mental afflictions to protect that self from others.

All the mental afflictions—aggression, jealousy, judgment,

pride, envy, and so on—develop on the basis of the separation of self and other. From the arising of mental afflictions comes our subsequent engagement in negative actions of mind, and it is right then that we accumulate karma. While we accumulate the seeds of both positive and negative actions, we are primarily accumulating negative seeds at this point. Through our involvement with such repetitive negative actions, we wander in samsara. The result of these negative seeds is the full manifestation of samsara.

It is clear how the fixation on a self causes suffering, how it becomes the root of all the suffering that we experience. We have many wonderful, beautiful illusions of the world, but when we do not realize that they are illusions and get caught in clinging to them as real and truly existent, we wander in samsara and experience all kinds of suffering. On the basis of this self-clinging, we create suffering not only for ourselves but also for others. It is said in the *Pramanavartika,* or *Commentary on Valid Cognition,* a classical Buddhist text by the great master Dharmakirti:

> If one conceives of the existence of a self, one will conceive
> of an other. From self and other arise clinging and aversion.
> Through thoroughly engaging in these, all faults arise.

"All faults" refers to suffering and mental afflictions. First, we have self-clinging and from there we have duality; the concept of "others" is automatically projected. Next arise the mental afflictions—aversion, attachment, anger, jealousy, and so on—and from there we have suffering.

This is evident in our own immediate experience. For example, we can easily see how much suffering we experience when we have strong anger or very strong attachment. We can see how much suffering we create as a result of the mental afflictions of jealousy or pride. We can also see that this doesn't happen only once and then pass; rather it happens again and again and again. This is what we call *samsara,* which has the connotation of a vicious circle.

Engaging in repetitive actions involving mental afflictions habituates us to these states of mind. It becomes so natural, so normal, to arouse anger. Certain environments create the conditions for us to give rise to strong anger. The first time, we experience anger as an irritation and feel just a little uncomfortable. The next time anger occurs, it becomes a bit stronger, like a small spark. Then it gets bigger and bigger and becomes like a flame to which the environment adds oxygen. The next time we find ourselves in the situation, our anger is very strong and we are ready to punch someone. The point is to see how the anger grows, especially over time when we become habituated to it.

Such habituation is our main problem because it creates a pattern. In fact, the main thing we are trying to transcend is our habitual patterns and tendencies. As for the mental afflictions, or *kleshas,* themselves, there is actually nothing to transcend. They are already gone. They come and they go. What we actually have to transform is that which is hanging on to all these kleshas—our habitual tendencies. We have to watch out for the habit of self-clinging.

How does self-clinging arise in every situation: at work, during dharma practice, or with our family? We can see how it destroys us and brings us a lot of suffering, but how does the self, or ego, come into existence? It is said that when we experience such habituation of self-clinging and the mental afflictions, it is like having a dream when we do not recognize that we are dreaming.

Samsara itself is a long dream. What we ordinarily call a "dream" is something much shorter, something that we wake up from every morning. But the dream of samsara continues, and when we are in the dream and do not recognize we are dreaming, we see everything as very real and very solid. We experience many kinds of suffering and pain, as well as some happiness. Between these alternating states, there is so much struggle. Yet, we do not see how we can transform that suffering. Not recognizing that we are dreaming, there is no way to imagine waking from that dream. Our experiences seem so real, just as our suffering does, and we do not see how we can free ourselves from such suffering.

In the same way, we are all in samsara right now, and our ego-clinging is so strong that it is very difficult to imagine how we could wake up, or what our experience might be like if we were to realize selflessness. We might wonder, How could I function in the world without this ego? How could I survive without clinging to myself?

From the Buddhist point of view, we would be much better off if we realized selflessness. We would function more efficiently and survive with less struggle; we would be stronger and benefit others much more than we can right now. Take, for example, the Mahayana masters, the bodhisattvas, and the great Hinayana arhats. These realized masters can manifest in the world and benefit sentient beings much more effectively than ordinary beings. Realizing egolessness does not mean that we forget how to do things. Rather, it means that we acquire the clarity and precision of mind that sees every detail of our actions in the world. One reason why our actions are often not so effective is that we do not have such clarity or insight; we lack the wisdom that sees our actions clearly in terms of cause and effect. When we realize the nature of selflessness, however, we see very clearly the subtleties of every movement of our body, speech, and mind.

Therefore, gaining certainty in the view of selflessness is very important and necessary. It is similar to what the great teacher of Madhyamaka, Chandrikirti, said in his text *Entrance to the Middle Way,* "First thinking 'me,' they fixate upon a self. Then thinking 'this is mine,' attachment to things develops." This shows indirectly how fixation on a self results in the development of other mental afflictions.

SELFLESSNESS OF PERSON

Three Incorrect Notions

Khenpo Tsultrim Gyamtso Rinpoche's next verse shows the Hinayana view of the selflessness of person, which is the first stage of meditation on emptiness.

> Because the observed objects of self-fixation are devoid of
>   inherent nature,

Because the mind of self-fixation is also devoid of inherent
    nature,
And because the self of past and future lives is like a moon
    reflected in the water,
Certainty in selflessness, the true nature, must be stabilized.

This verse looks at the notion of our self-clinging. When we cling
to the self as "I" or "me," we are generating several wrong ideas, which
can be summarized as three incorrect ways of perceiving the self.

The first incorrect notion is clinging to the self as being *permanent.* The second is clinging to the self as being *singular.* The third is
clinging to the self as being *independent.* Furthermore, each of these
three different types of clinging is associated with a corresponding
ignorance. Clinging to the self as being permanent arises due to ignorance with respect to time. Clinging to the self as being singular
arises due to ignorance with respect to the object observed as the
self. Clinging to the self as being independent arises due to ignorance with respect to causes and conditions.

The first incorrect notion is that we see ourselves as being permanent. Of course we never say to others in so many words, "I am
permanent," but this is how we basically think, and it comes from ignorance about time: past, present, and future, which are known as
"the three times." Not seeing the nature of our momentary existence, we lump all three times together as one and say, "This is me. I
am the same person I was yesterday, the day before, last year, twenty
years ago, thirty years ago. . . ." In the idea that "I am the same person," there is a sense of permanence: "I will do such-and-such in the
future. I will retire in a certain number of years. I will travel around
the world. I will go into three-year retreat." We do not see that the future is made up of moments that are yet to come; that every moment
we live is a separate, independent moment; and that there is not a
single self that exists throughout all these moments. All of this arises
from our ignorance with respect to time.

The second incorrect notion is that we cling to the self as being a
singular entity. When we say "I," we think it is one thing. But what is

this "self" or "I" when we actually look at it? When we look at the observed object of self-fixation, we find that the self is not singular but multiple because, from the Buddhist point of view, the basis of self-clinging is the five *skandhas,* or aggregates. The self is not singular but rather is composed of five different things. These five are the skandha of form, the skandha of feelings, the skandha of discrimination, the skandha of formation, and the skandha of consciousness.

The first of the five, the form skandha, relates to the physical body, and the next four are all related to the mind. So, in short, we can say that there are two observed objects of self-clinging: body and mind. Therefore, the self is not singular; it has at least two objects. And when we examine these two, we find that they, too, comprise many parts. We don't find just one form or one body. The body itself has many parts. It is not singular. The mind also has many parts; it is not a single entity either. Therefore the self is not singular. However, we have this ignorance with respect to the singularity of the self.

The third incorrect notion is that we think the self is independent. We believe that it is not dependent on anything when, in fact, the existence of the self is dependent on many causes and conditions. This is the ignorance about causes and conditions. The self cannot exist without many different causes and conditions coming together. Therefore its nature is not independent; rather, it exists dependently.

Our wrong ideas about the self can be summarized in these three incorrect notions, or mistaken ways, of fixating on or clinging to a perceived self. However, when we analyze these different ways of clinging, we see that our fixations are based on a very coarse understanding of the self. Through our analysis, we begin to develop a more subtle understanding. We begin to see how we cling to the self as permanent when it is impermanent, singular when it is multiple, and independent when it relies on causes and conditions. In this way, we discover that our original assumptions do not reflect reality.

Moreover, when we look at the self of person, we find two elements: the observed object and the mind of self-fixation.

The Observed Object and the Mind of Fixation

When we look for the observed object, or the basis of self-clinging, we discover that it is the five skandhas. They are the basis upon which we think, "This is me." So it is important to relate with these and analyze each one to see exactly *where* this "self" is located. Our sense of "I," of "me-ness," is so strong that we should be able to find this self if it truly exists. Therefore, in the first stage of our analysis, we should try to pinpoint the location of our self-clinging.

First, we look among these five skandhas. Is the self located in just one of the skandhas, such as the skandha of form or the skandha of feeling? Is it to be found in the skandha of discrimination, the skandha of formation, or the skandha of consciousness? Or we may conclude that the basis of the self is all five skandhas together.

Once we have reached a conclusion about the location of the self, then, in the second stage of our analysis we look to see exactly *what* this self is. What is it that this ego or "I" clings to as my "self," as "me"? If we think that the self is in the form skandha, for example, then we would ask: Is the self the whole body, or one of its parts? The skandha of form has many parts. What is the self among all those parts? Is it the brain? Is it the heart? If we conclude that there is no self, after all, in the skandha of form, then we apply the same line of investigation to the remaining skandhas. If we think the self is most likely to be located in the skandha of feeling, we would ask: Is the self the totality of feeling, or is it just one particular feeling? If it is one feeling, which one is it? And so on with the skandhas of discrimination, formation, and consciousness.

If we say that the self is the form skandha, the body, then it would follow that our body would be permanent, singular, and independent of causes and conditions. If that were so, then it would follow that the self, which is singular and is the skandha of form, could not include any of the other skandhas, such as consciousness. Therefore, self would exist as body alone and would lack the attributes of mind. Furthermore, each of the other skandhas would then become another, separate self. The result would be the existence of five different selves, which is not the case. This contradicts our experience and clearly shows that the self is neither singular nor permanent, because when we think of the self, we think not only of form but also of the mental attributes of the other four skandhas. In the same way, if we look at the self as being the skandha of consciousness, then consciousness would have to be singular, permanent, and independent. But this is not the case either.

We can also approach our analysis using simply these two—the body and the mind—as the main objects of focus. When we examine in this way, then where is self-clinging? Sometimes we perceive self-clinging, the sense of "I" or "me," as being body. For example, when we have a headache, we say, "I have a headache." We don't say, "The body has a headache." In this situation, we are perceiving our body as the self. Similarly, when we cut ourselves in the kitchen, we say, "I cut myself." Here again we are seeing the self as the body, the skandha of form. We can clearly see in these two examples how we perceive the body as the self. However, when we experience mental suffering, we might say, "I'm unhappy. I'm depressed." In this case, we are regarding mind as the self, and so our fixation is on the mind. In everyday life, we alternate between these fixations, this clinging onto the self as being either the body or the mind. Much of our confusion and suffering comes from not seeing this clearly; that is why we don't know who we are.

Therefore, we should analyze and gain some certainty about where and what the self is. Is it the body or is it the mind? If the self is the body, then, from hair to toes, where is it? If the self is the mind, then is it in our feelings, discriminations, formations, or consciousnesses? If it is within the consciousnesses, then which one is it? We have many types of consciousnesses. Generally, when we refer to our consciousness, we are referring to the sixfold collection of consciousness: the eye consciousness, the ear consciousness, the nose consciousness, the tongue consciousness, the body consciousness, and finally the mental consciousness. The sixth, the mental consciousness, has two aspects, a conceptual and a nonconceptual side.

So what and where is the self among the consciousnesses? It is important to analyze the object of fixation on the self in this way.

When we look at the self of person, as we discussed earlier, we find two elements: the observed object and the mind of self-fixation. These two, object and subject, exist only by way of their interdependent relationship. If we have thoroughly analyzed and found no self in any or all of the five skandhas, then it naturally follows that the mind that fixates on that self must also be empty. In other words, the mind of fixation—the subject that observes and fixates on the object—cannot exist either.

Once we have determined that there is no self anywhere in all these objects we have inspected, we can be certain that the self does not exist. As a consequence, we can also be certain that the mind that clings to that notion must also be free of existence. Therefore, there is absolutely no existence of self.

The Interdependent Self

From the Buddhist point of view, the self exists only on the level of relative reality and only on the basis of all five skandhas. That is why it is called the dependent or interdependent nature. We can illustrate this with the example of five matchsticks standing upright, leaning together to form the shape of a tent. Any one of these matchsticks could not stand up without relying on the support of the others. In the same way, the illusion of self can only exist on the basis of all five skandhas coming together, and that which is dependent on causes and conditions has no true existence of its own.

Whatever comes from a collection, such as a self, has no true, or self-existence. This can be illustrated by the example of a car. What we call a "car" is actually a collection of many different components: four tires, a body, an engine, a steering wheel, gas and break pedals, seats, windows, and so forth. If we look at it in this way, there is no separate entity called "car" beyond the coming together of these parts. We cannot find the car in any one of the individual mechanisms. These parts have their own designations, such as "tire," "seat," and "steering wheel." Each has a different name and is not the car.

Thus the illusion of "car," our notion of car, only appears as the result of the coming together of many causes and conditions. In the same way that there is no inherently existing car, there is no independently existing self. The self we experience conventionally is of the nature of interdependence. Accordingly, it is emptiness. In its own nature, it is devoid of anything permanent, singular, or independent—of anything truly existent.

Furthermore, it is said that the self we experience as coming from a past moment into the present moment and continuing on into a future moment is like the reflection of the moon in clear water. The reflection appears so vividly and clearly, yet it has no solid existence. It appears due to the coming together of certain causes and conditions: clear water, an absence of wind, the moon above, and a sky that is free of clouds. In the same way, the self, which appears to us so vividly and clearly, is just an empty form. When all its causes and conditions come together, we have the appearance of a self that continues from the past and into the future. However, that self is as illusory and empty as a reflection of the moon in water.

How Body and Mind Exist

When we analyze the two main aspects of the skandhas, body and mind, we must address the question of *how* they exist. How does the body exist? How does mind exist? When we look at the body, or the skandha of form, we are starting with physical matter. Conventionally speaking, we accept that matter exists on a subtle level as countless infinitesimal particles, or atoms, which then become the building blocks of larger, more coarse-level forms. However, according to Buddhist analysis, when we analyze these atoms using various reasonings, we cannot find any solid matter, any physical substance that truly exists. Regardless of how deep and refined our analysis is, we will not be able to find, finally, the particles of which coarser objects are composed. TVs, telephones, newspapers, as well as our own bodies, all of these are forms that can be broken down to an atomic level. When we arrive at that level, however, we find that these subtle particles are not solid entities either. They are not "the last remaining" thing. They can be further divided. We cannot find anything that is, in itself, partless. Thus, if we analyze thoroughly and do not find any truly existing particles on the subtlest of levels, then what is the basis for the tangible forms that we see and use every day?

We can combine our understanding arrived at through reasoning with the insights of scientists working in the field of contemporary physics. Many of these scientists are suggesting that the basic makeup of existence goes far beyond the atomic level; whatever it is that exists as a creative force is not solid matter but exists more as energy fields, to which names are given like "quarks" or "strings." Giving such names to these energy fields makes it all sound a little more substantial than if it were identified as "emptiness." Emptiness scares people, but quarks and strings are somehow more comforting. They may be nicer words, but in the end they actually say the same thing: emptiness. So modern science arrives, by it owns means, at the same conclusion as reasoning and logical analysis.

When we look at mind to see how it exists, we see that, like the body, the mind has many parts, and each part is momentary. When we look very carefully at this momentary nature of mind, we can isolate a single moment of thought, and this single moment can be regarded as the smallest unit of mind, akin to the atom. However, when we look further, we find that this single moment of thought has three parts: a beginning, a middle, and an end. Described another way, it is said that thoughts arise, abide, and cease. Therefore, each thought goes through a three-stage process. Nevertheless, when we examine what we actually mean by "a thought," we find that we are talking about the second stage, the moment of abiding. For most of us, that is the only perceptible moment. But when we look carefully at this abiding moment of thought, we find that it, too, has three parts: one that is just arising, one that is abiding, and another that is just ceasing. We begin to see that this very subtle moment of thought is actually nonexistent, and it is the same for all moments of consciousnesses, regardless of whether it is a moment of feeling, perception, or thought. Therefore when we look at the mind consciousness and try to find true existence—a solid existence that is permanent, singular, and independent—that nature of mind cannot be found.

Therefore the basis of self-clinging with regard to both the body and the mind is actually empty, appearing form. Unanalyzed, these forms seem quite real and solid, but when we analyze them, they are like mirages. This is what we call illusion, and all illusions are like that. Sometimes when you are driving on a highway, you may see water on the road ahead. You may even see the reflection of the lights of other cars in the water. But when you get closer, there is nothing but asphalt. In the same way, the body and mind seem very real and the world seems very solid when we don't analyze them. However, when we look closely at our experiences, we find only the arising, abiding, and ceasing of selfless, transitory states, whether these are states of happiness or states of suffering. This may be bad news if you have a happy mind, but it's good news if you have a suffering mind.

Understanding Selflessness in the Context of the Two Truths

It is important to remember that the analysis described here is presented from the point of view of absolute, ultimate reality, not from the point of view of relative truth or conventional reality. From the perspective of the absolute nature, we say that things do not have true existence but are empty in nature. However, from the relative or conventional point of view, things do have interdependent existence. Things exist, but only in a state of interdependence. There is the interdependent arising of self and the interdependent continuity of self, that is, a sense of self that continues from the past into the present and on into the future.

Because there is this sense of continuity in relative truth, the Buddha presented the teachings about karma—cause and effect—and about how an individual can transform his or her mental afflictions and achieve freedom. However, the sense of continuity is still relative, interdependent existence. Nothing exists solidly; there is nothing other than interdependent existence. Relatively speaking there is a world, but its nature is entirely interdependent. That is why Nagarjuna and other great masters who taught emptiness said very clearly that, when we study this view of egolessness, we must separate the relative truth and the absolute truth. If we mix them, we will become confused. Once, during a teaching on emptiness a student asked me, "If everything is empty, then isn't your chair also empty?" I said, "Yes, of course, my chair is also empty." The student then questioned, "Then how can you sit on it? Why don't you fall to the floor if it is empty?" This student was trying to put a relative, solid person on an absolute, empty chair. He was mixing the two truths. We must see that when the chair is empty, the person is empty too.

Interdependent existence is the nature of the relative truth, which we call "mere appearance," or mere existence. Everything merely appears to be real, much like in a dream. For example, in a dream, when you see fire and put your finger into it, it gets burned. But when you wake from that dream, you realize there was no fire, there was no person, and there was no action of burning. None of that existed on the ultimate level. In the same way, when we are confused about the appearances of relative truth, we have many vivid experiences—just as we do when we are dreaming—but when we realize emptiness, the absolute nature of reality, it is like waking from a dream. We are no longer confused about relative appearances. Therefore, distinguishing between the relative and absolute levels of truth is very necessary. We must understand that when we are talking about selflessness or emptiness, we are speaking from the perspective of absolute truth.

RESTING IN CERTAINTY

When we have thoroughly practiced analytical meditation, when we have reached the point in our investigation when we have looked deeply and extensively into both body and mind and have been unable to find the existence of a self, we will experience a sense of a gap. That is the beginning of certainty in selflessness. Certainty comes not only from hearing or reading words about selflessness but also from our personal experience of searching and analyzing, through which we reach our own conclusions. This is very important. When we reach that level of certainty, we should rest in it. We should relax and rest freely. Whether we feel we have achieved a complete experience of selflessness or only a glimpse, it does not matter. Just rest in that nature of emptiness.

This is the first stage of the meditation on emptiness, resting in the nonexistence of a self—of not finding that self—and then resting in that certainty. We reach this point through analysis. *Look* at your body, *look* at your mind—where is the self? Then *rest* in that moment, in that very moment, of not finding the self. It is very important not to miss that moment. Sometimes we get lost in the analysis. We don't find anything and we think, "Oh, I'll just go back over it again and maybe find something." Instead, at the point when we don't find anything, we should rest as much as we can. Sometimes, when we have come to the point of resting, we find the experience so beautiful that we want to hold on to it. Then grasping comes, and the thought process resumes. At that point we have to return to our analysis.

This is an important process, because repeatedly alternating our analyzing and resting minds leads us to greater and greater certainty. Certainty based on such direct experience is much stronger than the confidence we might have in someone else's experience. If we merely believe the words of gurus or other meditators who say, "Yes, it is all empty," then our meditation becomes very shallow. At some point we may be forced to acknowledge that we actually have no idea what we are doing. But if we reach certainty through our own analysis, then that certainty will be much deeper because it is our own conclusion. It is our own conclusion based on the Buddha's words, and when these two come together we have a much deeper and more valuable experience.

FINDING THE MIDDLE WAY

As our practice of meditation on emptiness matures, eventually we will be able to rest free of apprehending both existence and nonexistence, which are regarded equally as extreme beliefs. On the one hand, if we hold a solid belief in the inherent existence of things, then we are denying their empty, absolute nature. On the other hand, if we hold a solid belief in the utter nonexistence of things, then we are denying conventional appearances, which do have an interdependent existence on the level of relative reality. No matter which extreme we are fixated on, they are equal in their power to obscure the direct experience of emptiness, which is beyond all such conceptual fabrications.

In order to arrive at the middle way that is beyond these two extremes, sometimes we must first go to the extreme of nonexistence. In our practice, we should emphasize the empty or ultimate nature of mind and phenomena, and de-emphasize the relative, appearing aspect. We do this because right now we have such a strong clinging to existence altogether—to the existence of the self, to the existence of the skandhas, to the existence of mind and body. Because we cling to existence so strongly, we should throw our mind all the way to the other extreme of nonexistence. We should go in that direction as far as we can. However, no matter how far we go, our mind will always be pulled back toward existence. Our mind will never be completely stuck in the view of nonexistence because there is a kind of gravity that pulls us back. That gravity is the force of our clinging, our grasping at solid existence. Therefore, when we find ourselves drifting back, we throw our mind again toward the extreme of nonexistence. It is much like the swinging of a pendulum between two opposing points. We do this over and over until, at some point, we find the middle way that goes beyond existence and nonexistence. Therefore, at the beginning, resting in the complete opposite of existence, in nonexistence, is very important.

Once we are able to stabilize our certainty in nonexistence and rest within that for a long time, we should change the focus of our practice. We may find that we have become attached to the view of nonexistence, and that is also a fault. Then we should begin to dismantle the idea of nonexistence and try to transcend that fixation as well. In the beginning stage of our practice, however, we do not have to worry about that. We should simply rest in the nonexistence of self as much as we can.

Generally speaking, when you reach the level of analysis where you say, "Oh, I can't find the self," or, "There is no self!" at that point you should rest without any concepts. Just simply relax and let go of everything. Let go of all your thoughts, including the thought of the observer. Just let go. That is actually the point where the observer and the observed merge. They come together and there is no more separation. It is like rubbing two sticks together to create a fire. The fire that is produced will burn both sticks, not just one. In the same way, when you have realized selflessness, the fire of that wisdom will transcend both subject and object.

My Guru ⚌⟫

Tulku Urgyen Rinpoche

It has been argued that the Buddhist sangha, which began more than 2,500 years ago, is the oldest continuous institution in human history. That's more than a historical curiosity; it points to the very essence of Buddhism—as a living transmission from teacher to student going back in an unbroken lineage to the Buddha himself. All of the great Buddhist teachers, such as the late Tulku Urgyen Rinpoche, were once students themselves, and they remain forever grateful and devoted to their own teachers. Tulku Urgyen's extraordinary memoir, Blazing Splendor, *reveals the inner workings of the teacher-student relationship in tantric Buddhism, and offers a rare glimpse into the now-lost world of Old Tibet.*

My grandmother's eldest son, Samten Gyatso, was my root guru and ultimate refuge. He was also, of course, my uncle. I feel a bit shy telling stories about him, because I don't want to sound as if I'm indirectly praising myself by lauding a family member. A disciple who emphasizes signs of accomplishment, clairvoyant abilities, and miraculous powers in stories about his own guru, may—instead of honoring him—end up discrediting him. Yet though he was a relative, there is no way I can avoid praising him. I don't mean to be crude, but I'm related to him like excrement is related to fine cuisine.

Within the Barom Kagyü lineage, Samten Gyatso was regarded as an emanation of Four-Armed Mahakala, one of the more prominent guardians of the dharma. Moreover, the second Chokling of Tsikey once had a vision of Samten Gyatso in which he saw him as an emanation of Vimalamitra.

From the time I was young, I respected my guru deeply. In his conduct, Samten Gyatso kept the monastic precepts quite purely and strictly. He never tasted alcohol nor ate any meat. In his attitude, he was always in tune with the bodhisattva trainings.

Some of us who were with him every day could be quite blind to his qualities, just like the people in Lhasa who never go to see the Jowo statue of the Buddha, thinking there is plenty of time to get around to going. But if you paid attention to his personality, it was obvious that he was fully endowed with compassion, perseverance, and devotion.

Samten Gyatso never flattered others by playing up to them or telling them how wonderful they were. He spoke straightforwardly. If something was true, he would say so; if it was not, he would say it was not, without adding or subtracting anything. He never talked around a sensitive topic.

Samten Gyatso was so learned and skilled, so trustworthy and matchless, that people compared him to Marpa, the master translator who brought the Kagyü teachings from India. Yet my guru never postured nor put on the air of high realization, like those meditators who never lower their vacant, glaring gaze to the ground and who spout random "profound" statements such as "Everything in samsara and nirvana are equal!" What do you gain from such pretense?

Samten Gyatso would move about as if he were just an ordinary person. He kept to the hidden yogi style: he didn't flaunt his accomplishments and never behaved as if he were a grand lama. He would not bless people by placing his hand on their heads nor sit on a high seat. He didn't even let people bow to him—if anyone tried, he would jump up and move away. He avoided ostentatious displays, like erecting impressive temples or commissioning fancy statues. He kept a low profile: he never dressed up nor wore brocade, just the robes of an ordinary monk.

I heard a wonderful story about one of Samten Gyatso's prior incarnations, Ngaktrin of Argong. He was recognized as a tulku while still a small child and brought to Lachab, his predecessor's monastery. One day, when he was just eight, he was having fun with his friends, as children do. An old *gönla*—the lama in charge of the chants for the protectors—was beating a drum and chanting while the kids were playing boisterously around him.

"You are an incarnation of a lama. Don't behave like this," the gönla said suddenly, berating the young Ngaktrin. "A tulku should be a noble boy, but you are a spoiled brat! Why are you doing this? What's the use? Listen: don't wander! Don't wander!"

"What does that mean?" the little tulku asked. "What does it mean not to wander?"

"Don't let your mind wander," replied the old lama. "That's what it means!"

"How does one not wander?"

"Look at yourself. Look at your own mind!"

When the boy heard these words—"Don't wander; look at your own mind!"—he recognized mind nature right then and there. Despite all the great masters he met later in his life, he always said his insight occurred when he was a young child.

As I grew up, Samten Gyatso became my main meditation instructor. Though he was well aware that I was a small child and hence likely unable to comprehend all the teachings, he didn't hold anything back. I was about eleven when he clarified the details of the principal teachings.

Until then, my meditation was guided mainly by what felt right. As a child, I would go to nearby caves and "meditate," but what I experienced then as the meditation state and my practice right now seem to be exactly the same—don't ask me why. I must have had some habit of letting be in the natural state carried over from former lives. Yet in those early days, I wasn't that clear about what it was until Samten Gyatso instilled in me a certainty about the natural state. Up to that point, meditation experience had been more spontaneous, but with Samten Gyatso I could ask one question after another, and I discovered that what he was explaining was the same as what I had experienced as a child.

I don't have much to brag about in terms of realization, so the clarity I am talking about has more to do with demonstrating personal confidence. The faith and devotion I had as a kid were quite natural and not imposed on me by anyone. Along with my devotion, I also had an acute feeling that mundane aims were futile. The only thing that made sense was to be a tough guy—tough like my heroes Milarepa and Longchenpa.

When I look back on my life, it seems I haven't been very diligent; I have only been distracted day and night, letting life run out.

I remember well one particular instruction that Samten Gyatso gave me at an early age. It had to do with a teaching on the profound topic of *essence, nature, and capacity.* He said, "The word *capacity* refers to the unconfined basis for experience, as in the moment just before something takes place. Once the arising has occurred, it usually has already turned into a thought. Capacity means the basis for that to happen, an unimpeded quality of awareness.

"This unimpeded quality is extremely subtle and significant. Once you acknowledge this unimpededness, nothing more needs to be done. In this unimpededness, it is impossible to find any subject or object. The analogy for this is a bright mirror, a readiness for experience to unfold without any preconception whatsoever. So please understand very well the third of these three: essence, nature, and capacity."

This is an example of how Samten Gyatso would teach. I feel very fortunate to have been instructed by such a master when I was young, because there are many people who misidentify capacity as being not the basis, like the mirror, but the manifestation, like the reflection in the mirror. However, the reflection means that the mind and sense object have already linked up, and the attention has already been caught up in distraction.

"One should not identify the capacity with being caught up in subject, object, and the act of perceiving," he said. "An unconfined basis for experience means the readiness, being able to experience— just ready to be, but not yet involved in dualistic experience. If your training is in this readiness, rather than in conceptual thinking, you won't be caught up in duality during daily activities. This capacity, in essence, is the unimpeded omniscience of all buddhas, which is totally unlike the attention that focuses on one thing while eliminating everything else."

When I was around twenty, Samten Gyatso told me, "You appear to be someone who can give mind teachings. You are the kind of person who finds it all quite easy, not seeing how anyone could have problems understanding the nature of mind. You could end up too blasé; then again, maybe you simply will be very confident.

"Sometimes I think you assume too much. I must caution you that there is one thing you should watch out for: On the one hand, you could assume it is all so simple that everyone would understand. But then, on the other hand, that's not the way things are. People will often comprehend something totally different from what you mean, concluding that there is nothing to gain, so that they become careless and give up.

"You feel that realizing the nature of mind is simply a matter of course," he continued, "but I want you to understand that some people do not know the nature of mind, and there definitely *is* a reason for that. There are many people whose practice of 'mind essence' is nothing more than remaining absent-minded and unaware in the state of the all-ground.

"Nevertheless, for the time being, you should go ahead and test your confidence on a few old men and women. You might be able to benefit one or two, so it's fine for you to teach them."

In this way, he gave me the go-ahead to begin teaching. I started giving people advice on understanding the nature of mind because I was very talkative. I couldn't help it; it would just slip out! When I spent time with Samten Gyatso, I listened in on whatever instructions he gave. Often it would be the pointing-out instruction and advice on how to truly meditate in the simplest way. Afterward, there might be some people outside his room who couldn't quite understand what he had said. They would ask me, "How can it be that easy?"

And I would say, "Why do you think it has to be difficult? It really *is* so easy."

Then they would reply, "But I don't get it."

And I'd tell them, "What do you mean, you don't get it? Just let be!" I had that attitude because I'd heard what my uncle had said and I'd just parrot it.

My uncle would then call me in and repeat, "It seems you are the talkative type, as well as someone who thinks that recognizing mind nature is totally easy. I think that in the future you will be like this as well—you will be both talkative and somebody who acts like it is really simple!" And he was right.

On one hand, maybe with my teaching style I'm just fooling everybody, making it too simple. But on the other hand, this *is* really how it is! It is the truth. What is the use of trying to sit and push and struggle, when we can allow the three kayas of buddhahood to be naturally present? Why do we have to strain and contort ourselves into an uncomfortable posture and an uptight meditative state with some hope that in the future, after lots of effort, we may get there? We don't need to go through all that trouble and tension. All we need to do is totally let be and recognize our nature right now.

The Buddha realized that different beings have various capacities. So out of great compassion and skillful means, he gave an assortment of teachings, each right for different individuals. Although the essence of all teachings of all enlightened ones is to simply let be, in recognition of one's own nature, the Buddha taught a wide variety of complex instructions in order to satisfy people at their own level. Another reason the Buddha and the great masters taught the nine vehicles [*yanas*] is not just that they couldn't leave well enough alone, but to make everybody happy. It seems to be human nature to love complication, to want to build up a lot of concepts. Later on, of course, we must allow them to fall to pieces again.

The great variety of teachings that exist doesn't change the fact that the very essence of the dharma, the nature of mind, is extremely simple and easy. In fact, it's so simple and easy that sometimes it's hard to believe!

The general tradition for giving the pointing-out instruction to the nature of mind holds that we need to go step by step. First, we complete the reflections of the four mind-changings. Next, we go through the preliminary practices, and after that the yidam practice of deity, mantra, and samadhi. And indeed, these are all still necessary, even if we have already received teachings on mind essence. Don't get the idea that suddenly all the practices taught by the enlightened ones are unimportant. On the contrary, they are incredibly important.

Since it's not so easy nor very common for someone to ever have the opportunity to receive mind teachings, I felt that I should speak up and give it. Please remember that we can easily receive the other important teachings from various masters, so don't ignore them. Please be diligent in practice. In truth, perseverance makes the difference between buddhas and ordinary beings.

There is a story from Kham in which an old guy says to a lama, "When you talk about the benefits of recognizing mind essence, it's certain that *you* have no problem; in fact, even this old sinner will probably be safe from rebirth in hell. But when you talk about the consequences of our actions, there's no doubt I will end up in hell. In fact, I wonder if even you might not be in trouble, my lama!" A phony meditator might be able to fool others while alive, but there's no doubt he'll be caught unprepared when facing the bardo [the intermediate state between death and rebirth]. I am quite certain that, in the long run, the greatest benefit comes from simply trusting in the three jewels. Of course, if one also has authentic experience of mind essence, then, as the Kagyü saying tells us, "Though death is regarded with so much dread, a yogi's death is a small awakening."

I also feel that even if one still hasn't reached the splendid heights of experience and realization, some simple, sound comprehension is extremely beneficial. An understanding, even intellectually, of emptiness—the empty and awake quality of mind—will surely help you cross over to the other side in the bardo. When sentient beings pass on, it is their own mind that becomes bewildered—and it is their own mind that needs to come to their rescue, since no one else is going to do it at that time.

Therefore, a sound understanding of mind essence could become the reminder that liberates in the bardo. The most essential benefit, however, comes from *actually* training in mind essence while you are alive; this is the only thing that will ensure true success. First, liberate your own stream of being through realization, then liberate others through your compassionate activity. Proceeding in this way makes a human life meaningful.

When I taught, some understood and others didn't, but I kept at it just the same. This bold attitude has stuck with me and is now my style. I don't know if it helps others much. The teachings on mind essence may be the most precious and secret. They may also be "liberation through hearing," so that whoever hears them will be benefited. So I feel it's acceptable to give them from time to time. I don't claim that everyone to whom I explain the essence of mind recognizes and trains in the genuine experience. There are many different types of students. Those who don't recognize are inevitably preoccupied by fleeting phenomena and will get distracted. But even if they have not recognized the natural state of mind, anyone who has heard the essential teaching, even once, will slowly grow closer to realization so long as they don't abandon the attempt entirely but continue to practice. Those who *have* recognized, and so have some trust in mind essence, cannot give up the dharma, even if someone tells them to. This springs from confidence in their personal experience.

Like others, tulkus obviously have emotions too. Just look at Marpa the translator, with his incredibly strong emotions, blazing like flames. But the moment an experienced meditator looks into the nature of mind, every thought and emotion vanishes like snowflakes falling on a hot plate. At that moment a meditator is truly free of any attachment. Marpa may have treated Milarepa with a lot of abuse, harsh words, and beatings—but that was totally unlike the anger of an ordinary person, in that there wasn't even a shred of selfishness involved. You can't only judge people by their behavior.

Even though his kindness was boundless, Samten Gyatso could be quite wrathful at times. Once in a while, I saw him slap one of his attendants. Sometimes I even had to bring him the cane, and that scared me too, because even one whack would hurt—it was big! Occasionally, he gave more than a little tap. He could give a real thrashing, especially to his attendant Dudul, who often had it coming.

"With this guy, there is no other way," Samten Gyatso once said. "He's too dense, and a slap of the stick gets through to him; it's effective for at least five or six days." Afterward, Dudul would act like a real human being, bright, and gentle—at least at first. Then he would start to be argumentative again, finding fault and loudly complaining about every little thing.

"Why don't you just let it drop?" I often told him, "Nothing is that bad. Don't you remember what happened to you last time?"

But the story would always end with Samten Gyatso sending me to fetch the cane one more time. Oh my! Once, Samten Gyatso smacked him so many times I thought he wouldn't be able to walk the next morning, but when I met Dudul afterward, he was carrying on with his duties as if nothing had happened. The story often repeated itself, but he just wouldn't listen. Once, I asked him about it and he said, "That was nothing. I don't care that much. It hurts for a moment and then passes." He too had a lot of devotion for Samten Gyatso.

· · ·

Shortly before Samten Gyatso died, I spent many evenings with him. He would lie in his bed and I would sleep on the floor beside him. One night, as we were talking, Samten Gyatso began to speak, for the first time, about his innermost realization.

"I never had special experiences," he told me, "but as the years passed by, my trust in the authenticity of the dharma has grown. I am now confident in the truth of the three kayas. At the age of eight, I recognized the nature of mind and since then I have never forsaken it. Of course my diligence varied and I got distracted at times, but mostly I kept to the practice of mind's natural state." I heard him say this only once. Other than this, he never discussed such personal matters.

No matter where he was, Samten Gyatso had a certain influence on people. There was no small talk; he didn't leave any room for superficial conversation, just sincere questions about practice, for which he never lacked an answer. When he gave instructions, Samten Gyatso would foresee how his words would end up—whether they would be put to good use or not.

To laypeople, whose main aim was mundane success and raising families, he would give the mantra of Avalokiteshvara—*Om Mani Padme Hum*—and teachings on trust and devotion. But he gave special attention to people who had dedicated their lives to deepening their experience and realization. With a sincere practitioner, he would truly share his heart.

In either case, whenever someone left an interview with him, they were deeply inspired and full of admiration.

Many old *ngakpas* [tantric yogis] lived around Lachab monastery and whenever they heard that Samten Gyatso had come home, they would immediately flock to his room to receive teachings on the Dzogchen view. Sometimes they stayed throughout the night, not leaving until morning. These meditators, his closest disciples, marveled at the clarity of his teachings—and such seasoned meditators were very hard to impress.

These old ngakpas loved Samten Gyatso and felt that his mind was completely unimpeded. In fact, anyone who had a chance to discuss their meditation practice with him always came out amazed—no matter who, no matter how learned. Even knowledgeable scholars who had oceans of learning behind them became humbled on the topic of meditation experience in any discussion with Samten Gyatso. Finally, their initial air of self-assurance would dissipate altogether and they couldn't help requesting teachings from him, asking one question after another.

As Samten Gyatso imparted the essential meditation practice, his majestic presence would shine through ever stronger, intimidating even the most learned khenpo. The more anyone talked with Samten Gyatso, the more clearly they discovered how invincible his self-confidence was. This unshakable assurance signifies profound practice and personal experience.

That's the kind of guru I had.

The Perfect Love We Seek, The Imperfect Love We Live

John Welwood

Love is what we most long to give and to receive, yet our intimate relationships are often conflicted and painful. Psychologist John Welwood says that one of our problems is failing to distinguish between absolute and relative love. Seeking perfect, unconditional love, we are wounded by the imperfect and variable love we receive, beginning with our parents. But what we are looking for is not found through others, but in our own capacity to love.

> Again and again it defeats me–
> This reliance on others for bliss.
> —*from a poem by the author*

While most of us have moments of loving freely and openly, it is often hard to sustain such love where it matters most—in our intimate relationships. This creates a strange gap between absolute love—the perfect love we can know in our heart—and relative love, the imperfect ways it is embodied in our relationships. Why, if love is so great and powerful, are human relationships so challenging and difficult? If love is the source of happiness and joy, why is it so hard to open to it fully?

What lies at the root of every relationship problem is a core "wound of the heart" that affects not only our personal relations, but the quality of life in our world as a whole. This wounding shows up as a pervasive mood of unlove, a deep sense that we are not intrinsically lovable just as we are. We experience ourselves as separated from love, and this shuts down our capacity to trust. So even though we may hunger for love or believe in love, we still have difficulty opening to it and letting it circulate freely through us.

ABSOLUTE LOVE

If the pure essence of love is like the sun in a cloudless sky, this clear and luminous light shines through relationships most brightly in beginnings and endings. When your baby is first born, you feel so graced by the arrival of such an adorable being that you respond to it totally, without reserve, demand, or judgment. Or when you first fall in love, you are so surprised and delighted by the sheer beauty of this person's presence that it blows your heart wide open. For a while the bright sunlight of all-embracing love pours through full strength, and you may melt into bliss.

Similarly, when a friend or loved one is dying, all your quibbles with that person fall away. You simply appreciate the other for who he or she is, just for having been here with you in this world for a little while. Pure, unconditional love shines through when people put themselves—their own demands and agendas—aside and completely open to one another.

Absolute love is not something that we have to—or that we even can—concoct or fabricate. It is what comes through us naturally when we fully open up—to another person, to ourselves, or to life. In relation to another, it manifests as selfless caring. In relation to ourselves, it shows up as inner confidence and self-acceptance that warms us from within. And in relation to life, it manifests as a sense of well-being, appreciation, and *joie de vivre.*

When we experience this kind of openness and warmth coming from another, it provides essential nourishment: it helps us experience our own warmth and openness, allowing us to recognize the beauty and goodness at the core of our nature. The light of unconditional love awakens the dormant seed potentials within us, helping them ripen, blossom, and bear fruit, allowing us to bring forth the unique gifts that are ours to offer in this life. Receiving pure love, caring, and recognition from another confers a great blessing: it affirms us in being who we are, allowing us to say yes to ourselves.

What feels most affirming is not just to feel loved but to feel loved as we are. As-we-are means in our very being. Absolute love is the love of being.

Deeper than all our personality traits, pain, or confusion, our being is the dynamic, open presence that we essentially are. It is what we experience when we feel settled, grounded, and connected with ourselves. When rooted in this basic ground of presence, love flows freely through us, and we can more readily open up to others. When two people meet in this quality of open presence, they share a perfect moment of absolute love.

However—and this is an essential point—the human personality is not the source of absolute love. Rather, its light shines through us, from what lies altogether beyond us, the ultimate source of all. We are the channels through which this radiance flows. Yet in flowing through us, it also finds a home within us, taking up residence as our heart-essence.

We have a natural affinity for this perfect food that is also our deepest essence, our life's blood. That is why every baby instinctively reaches out for it from the moment of birth. We cannot help wanting our own nature.

When the value and beauty of our existence is recognized, this allows us to relax, let down, and settle into ourselves. In relaxing, we open. And this opening makes us transparent to the life flowing through us, like a fresh breeze that enters a room as soon as the windows are raised.

This is the one of the great gifts of human love, this entry it provides into something even greater than human relatedness. In helping us connect with the radiant aliveness within us, it reveals our essential beauty and power, where we are one with life itself because we are fully transparent to life. When life belongs to you and you belong to life, this sets you free from hunger and fear. You experience the essential dignity and nobility of your existence, which does not depend on anyone else's approval or validation. In this deep sense of union with life, you realize you are not wounded, have never been wounded, and cannot be wounded.

This is the bottom line of human existence: Absolute love helps us connect with who we really are. That is why it is indispensable.

RELATIVE LOVE

Yet even though the human heart is a channel through which great love streams into this world, this heart channel is usually clogged with debris—fearful, defensive patterns that have developed out of not knowing we are truly loved. As a result, love's natural openness, which we can taste in brief, blissful moments of pure connection with another person, rarely permeates our relationships completely. Indeed, the more two people open to each other, the more this wide-openness also brings to the surface all the obstacles to it: their deepest, darkest wounds, their desperation and mistrust, and their rawest emotional trigger-points. Just as the sun's warmth causes clouds to arise, by prompting the earth to release its moisture, so love's pure openness activates the thick clouds of our emotional wounding, the tight places where we are shut down, where we live in fear and resist love.

There is good reason why this happens: Before we can become a clear channel through which love can freely flow, the ways we are wounded must come to the surface and be exposed. Love as a healing power can operate only on what presents itself to be healed. As long as our wounding remains hidden, it can only fester.

This, then, is relative love: the sunlight of absolute love as it becomes filtered through the clouds of our conditioned personality and its defensive patterns—fearfulness, distrust, reactivity, dishonesty, aggression, and distorted perception. Like a partly cloudy sky, relative love is incomplete, inconstant, and imperfect. It is a continual play of light and shadow. The full radiance of absolute love can only sparkle through in fleeting moments.

If you observe yourself closely in relationships, you will see that you continually move back and forth between being open and closed, clear skies and dark clouds. When another person is responsive, listens well, or says something pleasing, something in you naturally starts to open. But when the other is not responsive, can't hear you, or says something threatening, you may quickly tense up and start to contract.

Our ability to feel a wholehearted yes toward another person fluctuates with the changing circumstances of each moment. It depends on how much each of us is capable of giving and receiving, the chemistry between us, our limitations and conditioned patterns, how far along we are in our personal development, how much awareness and flexibility we each have, how well we communicate, the situation we find ourselves in, and even how well we have each slept the night before. *Relative* means "dependent on time and circumstance."

Ordinary human love is always relative, never consistently absolute. Like the weather, relative love is in continual dynamic flux. It is forever rising and subsiding, waxing and waning, changing shape and intensity.

So far all of this may seem totally obvious. Yet here's the rub: We imagine that others—surely someone out there!—should be a source of perfect love by consistently loving us in just the right way. Since our first experiences of love usually happen in relation to other people, we naturally come to regard relationship as its main source. Then when relationships fail to deliver the ideal love we dream of, we imagine something has gone seriously wrong. And this disappointed hope keeps reactivating the wound of the heart and generating grievance against others. This is why the first step in healing the wound and freeing ourselves from grievance is to appreciate the important difference between absolute and relative love.

Relationships continually oscillate between two people finding common ground and then having that ground slip out from under them as their differences pull them in different directions. This is a problem only when we expect it to be otherwise, when we imagine that love should manifest as a steady state. That kind of expectation prevents us from appreciating the special gift that relative love does have to offer: personal intimacy. Intimacy—the sharing of who we are in our distinctness—can happen only when my partner and I meet as two, when I appreciate the ways she is wholly other, and yet not entirely other at the same time.

If we look honestly at our lives, most likely we will see that no one has ever been there for us in a totally reliable, continuous way. Though we might like to imagine that somebody, somewhere— maybe a movie star or a spiritual person—has an ideal relationship, this is mostly the stuff of fantasy. Looking more closely, we can see that everyone has his or her own fears, blind spots, hidden agendas, insecurities, aggressive and manipulative tendencies, and emotional trigger-points—which block the channels through which great love can freely flow. Much as we might want to love with a pure heart, our limitations inevitably cause our love to fluctuate and waver.

Yet our yearning for perfect love and perfect union does have its place and its own beauty. Arising out of an intuitive knowing of the perfection that lies within the heart, it points toward something beyond what ordinary mortals can usually provide. We yearn to heal our separation from life, from God, from our own heart. When understood correctly, this longing can inspire us to reach beyond ourselves, give ourselves wholeheartedly, or turn toward the life of the spirit. It is a key that opens the doorway through which absolute love can enter fully into us.

We invariably fall into trouble, however, when we transfer this longing onto another person. That is why it's important to distinguish between absolute and relative love—so we don't go around seeking perfect love from imperfect situations. Although intimate connections can provide dazzling flashes of absolute oneness, we simply cannot count on them for that. The only reliable source of perfect love is that which is perfect—the open, awake heart at the core of being. This alone allows us to know perfect union, where all belongs to us because we belong to all. Expecting this from relationships only sets us up to feel betrayed, disheartened, or aggrieved.

The Genesis of the Wound

Riding the waves of relationship becomes particularly difficult when the troughs of misunderstanding, disharmony, or separation reactivate our core wound, bringing up old frustration and hurt from childhood. In the first few months of our life, our parents most likely gave us the largest dose of unconditional love and devotion they were capable of. We were so adorable as babies; they probably felt blessed to have such a precious, lovely being come into their lives. We probably had some initial experiences of basking in love's pure, unfiltered sunshine.

Yet this also gives rise to one of the most fundamental of all human illusions: that the source of happiness and well-being lies outside us, in other people's acceptance, approval, or caring. As a child, this was indeed the case, since we were at first so entirely dependent on others for our very life. But even if at the deepest level our parents did love us unconditionally, it was impossible for them to express this consistently, given their human limitations. This was not their fault. It doesn't mean they were bad parents or bad people. Like everyone, they had their share of fears, worries, cares, and burdens, as well as their own wounding around love. Like all of us, they were imperfect vessels for perfect love.

When children experience love as conditional or unreliable or manipulative, this causes a knot of fear to form in the heart, for they can only conclude, "I am not truly loved." This creates a state of panic or "freak-out" that causes the body and mind to freeze up. This basic love trauma is known as "narcissistic injury" in the language of psychotherapy, because it damages our sense of self and our ability to feel good about ourselves. It affects our whole sense of who we are by causing us to doubt whether our nature is lovable. As Emily Dickinson describes this universal wound in one of her poems: "There is a pain so utter, it swallows Being up."

This wounding hurts so much that children try to push it out of consciousness. Eventually a psychic scab forms. That scab is our grievance. Grievance against others serves a defensive function, by hardening us so we don't have to experience the underlying pain of not feeling fully loved. And so we grow up with an isolated, disconnected ego, at the core of which is a central wound, freak-out, and shutdown. And all of this is covered over with resentment, which becomes a major weapon in our defense arsenal.

What keeps the wound from healing is not knowing that we are lovely and lovable just as we are, while imagining that other people hold the key to this. We would like, and often expect, relative human love to be absolute, providing a reliable, steady flow of attunement, unconditional acceptance, and understanding. When this doesn't happen, we take it personally, regarding this as someone's fault—our own, for not being good enough, or others', for not loving us enough. But the imperfect way our parents—or anyone else—loved us has nothing to do with whether love is trustworthy or whether we are lovable. It doesn't have the slightest bearing on who we really are. It is simply a sign of ordinary human limitation, and nothing more. Other people cannot love us any more purely than their character structure allows.

SEARCHING FOR THE SOURCE OF LOVE

Fortunately, the storminess of our relationships in no way diminishes or undermines the unwavering presence of great love, absolute love, which is ever present in the background. Even when the sky is filled with thick, dark clouds, the sun never stops shining.

The problems in relationships begin when we imagine that the warmth ignited in our heart isn't really ours, that it is transferred into us by the other person. Then we become obsessed with the other as the provider of love, when in truth the warmth we feel comes from the sunlight of great love entering our heart.

"Those who go on a search for love," D. H. Lawrence writes, "find only their own lovelessness." Here is a simple way to experience for yourself what Lawrence means. Fix your attention on someone you'd like to love you more, and notice how it feels to want that. If you observe this carefully, you will notice that looking to another for love creates a certain tension or congestion in your body, most noticeably in the chest. It constricts the heart. And as a result you feel your own lovelessness.

Imagining others to be the source of love condemns us to wander lost in the desert of hurt, abandonment, and betrayal, where human relationship appears to be hopelessly tragic and flawed. As long as we fixate on what our parents didn't give us, the ways our friends don't consistently show up for us, or the ways our lover doesn't understand us, we will never become rooted in ourselves and heal the wound of the heart. To grow beyond the dependency of a child requires sinking our own taproot into the wellspring of great love. This is the only way to know for certain that we are loved unconditionally.

In emphasizing the importance of not looking to others for perfect love, I am not suggesting that you turn away from relationships or belittle their importance. On the contrary, learning to sink your taproot into the source of love allows you to connect with others in a more powerful way—"straight up," confidently rooted in your own ground, rather than leaning over, always trying to get something from "out there." The less you demand total fulfillment from relationships, the more you can appreciate them for the beautiful tapestries they are, in which absolute and relative, perfect and imperfect, infinite and finite are marvelously interwoven. You can stop fighting the shifting tides of relative love and learn to ride them instead. And you come to appreciate more fully the simple, ordinary heroism involved in opening to another person and forging real intimacy.

LOVING OUR HUMANNESS

Although perhaps only saints and buddhas embody absolute love completely, every moment of working with the challenges of relative human love brings a hint of this divine possibility into our life. As the child of heaven and earth, you are a mix of infinite openness and finite limitation. This means that you are both wonderful and difficult at the same time. You are flawed, you are stuck in old patterns, you become carried away with yourself. Indeed, you are quite impossible in many ways. And still, you are beautiful beyond measure. For the core of what you are is fashioned out of love, that potent blend of openness, warmth, and clear, transparent presence. Boundless love always manages somehow to sparkle through your limited form.

Bringing absolute love into human form involves learning to hold the impossibility of ourselves and others in the way that the sky holds clouds—with gentle spaciousness and equanimity. The sky can do this because its openness is so much vaster than the clouds that it doesn't find them the least bit threatening. Holding our imperfections in this way allows us to see them as trail markers of the work-in-progress that we are, rather than as impediments to love or happiness. Then we can say, "Yes, everyone has relative weaknesses that cause suffering, yet everyone also possesses absolute beauty, which far surpasses these limitations. Let us melt down the frozen, fearful places by holding them in the warmth of tenderness and mercy."

In his book *Works of Love,* the Danish philosopher Søren Kierkegaard points out that true love doesn't embrace others in spite of their flaws, as if rising above them. Rather, it finds "the other lovable in spite of and together with his weaknesses and errors and imperfections. . . . Because of your beloved's weakness you shall not remove yourself from him or make your relationship more remote; on the contrary, the two of you shall hold together with greater solidarity and inwardness in order to remove the weakness."

The same holds true for loving yourself. When you recognize that the absolute beauty within you cannot be tarnished by your flaws, then this beauty you are can begin to care for the beast you sometimes seem to be. Beauty's touch begins to soften the beast's gnarly defenses.

Then you begin to discover that the beast and the beauty go hand in hand. The beast is, in fact, nothing other than your wounded beauty. It is the beauty that has lost faith in itself because it has never been fully recognized. Not trusting that you are loved or lovable has given rise to all the most beastly emotional reactions—anger, arrogance, hatred, jealousy, meanness, depression, insecurity, greedy attachment, fear of loss and abandonment.

The first step in freeing the beast from its burden is to acknowledge the hardening around our heart. Then, peering behind this barrier, we may encounter the wounded, cut-off place in ourselves where the mood of unlove resides. If we can meet this place gently, without judgment or rejection, we will uncover the great tenderness that resides at the very core of our humanness.

Our beauty and our beast both arise from one and the same tenderness. When we harden against it, the beast is born. Yet when we allow the tenderness, we begin to discern the contours of a long-lost beauty hidden within the belly of the beast. If we can shine warmth and openness into the dark, tender place where we don't know we're lovable, this starts to forge a marriage between our beauty and our wounded beast.

This is, after all, the love we most long for—this embracing of our humanness, which lets us appreciate ourselves as the beautiful, luminous beings we are, housed in a vulnerable, flickering form whose endless calling is to move from chrysalis to butterfly, from seed to new birth. As earthly creatures continually subject to relative disappointment, pain, and loss, we cannot avoid feeling vulnerable. Yet as an open channel through which great love enters this world, the human heart remains invincible. Being wholly and genuinely human means standing firmly planted in both dimensions, celebrating that we are both vulnerable and indestructible at the same time.

Here at this crossroads where yes and no, limitless love and human limitation intersect, we discover the essential human calling: progressively unveiling the sun in our heart, that it may embrace the whole of ourselves and the whole of creation within the sphere of its radiant warmth. This love is not the least bit separate from true power. For, as the great Sufi poet Rumi sings:

When we have surrendered totally to that beauty,
Then we shall be a mighty kindness.

I'm Breathing, Are You?

Nancy Hathaway

Parenthood is a time of heightened love, heightened stress, and heightened opportunity to display our neurosis and sanity. Perhaps reflecting the concerns of baby boomers, Buddhism in the West has devoted far more attention to death and dying than it has to parenting. Yet parenting, too, is an ideal—and vital—time to work with our own state of mind. Nancy Hathaway is a mother of two and a Zen teacher. Here's what she has learned about applying Buddhist practice to the challenges of raising a young child.

It began as a quiet, peaceful day, as mornings with mothers and children at home often begin. But as the day went on, the activity and energy of the household increased. Grandmother came to visit, friends came to play with treasured toys, tiredness came on, and hunger appeared. So, he lost it. Five years old and screaming, a full-blown temper tantrum. Grandmother (my mother) began getting uncomfortable with his behavior, saying: "If he doesn't stop screaming, I will need to go home." This was the beginning of her three-day visit.

I lead my child into our little at-home meditation room. This room is bare and full of space—loving, attentive, nonjudgmental space. It has been furnished over time with breath and posture, with attention and chanting. I sit with him on a pile of bed pillows and hold the flailing, screaming mind for ten minutes, for twenty minutes, for thirty minutes. What a meditation retreat! How long will this mind go on? I hang in, mindful of my breath, posture, and body sensations, mindful of us both. Staying with my breath, I keep an upright posture, and quietly chant *Kwan Seum Bosal* (a Korean Zen chant that invokes love and compassion). Finally, at sixty minutes, the flailing quiets and disappears; the mind of smiles and hugs and cuddles appears. We sit quietly breathing together.

A week later the screaming mind appears again in my five-year-old. This time he takes me by the hand and leads me into the safe space. On this day the screaming mind only needed ten minutes. And the next time only four. And the next time only. . . . Now, at eighteen years old, when this young adult/child who knows me so well sees any tension in my face, he says lovingly, with a relaxed, strong posture, full of confidence, and with a smile, "I'm breathing, are you?"

Parenting is a challenge. Our children cry. Our children throw temper tantrums—in supermarkets, in quiet spaces, in the most embarrassing of places. Our children whine, fight, say sassy things. They push our buttons. They want dinner when we're not ready to make dinner, and they don't want dinner when it is ready. Our children want one more story, just when we are beat, exhausted, and need to do just a few more things before hitting the sack ourselves. Our children look into our eyes and with the sweetest of faces say, "Mommy, will you play with me?" while we are in the middle of something, whatever it is, and it's hard to let go of what we're doing or it's not appropriate to let go of what we're doing. Perhaps dinner is burning and the phone is ringing and someone is at the door while at the same time our children want our attention—and they want it RIGHT NOW!

We want the best for our children, our families, ourselves; we want family life to be peaceful and happy. But family life is often uncomfortable and filled with intense feelings. The question is: What do we do with this discomfort? What do we do with our feelings? How do we relate to the strain of wanting something other than this?

Many of us have come to expect family life to look like images from *Martha Stewart Living*. Magazine pictures begin to seem like the norm. If our life doesn't look like that, we think something is wrong. The few of us who do have the Martha Stewart house realize that something is missing. We spend much of our time and energy trying to get it all together. We put a lot of time into our makeup, but our faces have frowns; our clothing is well thought out, but our posture is bent over; our kitchens are big and glamorous, but the warmth of the hearth is missing. We have romanticized the material world, thinking that it brings happiness. We are surrounded by messages from the media that tell us if we have this or that, we will have it all. But what is it all? Do we take the time to ask ourselves what it is that we are *really* looking for?

The simple answer is, we're looking for happiness. We have come to believe that happiness will come from stopping the crying child, the temper tantrum, the whining, the sassy talk, the loud music. We try to avoid pain, and we seek comfort—often by acquiring more and more of something, anything—instead of wanting, accepting, appreciating, and receiving what we actually have.

There is another way. As a longtime student of Zen and the mother of two sons, I have found certain Buddhist teachings and practices to be extremely helpful in working with the inherent challenges and discomforts of raising children. In particular, the core Buddhist teachings of the Four Noble Truths and the practice of meditation—in the midst of regular, everyday life—have guided and supported me through the parenting years. These teachings have no religious boundaries; they are remarkably universal— mothers of any background can draw on them for insight and guidance.

Meditation and the Four Noble Truths point us in the direction that we all long for as human beings on this planet together: they point us in the direction of freedom from suffering.

THE FOUR NOBLE TRUTHS OF PARENTHOOD

1. Parenthood will always include discomfort and pain.

The First Noble Truth of Buddhism is that life often fails to meet our hopes and expectations. As parents, we face this essential fact when our children cry, lose a favorite toy, feel left out, get sick. When pain arises, more often than not we get tight, we turn off, we resist. We try to push it all away. Many mothers think that if they are "good mothers," their children will not be uncomfortable, will not cry, will not feel angry, will not have any real problems. But the First Noble Truth reminds us that difficulty and pain will always be part of life, whether we are young or old, rich or poor, whether we are the haves or the have-nots.

2. Suffering is caused by wanting life to be other than the way it is.

Suffering arises when we want something other than what we are presented with. And, of course, we often want something other than what we get. Our children are crying, and we want them to be smiling. They are throwing a temper tantrum in the grocery store, and we want them to be cute and make it easy for us to do our shopping. Our child wets the bed or the house is a mess, and we yell out of frustration.

The way we usually try to find happiness—by controlling or forcing the situation to be the way we want it to be—is, in fact, the route to more suffering. Of course we want peaceful situations, happy children, a clean house. But if this is not the reality, how do we deal with it? How do we relate to the inherent challenges, frustrations, and pain of daily life with children? So often we create more unnecessary suffering by insisting that our children be different from who they are, that this moment be different than it is. We create more suffering when we try to ignore the pain, the discomfort, or when we get angry at it. In short, whenever we try to get rid of what *is*, we get into trouble.

3. *Freedom from suffering is possible.*

The Third Noble Truth is fairly simple. Since we know the cause of suffering (wanting things to be other than they are), we can find a solution. There is a way out of this trap. Then we ask, what is this way out of suffering? How can we create true happiness instead of being led down the old, worn path of creating more suffering?

4. *The way out of suffering is learning to be with life as it is and making that our practice.*

More traditionally, the Fourth Noble Truth of Buddhism outlines a specific way out of suffering known as the Eightfold Path (right view, right thought, right speech, right action, right livelihood, right effort, right mindfulness, and right meditation). In broad terms, the Eightfold Path consists of powerful daily practices for learning to live in harmony with life as it is, rather than constantly trying to force life into being what we want it to be. Parenthood provides countless opportunities to do just that—to drop our expectations, our hopes, our preconceptions, and to learn to be with life just as it is, in *this* moment.

The first step is to become fully aware of what *is*. For example, I am in the supermarket and my child is crying. Embarrassment arises within me and the look of the woman next to me suggests to me that I am committing a mortal sin by having a screaming child. I feel tightness in my chest. I hear the voice in my head that says my child shouldn't be screaming!

This is my experience, this is the pain of *this* moment. I breathe and take a moment to notice my thoughts, feelings, and physical sensations. I let them in. This is what *is*. You might ask how I can do this in the middle of such a situation, feeling harassed and under pressure. It takes practice and courage and faith. The more we do it, the more we open to the fullness of the moment, the more we know in our mind and body that it works. It doesn't take long before the situation starts to shift. We begin to feel a little space, and coolness arises. Then from a calmer, more balanced place, where we are aware of what is and accept what is, we find that we know what to do. We know how to set limits for our child or we know that we must let go of our own expectations. We act with greater compassion and wisdom for all.

Too often, when the going gets tough with our children, we try to escape our reality. We lose our courage to live in the moment. When our feelings start to intensify, we try to run away from them by blaming the situation on someone else, usually someone closest to us like our spouse or our children. As strange as it sounds, if we open to discomfort and experience it 100 percent, then we experience freedom, liberation, true love.

By opening to the moment, we are able to slow down and breathe into the middle of our discomfort. We are able to be with our children, see their discomfort fully, see their pleasure fully, smell the flowers, really see the smiles on their faces. We notice the I-want-a-perfect-child dream, the I-want-a-bigger-house dream, the I-want-you-to-be-other-than-you-are dream. By noticing the dream, we acknowledge it; by acknowledging it, we sometimes don't have to act on it. The essential point is that the way out of suffering is to practice accepting what *is*—accepting the whole realm, accepting discomfort, ours, theirs—accepting it all.

PUTTING THE TEACHINGS INTO PRACTICE

As mothers, how do we use the Four Noble Truths to help us to become more present with our children? How do we start to live in the real moment right here, right now, rather than in the dream, whatever dream it is? The idea of living in the moment is simple, but attaining it is not so easy. Old habits die hard—old patterned ways of being, of doing things, of living life. To change these old habits, we need to practice. We need to practice making a choice that is not based on feelings of fight-or-flight, not trying to change what *is*, not trying to control the situation, but rather choosing to live *with* discomfort. So how do you actually do this in the real world, in daily life? How do you turn this vision of wakeful parenting into a reality? In Zen, we begin with the body.

Posture

In Zen, proper meditation posture is the basis of enlightenment—some say it's all you need. What is proper posture for the practice of parenthood? It is to stand erect in the middle of life, with dignity, grace, and an open heart. The practice is to do this at the kitchen sink, behind the wheel of the car, pushing the grocery cart, changing diapers. The other choice is to stand rounded over, chest hollowed in as we sink in and try to cover or hide our pain, oftentimes subconsciously. If we stand straight, or sit upright, with shoulders back, chest and heart open, and head upright, we automatically become more aware and awake.

In traditional Zen meditation, proper posture also includes how we hold our faces. Zen practitioners are sometimes instructed to do sitting meditation with a slight smile on their faces. Not a fake, wide smile, but a gentle, half-smile. A simple practice for mothers is to bring this kind of smile into the daily life of parenting.

Many of us have always wanted to be a mother. We knew that this would involve making dinner for our families, changing diapers, getting up early, and so on, and yet here we are making dinner and wishing that we were somewhere else, "Oh, the sunny, warm Caribbean . . ." Yet this same exact experience, including the Caribbean dream, can change from an expression of our suffering into a moment of true happiness if we put a small smile on our faces. It is that simple. The same exact scenario of wanting to escape from our lives can bring us happiness, if we are fully present to it, aware of the longing, and aware of exactly what this present moment brings.

Doing so, we become less attached and have more distance, seeing this scenario as manifesting on its own. The practice of the half smile takes the ego out of the situation, adds some space, and brings gentle awareness of what *is*. Try it. Change a messy diaper mumbling, grumbling, complaining—then add a smile, being aware of it all. This small, relaxed smile can make a surprisingly big difference.

Breath

The next helpful step in becoming a more wakeful and compassionate parent is being with the breath, especially when the going gets tough. Feel the breath as it comes in and as it goes out. Follow the breath with your attention. The breath is always with you. Notice how the in-breath has a beginning, middle, and end to it. Then the out-breath has a beginning, middle, and end, going out and out until it stops. Notice the small pause between the out-breath and the in-breath. The breath is always with us, the gift of life.

Breathing within the chaos of parenting brings us balance and perspective, and it reconnects us with our loving nature. As a parent, conscious breathing was not so easy for me within the hectic pace of daily life. When I just couldn't give my breath attention, I would use a word that would help me to be in the present moment.

Any word is fine. I would often use the name of the bodhisattva of compassion, Kwan Seum Bosal (also known as the goddess Kwan Yin). Repeating a special word over and over again can be very powerful and enjoyable. It cuts down on thinking, which helps us to live in the moment. Our excess mental energy quiets, and we open more to our children, to what is at hand, in a gentler, more peaceful and relaxed way. Try it, you might like it. You can use any word: *one, peace, now, here,* or as my Zen teacher would say, even *Coca Cola* is okay. It's not the word itself but what the saying of the word does to quiet the racing mind.

The Bell of Attention

Ringing a bell in the home is a wonderful way to remind ourselves to breathe, straighten our posture, and come back to the present moment. Find a bell that is attractive and easy to ring. Create a special table that invites attention, presence, and respect as the setting for the bell. This table could include seasonal flowers or objects that your children might collect, such as horse chestnuts or acorns. This should not be a place of forgetfulness, but a place that is alive with change. You could add a frame to display school papers for a few days at a time. Place the bell on the table so that it invites people to ring it.

Anyone in the family, child or adult, may ring the bell at any time. When the bell is rung, everyone stops what they are doing and takes three conscious breaths (and perhaps the parents remember to smile). This bell can give children a wonderful sense of power. They can do something that makes everyone stop—for a positive reason. Children are sensitive, more so than we realize. When they need attention they can ring this bell, and sometimes their need will be satisfied by taking three breaths . . . sometimes.

My Zen teacher taught me to continually come back to my breath, straighten my posture, and ask myself, "Right now, what is *this*?" This simple, skillful technique is always within our reach. When someone rings this bell, it will be a reminder for all to return to, "Right now, what is *this*?" The bell also reminds us that the direction of our home is to inhabit the present moment, because the present moment is the only place where we can deeply connect with our children and find real happiness.

Knowing that this is your direction, your children may start to notice when you are stressed and may know that if you raise your voice, it's because you've temporarily lost your openness, not because they are bad. They may also see when they are not acting compassionately and may develop a skill for coping with their own stressful situations—breathing before an exam, straightening their posture as they get up in front of the class while giving a report, or taking a quiet moment before a foul shot in front of the whole school.

As mothers, we must make a conscious choice about how we want to live. The swirl of the society is rushing around us. Do we want to live in a dream or do we want to experience reality? As we experience what it really means to be a mother, we begin to connect to all mothers, for we all want to end suffering and find true happiness for ourselves, for our children, and for all beings. I call this realizing "mother's mind."

As we learn through our experience what it means to be a loving, compassionate mother, we encounter each situation as our child. Using the resources of the present moment, we become fulfilled and truly happy even as we face our biggest challenges because we know that this, too, is part of being a mother in this universe. As we practice on this path of awareness, we expand our love to include more and more of the pleasures and pains of what it means to be human. This is the way things are as a parent.

Motherhood is the perfect path for spiritual practice, for enlightenment. It puts us right in the guts of this life: we love our children to death, we want the very best for them. We do so much for them, making great efforts to get them what we think they need. But what our children really need is for their mothers to be present with them. You can give them the tiniest of birthday cakes, the smallest of presents, and if it is done with real attention and wakefulness, what could be better?

And when they cry, over the loss of a toy or the loss of a friend, what is it that they really want? Yes, they want this particular thing, this or that, but on a basic level they want their mothers to be present with them while they cry. They want a mother who can stand in the middle of chaos and breathe, and have a slight smile on her face, because chaos is the way it is. So please be present in it, and give them what they—and you—really want.

Passing It On

Mark Magill

Wisdom and compassion are part of our human nature; they are not the property of any one religion, group, or generation. The basic goodness of human nature is being expressed around us all the time; sometimes we recognize it and often we don't. Here Buddhist writer Mark Magill talks about the inheritance of character he received from his father and how much he would like to pass it along to his son.

A cookie works for a few minutes. An animated sponge and a couple of well-meaning monsters pass the time until the final credits bring a howl of despair. The stuffed pig from FAO Schwarz provides some comfort, though a fruitless search for a duplicate since Schwarz went bankrupt only magnifies the dreaded day when the pig goes missing for good.

I want my son to be happy. But cookies and missing pigs only prove how fitfully temporal these measures are. So what will it take? I'm quite sure the answer doesn't lie at Toys R Us.

My father was a quiet man who spent thirty years working at a bookstore and volunteering at a local nature preserve. But from 1943 to 1945 he was a lieutenant with the Thirty-sixth Division as it fought its way through Italy and France into the heart of Germany. Though he did not speak much of the war when we were children, the medals he gave my mother when they married hinted at bravery. An officer who served with him told me a story when I called to inform him of my father's death. Their company was in the Vosges Mountains, on the border between Germany and France. They knew the Germans would put up a fierce fight, since the mountains were the last line of defense before the Allies entered Germany. My father's unit waited in their foxholes for the attack. Then, in the first gray light of dawn, they saw a vast line of Germans advancing toward them in the mist. "Oh, to be in England, now that the Germans are here," my father said, and soldiers laughed at his lift from Robert Browning.

He came home from the war to his job in the bookstore, where, for a while, he was responsible for hiring and firing. Having seen firsthand what Nazi bigotry had wrought, he had no room for anything but quiet tolerance. Though he never once preached it, I think the fact that I am physically unable to utter a racial epithet came from his determination to view people according to their abilities.

Courage. Resourcefulness. Grace under fire. An open mind. When I think of what would be of value to my son's happiness, these are the qualities that come to mind. But how to deliver them?

It might help to know what happiness is. Buddha said, "Those who practice the diminishing of desires thus achieve a mind of contentment having no cause for either grief or fear and, finding the things they receive are sufficient, never suffer from want. . . . Those who are contented are happy even though they have to sleep on the ground. Those who are not contented would not be so though they lived in celestial mansions."

The First Panchen Lama said, "The naive work for their aims alone, while the buddhas work solely for the benefit of others." Who do you suppose is better off?

Contentment and a casting off of naive self-indulgence seem to be part of the formula for happiness. How can I foster contentment in a town where spiraling real estate prices and celestial mansions seem the order of the day? We could go to sleep on the ground, but my son's only two, and I'd likely wake up with a backache. It's obviously the attitude that makes the difference. Now we're getting somewhere.

I used to wonder what love and compassion had to do with enlightenment. One seemed to rest entirely on feeling, while the other was a question of reasoned insight. What business did one really have with the other? But if the Buddha were indifferent to our suffering, why would he bother to explain the path to contentment? When I see my little fellow with his tears and smiles, indifference seems an insult to intelligence. How can I be happy while he is suffering? Clearly, we're in this together.

I've served for a number of years as a volunteer fireman in the little town where I spend part of each week. I've walked or, more often, crawled into a number of burning buildings. There is a moment when I'm geared up outside, with the smoke pouring out the windows, when it's clear to me that if someone has to go in, it might as well be me. It has always been an oddly peaceful feeling. Whenever that happens, I think of my father and his wry remark as the Germans approached—ready to meet his fate. Maybe it's something I can pass along to my son.

To Drink a Glass of Water

Noelle Oxenhandler

Noelle Oxenhandler finds the roots of fundamentalism in the urge for simplicity. For many people, this expresses itself in the need for strongly held, black-and-white views of the world. Oxenhandler suggests that another approach—that of being present in the ordinary acts of our lives— is a deeper, more humble, and ultimately less dangerous type of simplicity.

Once, long ago, in the midst of a Zen retreat, I stood in a darkened hallway and drank a glass of water.

That's a lie.

The truth is: I stood in a darkened hallway and discovered that I couldn't even drink a glass of water! Of course, I could lift the glass, open my mouth, and swallow the water. But I couldn't perform this simple activity simply, wholly—with each gulp, my mind splintered into myriad thoughts of past and future, each one of them bearing its weight of self-consciousness, its little tag marked *me, me, me.*

For years thereafter, if anyone had asked me, "Why do you study Zen?" the answer would have been: *I just want to be able to drink a glass of water.* Still today, those words express both my greatest happiness and my deepest aspiration. Lately, I've discovered something quite startling within this aspiration, something that has helped me to understand the form of religion that has long seemed most alien to me: fundamentalism.

Here I'm defining the term in its broadest sense, as any form of religion that takes a particular interpretation of its historical doctrine to be the absolute and literal truth. What connection could there possibly be between such a rigidly dogmatic stance and the aspiration just to drink a glass of water?

The connection is to be found in the desire for simplicity, for clarity. The desire to be free from doubt, to feel as though I am simply doing the right thing, fulfilling my role as a human being and acting in harmony with the very ground of existence. The desire to be part of something vaster than myself, something that relieves me from the pain and uncertainty of being trapped inside a separate *me, me, me.*

Let's face it: it isn't easy to be human. Look at our closest primate relatives: their behavior has scarcely changed in thousands of years. When undisturbed in his natural habitat, the chimpanzee—with whom we share 98 percent of our DNA—gathers his food, swings from his trees, and interacts with his chums in much the same way as did his distant ancestors. Governed by instinct and tightly patterned behavior, other animals aren't faced with the nearly limitless possibilities that confront our species. They don't have to find their way among the ten thousand ways of uttering meaningful sounds, claiming territory, creating shelter, expressing sexuality, or rearing offspring.

It's a great irony that fundamentalism in America was galvanized by resistance to Darwin, to what was considered the blasphemous put-down of being called "animal." For at its root, the fundamentalist impulse may be seen as one way of finding relief from the burden of human choice, complexity, self-consciousness. And in this sense, the impulse toward simplicity, clarity, certainty may be seen as a desire to be *more* like an animal. Isn't it remarkable that while some people would fiercely deny such desire, others honor it? In her poem "Come into Animal Presence," Denise Levertov gazes with admiration and longing at a snake, a rabbit, a llama, and an armadillo, who radiate such a natural ease and dignity in their being. She asks, "What is this joy? That no animal / falters, but knows what it must do?"

Fundamentalism is one answer to the human fear of faltering. It answers this fear through appealing to the fundament, a word that derives from the Latin *fundus,* or "bottom." The fundament is the base, the bottom layer—and that's where all the trouble begins. For one man's base is another man's pinnacle; one man's pure, absolute, divinely revealed and unshakable foundation is another man's leaning tower of stories.

I first learned to meditate in a basement in Ohio, when a monk from Thailand came to my college. Sitting with my rump on the floor and my legs crossed, I was struck by the way the practice trained my attention downward: to my lower abdomen where the breath went, and lower still, to the level of hems, ankles, feet, baseboards, and outlets. Often, when the bell rang at the end of the sitting, I would feel a rush of affection for these lowly things.

Think of Jesus, at the Last Supper, washing his disciples' feet: this is tending to the lowly, an ancient way of expressing devotion, of practicing humility. *Humility:* the word contains the same root as the word *humus,* which refers to soil, earth, the ground. It is also linked to the word *human,* for we are earthlings; we are creatures whose feet touch the ground. When I am able—even for one moment—to drink a glass of water without being preoccupied by the leaning tower of stories, the elaborate edifice of *me, me, me,* then I am refreshed by an experience of true humility, I am restored to simple humanness, I know where I stand.

Though they share the same root, how different *humiliation* is from *humility.* For if humility is a state that blossoms from within, a state of true affection for and kinship with the lowly, humiliation is a state that is imposed from without. To be humiliated is to be brought low, to feel ashamed of being one-downed, of being made to "eat dirt." The combination of humiliation and religious fundamentalism is, as we have so grievously learned, one potent formula for terrorism. Nowhere is this more apparent today than in our encounter with radical Islam and its immense resentment of Western power—stretching all the way from the Crusades, through French and British colonialism and the creation of Israel, to American support for corrupt regimes and its current occupation of Iraq. In the deadly blend of humiliation and religious fundamentalism, two permutations of the bottom layer—*humus* and *fundament*— rub against each other like tectonic plates, releasing an enormous pent-up pressure.

One of the things that is remarkable about terrorism is its economy. For a small dose—a single act of brutal, unpredictable violence— easily becomes pervasive. It spreads like dye in a bowl of water. In the face of this lethal economy, I find it very heartening to remember that the Buddha, too, was a great believer in the small dose. *Look how a drop of water, over time, can wear away the hardest rock,* he said. *So it is that a moment of awareness, rekindled again and again, can wear away the hardest rock of ignorance.*

And so it is that I pose this question: If we were making a tincture, and using awareness as the base, what other ingredients might we add to create the small dose, the remedy for this terrifying time of clashing fundamentalisms? If the opposite of spreading fear is spreading courage, then how can we make a medicine to en-courage?

First, taking to heart the injunction "Physician, heal thyself," it seems important to search inside oneself for any susceptibility to fundamentalism, wherever it manifests as an attachment to particular forms, a tendency to mistake the finger for the moon. When I think, for example, of the sort of militant *oryoki,* the monastic practice of mindful eating, that I have witnessed at more than one Zen center, I feel grateful for my two left thumbs. Were I more dexterous, I could easily have joined the ranks of those who glowered at the poor clods who hadn't perfected the art of bowl-wiping, as if they were infidels. And how many times have I caught myself in the supreme paradox of arrogant bowing? (*What a good bow-er I am!* she said to herself, *So much better than that woman over there, who hasn't got the rhythm down and whose sash is unwinding.*)

While staying alert to the many forms that arrogant bowing takes, we can mix in the other ingredients of our potion. Of these, the first and foremost is not-knowing. Buddhism is *fundamentally* a path of inquiry, a practice of looking at the mind's tendency to cling—to adhere to opinions, beliefs, memories, emotions, moods. This is a remarkable foundation, because it's fathomless. For as every moment gives way to the next, we come face-to-face with an infinite freshness of experience—a freshness that, if we have truly surrendered to the practice, cannot be solidified into a doctrine.

Inextricably intertwined with the practice of not-knowing is the primacy of direct experience. "Don't take my word for it," the Buddha said, and also, "Seek out your own salvation." Though there is always room for distortion ("*I've* had an insight and *you* haven't!"), the insistence on direct experience is *fundamentally* an antidote to fundamentalism. For to be genuinely focused on discovering for oneself what is true or not true is inherently different from attempting to conform—and getting others to conform—to someone else's record of the truth.

Compassion: this is the most important element of all. And here, too, there's wisdom in the word's roots, for *com*-passion, to suffer *with,* expresses a mutuality, an equality that is a world away from the humiliation that is such a powerful catalyst for terrorism.

Laughter, humor—these, too, belong in the tincture. Once, in an almost unspeakably uptight zendo in southern France, a monk was demonstrating to me and another woman how to enter through the doorway. "*Vous entrez toujours avec le pied gauche,*" he told us. "You always enter with the left foot." He lifted his foot over the threshold, and the other woman and I looked at each other. Finally she dared to speak. "*Ce n'est pas votre pied droite?*" she asked, almost apologetically. "Isn't that your right foot?" He burst into laughter, and I saw that the monk's reverence was spacious enough to encompass the right foot and the left foot, the right way and the wrong way. Okay, I thought to myself, I can sit here.

When I look up *fundament,* the very first word in my dictionary is *buttocks*—and I feel like giving a whoop of delight! Suddenly, as if

I'd fallen through a time tunnel, it is thirty years ago and I am standing in the central square in Freiburg, Germany, staring up at a cathedral of carved pink stone. My eyes travel up past the saints, the angels, the Virgin Mary to where—high on a spire—I see a very prominent rear end sticking straight out into the sky. It's a gargoyle, offering not a mouth but an anus as the opening through which evil spirits exit and water rushes when it rains. What a humorous, irreverent way to conduct the unwanted away from the holy place! No judgment, no condemnation: just a drainpipe and a joke.

Humor is a word linked to *humid*, to what is fluid. In our fear of faltering, of being brought low, we earthbound humans get so identified with our sky gods, our lofty roofs, our metaphysical absolutes, that we need the fluid of humor to wash away the effluvia of pride, of arrogance, of dogmatic certainty.

From the butt passing rainwater from the spire, my mind leaps to the Zen dog who "outside the ancient temple, is pissing to the skies." In this image, I see the antidote to a terrible image from the recent past: a U.S. soldier pissing on a cowering Iraqi prisoner. For the dog pissing outside the temple reminds us that the truest reverence is that which doesn't carve the world up into sacred/profane, faithful/infidel, saved/unsaved—or even myself and other.

Now my tincture is complete. I remember my Zen teacher saying, "The rain falls on all things equally," and I take this as the fundament, the true Ground Zero: that I alone must see for myself that all things on earth are equally holy/unholy under the holy/unholy sky. Standing with my bare feet on the ground, I vow to drink a glass of water.

A Century of Spirituality

Thich Nhat Hanh

Lest we think that all this discussion of wisdom, compassion, and mindfulness is academic, or purely personal, Thich Nhat Hanh reminds us of the terrible century the world has just suffered through, and suggests that the best hope—perhaps the only one—for the twenty-first century is spirituality.

I have heard some people predict that the twenty-first century will be a century of spirituality. Personally, I think it *must* be a century of spirituality if we are to survive at all. In our society, there is so much suffering, violence, despair, and confusion. There is so much fear. How can we survive without spirituality?

The Kingdom of Heaven is like the blue sky. Sometimes the blue of the sky reveals itself to us entirely. Sometimes it reveals half of itself, sometimes just a little bit of blue peeks through, and sometimes none at all. Storms, clouds, and fog hide the blue sky. The Kingdom of Heaven can be hidden by a cloud of ignorance or by a tempest of anger, violence, and fear. But for people who practice mindfulness, it is possible to be aware that even if it is very foggy, cloudy, or stormy, the blue sky is always there for us above the clouds. Remembering this keeps us from sinking into despair.

In this very moment, a number of our Israeli and Palestinian friends are practicing walking meditation in Israel and Palestine. It is much easier to practice touching the Kingdom of God with every step here at our Buddhist center in Plum Village than it is over there in those territories occupied by anger, discrimination, and violence. I trust that our friends over there are practicing well so that they do not sink into despair. Despair is the worst thing that can happen to us. Our friends in the Middle East need to know that we are here, practicing for them. There is always something we can do to help the sky clear up, to help the Kingdom of Heaven reveal itself to us, just a little, so that we will not lose hope entirely.

While preaching in the wilderness of Judea, John the Baptist urged people to repent because "the Kingdom of God is at hand." I understand "to repent" here as "to stop": to stop engaging in acts of violence, craving, and hatred. To repent means to wake up and to be aware that the direction we are going as a society is crazy; it is covering up the blue sky. To repent means to begin anew. We admit our transgressions and we bathe ourselves in the clear waters of the spiritual teachings to love our neighbor as ourself. We commit to let go of our resentment, hatred, and pride. We begin anew; we start over with a fresh mind, a fresh heart determined to do better. After being baptized by John, Jesus taught the same thing. And this teaching goes perfectly well with the teaching of Buddhism. Here is the Pure Land, the Pure Land is here. The Pure Land is in our heart. The Pure Land is at hand.

If we know how to begin anew, if we know how to transform our despair, violence, and fear, the Pure Land will reveal itself to us and to those around us. The Pure Land does not belong to the future. The Pure Land belongs to the here and now. In Plum Village we have a very strong expression: "The Pure Land is now or never." Everything we are looking for we can find in the present moment, including the Pure Land, the Kingdom of God, and our buddhanature. It is possible for us to touch the Kingdom of God with our eyes, our feet, our arms, and our mind. When you are mindful, you are concentrated. When your mind and body become one, you need only make one step and there you are in the Kingdom of Heaven. When you are mindful, when you are free, anything you touch, whether it is the oak leaves or the snow, is in the Kingdom of Heaven. Everything you hear, the sound of the birds or the whistling wind, all belong to the Kingdom of Heaven.

The basic condition for touching the Kingdom of God is freedom from fear, despair, anger, and craving. Mindfulness practice allows us to recognize the presence of the cloud, the fog, and the storms. But we can also recognize the blue sky behind it all. We have enough intelligence, courage, and stability to help the blue sky reveal itself again.

People ask me, "What can I do to help the Kingdom of Heaven to reveal itself?" This is a very practical question. It is the same as asking, "What can I do to reduce the level of violence and fear that is overwhelming our society?" This is a question that many of us have asked. When you make a step with stability, solidity, and freedom, you help clear the sky of despair. When hundreds of people walk mindfully together, producing the energy of solidity, stability, freedom, and joy, we are helping our society. When we know how to look at another person with compassionate eyes, when we know how to smile at him with that spirit of understanding, we are helping the Kingdom of Heaven to reveal itself. When we breathe in and out mindfully, we are helping the Pure Land to reveal itself.

In our daily lives, every single moment we can do something to help the Kingdom of God reveal itself. Don't allow yourself to be overwhelmed by despair. We can make use of every minute and every hour of our daily life.

Go as a River

When we act as a community of practitioners, infused with the energy of mindfulness and compassion, we are powerful. When we are part of a spiritual community, we have a lot of joy and we can better resist the temptation to be overwhelmed by despair.

Despair is a great temptation in our century. Alone, we are

vulnerable. If we try to go to the ocean as a single drop of water, we will evaporate before we even arrive. But if we go as a river, if we go as a community, we are sure to arrive at the ocean. With a community to walk with us, support us, and always remind us of the blue sky, we'll never lose our faith. As a political or business leader, a social worker, teacher, or parent, you need to be reminded that the blue sky is still there for you. We all need a community, a sangha, to prevent us from sinking in the swamp of despair.

Community-building is the most important action of our century. How can the twenty-first century be a century of spirituality if we do not take up the work of building and strengthening spiritual communities? As individuals, we have suffered tremendously. Individualism is predominating, families are breaking down, and society has become deeply divided as a result. For the twenty-first century to be a century of spirituality, we must be guided by the spirit of togetherness. We should learn to do things together, to share our ideas and the deep aspiration in our hearts. We have to learn to see the sangha, our community, as our own body. We need each other in order to practice solidity, freedom, and compassion so that we can remind people that there is always hope.

Building Safety through Communication

If we want to be safe, we have to build safety. What do we build it with? We can't use fortresses, bombs, or airplanes. The United States of America has a very powerful military and the most advanced weapons in the world, but the American people don't feel safe; they feel very afraid and vulnerable. There must be some other kind of practice to take refuge in so that we can really feel safe. We have to learn to build safety with our in-breath and our out-breath. We have to learn to build safety with our steps, with our way of acting and reacting, with our words and our efforts to build communication.

You can't feel safe if you're not in good communication with the people you live with or see regularly. You can't feel safe if those around you don't look at you with sympathy and compassion. In the way you speak, sit, and walk, you can show the other person that she is safe in your presence, because you are coming to her in peace. In this way, you build confidence. Your peace and compassion help the other person feel very safe. This allows her to react to you with compassion and understanding, and you, too, will feel safer. Safety is not an individual matter. Helping the other person feel safe guarantees your safety.

Your country can't be safe if you don't do anything to help other countries feel safe as well. If the United States wants safety, it has to take care of the safety of other nations also. If Great Britain wants safety, it has to think of the safety of other groups of people. Any of us could be victims of violence and terrorism. No country is invulnerable. It's so clear that violence and weapons can't guarantee us real safety. Maybe the first thing we have to do is to say, "Dear friend, I am aware that you want to live in safety. I, too, want to live in safety, so why don't we work together?" This is a very simple thing for us to do—but we don't do it.

Communication is the practice. We live in a time when there are so many sophisticated means for communication: e-mail, telephone, fax. Yet it is very difficult for individuals, groups, and nations to communicate with each other. We feel we can't use our words to speak and so we use bombs to communicate.

When we arrive at the point when we can't communicate with our words and we have to use guns, we have succumbed to despair. We have to learn how to communicate. If we can show a group we are in conflict with that they have nothing to be afraid of, then we can begin to trust each other. In Asian countries, people often greet each other by bowing and joining their palms to form a lotus flower. In the West, when people meet each other, they shake hands. I learned that this tradition comes from medieval times when people were afraid of each other, and every time they met they wanted to show that they had no weapons in their hands. Now we have to do the same thing. With our actions, we can say, "Dear friend: I have no weapons. See? Touch for yourself. I am not harmful, there are no guns hidden on me." This is the kind of practice that can begin to build trust. With trust and communication, dialogue becomes possible.

While our friends from the Middle East were visiting Plum Village a few years ago, I asked them whether they would accept an international peacekeeping force in the area to stop the violence. Such a force would help us proceed with negotiations to find peaceful solutions for both the Israelis and the Palestinians. Some of our Israeli and Palestinian friends said they can't trust anyone. They don't trust the United Nations and they wouldn't trust an international peacekeeping force because they don't believe either would be neutral. Fear goes together with suspicion. Fear and suspicion are what prevent us from being together as friends, as a community of nations.

Since the so-called War on Terror began, we have spent billions of dollars but we have only created more violence, hate, and fear. We have not succeeded in removing terrorism, neither in its expression nor, most importantly, in the minds of the people. It's time to come home to ourselves and find a better way to bring peace to ourselves and to the world. Only with the practice of deep listening and gentle communication can we help remove wrong perceptions that are at the foundation of anger, hate, and violence.

You cannot remove wrong perceptions with a gun. We are all aware that the U.S. is having a difficult time in Iraq. The U.S. is caught in Iraq as it was caught in Vietnam not very long ago. In North Vietnam and Cambodia, the United States tried to search-and-destroy the communists. But the more they bombed, the more communists they created. Finally the U.S. had to withdraw.

The U.S. often has many good intentions. But in their course of action, they cause tremendous suffering. For example, in the war with Vietnam, the Americans had the intention to save Vietnam from Communism. It was a good intention, but this desire to save us destroyed us. That's why I have said, "Save us from your salvation." Your intention to help us ruined us. The intention to love is not yet love. We must know *how* to love. True love doesn't destroy the object of its love.

I am afraid that the U.S. is doing exactly the same thing in Iraq.

The more we strike against terror the more terrorists we create. The U.S. has invested a lot of money, human lives, time, and resources in Iraq. It is very difficult for America to withdraw from Iraq now, even if the government wanted to leave; it's very difficult to get out of the mess. The U.S. believes that there are countries that sponsor terrorism around Iraq. The State Department lists a number of Middle Eastern countries as sponsors of terrorism. If we continue to use the search-and-destroy model, we will end up bringing troops into these countries as well. This is very dangerous.

I think the only way for the U.S. to change this situation is to invest in making the United Nations into a real peace organization and transfer power to the U.N. so that it can take over the problems of Iraq, Afghanistan, and the Middle East. America could allow other nations to participate actively in building the United Nations into a true community of nations with enough authority to do her job. To me this is the only easy and honorable way out of the situation, and doing this would be applauded around the world. Using violence to suppress violence will not lead to lasting peace. America is powerful enough to wake up to this reality. The U.S. is powerful enough to find a solution through peaceful communication and reconciliation, forsaking violence.

THE FAMILY OF NATIONS

How can we make the United Nations into a true family of nations? The United Nations was meant to be a community, a sangha of nations. But we don't really trust it and we try to make the United Nations into an international instrument to serve our own national interests.

When there is trouble within a nation, the whole global community must come and help. For instance, in Plum Village if one person is sick, we come and help him, because that person is part of our body and we have to take good care of our body. If there is a member of the community who has difficulties, the whole community has to take care of that member. When there is a conflict between two members of our community, it's not only their problem, it's all of ours. In a family, if two brothers are fighting each other and trying to kill each other, other members of the family have to intervene to prevent this fratricide. The United Nations, representing the human family, hasn't done that. In a community, a sangha, each person trains to see beyond their individual point of view and to look with the eyes of collective wisdom, the sangha eyes. It is entirely possible to solve problems using our sangha eyes, for they are always clearer than the eyes of the individual.

The European Union aspires to act as a family, as one body. I'm very inspired that countries have acted on the wisdom of nondiscrimination. They've put aside national interest to a large extent and have understood that the well-being of the whole of Europe is their own well-being. I've heard that countries in Southeast Asia are considering forming a similar union. Now, we could come together on a global level, seeing that all countries' well-being is interconnected and that when we help other countries, we are helping ourselves.

If the United Nations could become a true community, the tensions between various countries could be taken care of by the sangha of the United Nations. The United Nations' General Assembly could also be a place where people learn to listen to each other as brothers and sisters. We could stop acting in the name of national interest. In a true sangha, you can't operate on the basis of your ego. You surrender your individual self that you believe to be separate from everyone else, and use the sangha eyes as your eyes. You learn to profit from the collective wisdom and insight of the sangha. It can be much stronger than each country's own individual insight. Speak out to help others in your community, city, and nation. We have to help the United Nations become a true sangha of nations.

We can't allow things to continue as they are. Every day people die; every day bombs explode. If people don't believe in the United Nations as a true sangha, it's because it's not functioning that way. Instead, each country wants to use it to their own advantage. And mass violence continues without intervention. If the United Nations can become a real sangha body and if the Security Council can become a true instrument of peace, we could act quickly and solve many of the problems of violence around the world. Some people say the U.N. is hopeless, and that we should destroy it and start with something new. But the U.N. is already there and it is what we have. The U.N. is our hope.

The sangha body of the United Nations can tell the governments of Pakistan and India, of Israel and Palestine, of the United States and Iraq, "You are friends, you are family. Please hold hands with each other and serve the sangha body." This may sound naive, but it is exactly in accord with the ancient wisdom of all our ancestors. Whenever there are conflicts between people in Plum Village, this is what we do and it may take only a few hours. Instead of fighting each other, we become allies to serve the common cause of peace and stability in the world. It is possible for countries to act as siblings instead of enemies. This is sangha-building in the twenty-first century.

If you're a journalist, if you're a writer, if you're a professor, if you're a parent, please speak out. Articulate your deep desire for peace and reconciliation and affirm your commitment to making it happen. Sangha-building has to be done at every level, local, national, and international. Sangha is our hope.

Displaying the Light of Wisdom

Whether or not the twenty-first century becomes a century of spirituality depends on our capacity of building community. Without a community, we will become victims of despair. We need each other. We need to congregate, to bring together our wisdom, our insight, and our compassion. The Earth is our true home, a home for all of us. We invite everyone to look deeply into our collective situation. We invite everyone to speak out to spread the message. If we fail in this task of sangha-building, then the suffering of the twenty-first century will be indescribable.

We can bring the spiritual dimension into our daily life, as well as our social, political, and economic life. This is our practice. Jesus had this intention. Buddha had this intention. All of our spiritual ancestors, whether Christian, Jewish, Muslim, Hindu, or Buddhist, had this intention. We can display the light of wisdom and come together in order to create hope and to prevent society and the younger generation from sinking into despair.

We can learn to speak out so that the voice of the Buddha, the voice of Jesus, the voice of Mohammed and of all our spiritual ancestors can be heard in this dangerous and pivotal moment in history. We offer this light so that the world will not sink into total darkness. Everyone has the seed of awakening and insight within her heart. Let us help each other touch these seeds in ourselves so that everyone will have the courage to speak out. We must ensure that the way we live our daily lives doesn't create more terrorism in the world. Only a collective awakening can stop this course of self-destruction.

Contributors

TENSHIN REB ANDERSON is a lineage-holder in the Soto Zen tradition. Born in Mississippi, he grew up in Minnesota and left advanced study in mathematics and Western psychology to go to the San Francisco Zen Center in 1967. He received dharma transmission from Shunryu Suzuki Roshi in 1983. Anderson served as abbot of San Francisco Zen Center's three training centers, City Center, Green Gulch Farm, and Tassajara Zen Mountain Center, from 1986 to 1995. Anderson continues to teach at Zen Center, living with his family at Green Gulch Farm. He is the author of *Warm Smiles from Cold Mountains: Dharma Talks on Zen Meditation* and *Being Upright: Zen Meditation and the Bodhisattva Precepts*.

DIANA ATKINSON's life was shaped by acute chronic ulcerative colitis, diagnosed at age four. She spent much of her childhood in Vancouver General Hospital, in British Columbia, having surgeries at ages twelve, fourteen, and fifteen. After dropping out of high school, she ran off with a one-eyed biker and became a stripper, taking buses and small planes all over British Columbia and western Alberta. Her novel recounting this period, *Highways and Dancehalls*, was nominated for the Governor General's Award and the Commonwealth prize for Best Book. She came to Buddhism in her thirties to help her cope with continuing surgery. Recently married, she is at work on an autobiography chronicling her long struggle with illness.

MARC IAN BARASCH is the author of *The Healing Path*, *Healing Dreams*, and *Remarkable Recovery*, a literary trilogy inspired by his own journey through serious illness, as well as *Field Notes on the Compassionate Life*, excerpted here. A former student of Chögyam Trungpa Rinpoche, Barasch has taught psychology at Boulder's Naropa University. He served as an editor at Psychology Today and Natural Health, and was editor-in-chief of New Age Journal. He is also a television producer and writer whose environmental special, "One Child, One Voice," was broadcast in 150 countries and nominated for an Emmy. As a hobby, he plays and records with Stephen King and Amy Tan in the "lit-rock" band the Rock Bottom Remainders.

KATY BUTLER writes regularly for the Science Times section of *The New York Times*, *Tricycle*, *More*, and *Psychotherapy Networker*. Her writing often explores how people transform themselves and their lives, especially at the boundary of psychology and spiritual practice. She was a finalist in 2004 for the National Magazine Award for Personal Service, and her AIDS reporting for *The San Francisco Chronicle*, in collaboration with Randy Shilts, was nominated for the Pulitzer Prize. Butler lives in Mill Valley, California, where she works as a writer, teacher, and editor.

MARIANA CAPLAN, PH.D., is a long-term student of the Western Baul tradition, a synthesis of Vajrayana Buddhism and Vaisnava Hinduism. Her prior spiritual studies were in Judaism, indigenous shamanism, and Vipassana Buddhism. Caplan has a private practice in spiritual guidance and counseling, and is an adjunct faculty member at the California Institute of Integral Studies, Naropa University (online), the Institute of Transpersonal Psychology, and John F. Kennedy University. She is the author of seven books, including *Halfway Up the Mountain: The Error of Premature Claims to Enlightenment*; *Do You Need a Guru?: Understanding the Student-Teacher Relationship in an Era of False Prophets*; and *To Touch is to Live: The Need for Affection in an Impersonal World*.

PEMA CHÖDRÖN is an American Buddhist nun whose root teacher was the renowned meditation master Chögyam Trungpa. Since his death in 1987, she has studied with Trungpa Rinpoche's son, Sakyong Mipham, and with her current principal teacher, Dzigar Kongtrül. Pema Chödrön is resident teacher at Gampo Abbey in Nova Scotia, the first Tibetan monastery in North America established for Westerners. Her many popular books include *The Places that Scare You*, *When Things Fall Apart*, and *Start Where You Are*. Her most recent book is *No Time to Lose: A Timely Guide to the Way of the Bodhisattva*, excerpted here.

PETER CONRADI took early retirement from academic life in 1996 in order to write freelance, and since then has published *Iris Murdoch: A Life*, an authorized biography nominated as Best Book of the Year in 2001 by ten reviewers, and *Going Buddhist: Panic and Emptiness, the Buddha and me*, excerpted here. In earlier life he taught English literature at the University of Colorado in Boulder, the Jagiellonian University in Krakow, and Kingston University, London, where he is now Professor Emeritus. He has also been both a medical student and lived for one year as a kibbutznik in Israel. He has been a student of Chögyam Trungpa Rinpoche for more than twenty years and is now also a student of Sakyong Mipham Rinpoche.

GEORGE CRANE is a poet, translator, and author of the internationally acclaimed memoir/travel book *Bones of the Master: A Buddhist Monk's Search for the Lost Heart of China*. "A Saint Beyond My Understanding" is excerpted from his most recent book, *Beyond the House of the False Lama*, another tale of spiritual travel. With Tsung Tai, Crane translated *A Thousand Pieces of Snow*.

ANNE CUSHMAN is committed to the spiritual path of ordinary life, for which her son, Skye, is her most important teacher. She lives with Skye and their cat, Tahini, in Fairfax, California, where she spends her time doing yoga, hiking, reading, teaching, baking, biking, writing personal essays, completing her first novel, and answering Skye's questions about chess, love, yeast, war, biology, and the origins of the universe. She is a contributing editor to both *Tricycle* and *Yoga Journal*, and is the director of the Mindfulness Yoga training program at Spirit Rock Meditation Center.

CHRISTINA FELDMAN has been training in the Tibetan, Mahayana, and Theravada Buddhist traditions since 1970, and has been teaching meditation throughout the world since 1974. She is the cofounder and a guiding teacher at Gaia House, a Buddhist meditation center in Devon, England, and is a guiding senior dharma teacher at the Insight Meditation Center in Barre, Massachusetts. She also coteaches Women in Meditation, an annual retreat at the Spirit Rock Meditation Center, in Woodacre, California. Feldman is the coauthor of *Soul Food* and *Stories of the Spirit, Stories of the Heart* (both with Jack Kornfield), and the author of a number of books, including *The Buddhist Path to Simplicity* and *Woman Awake*. Her most recent book is *Compassion: Listening to the Cries of the World,* excerpted here.

NORMAN FISCHER is a father, poet, and Zen priest. For many years he has taught at the San Francisco Zen Center, where he served as co-abbot from 1995 to 2000. He is currently a senior teacher there, as well as the founder and spiritual director of the Everyday Zen Foundation, an organization dedicated to adapting Zen Buddhist teachings to Western culture. His interests include the adaptation of Zen meditation and understanding to the worlds of business, interreligious dialogue and practice, care of the dying, and mentoring youth. His written works include collections of poetry, frequent essays in Buddhist publications, a Zen-inspired translation of the Psalms, a memoir about Buddhism and Judaism, and a book on the nature of maturity.

CAROLYN ROSE GIMIAN, PH.D., is a freelance editor and writer who edited many of the books of Chögyam Trungpa Rinpoche, including such classics as *Shambhala: The Sacred Path of the Warrior,* and the recent *Collected Works of Chögyam Trungpa*. She was the founding director of the Shambhala Archives, a repository of paper, photographic, and audio-visual records that document the lives and teaching activities of a number of Tibetan Buddhist teachers who came to North America in the twentieth century. She is the co-author of *Dragon's Thunder*, the memoirs of Trungpa Rinpoche's widow, Diana Judith Mukpo. Gimian has a doctorate in child psychology from Union Graduate School in Cincinnati.

Tenzin Gyatso, the 14th Dalai Lama, is the spiritual and temporal leader of the Tibetan people and a winner of the Nobel Peace Prize. He is a world statesman, national leader, spiritual teacher, and deeply learned theologian.

Thich Nhat Hanh is, along with His Holiness the Dalai Lama, one of the leading exponents of a Buddhist approach to politics and social action. He is a Zen master, poet, and founder of the Engaged Buddhist movement. A well-known antiwar activist in his native Vietnam, he was nominated for the Nobel Peace Prize by Martin Luther King, Jr. The author of more than forty books, he resides at Buddhist practice centers in France and Vermont.

Erik Hansen graduated from UC Berkeley, lived the writer's life in Europe, taught English, learned Spanish, became a screenwriter (*Heart & Souls*), got rich, lost it all on the stock market, and studied Zen meditation with the late Dr. Edward Wortz. Now back in New Orleans after Hurricane Katrina, Hansen is endlessly fascinated by (and grateful for) all of the ways that Zen practice can be applied to the twists and turns of an everyday American life.

Nancy Hathaway, MEd., is a therapist who has developed a popular training program for parents called Being Present with Our Children. She began studying meditation in Kopan Monastery in Kathmandu, Nepal, in 1974. Returning to the United States, she continued her Buddhist studies with numerous teachers in the Zen,

Tibetan, and Vipassana traditions. For six years she lived in a Zen Temple, where her two sons were raised in their early years. In 1985, she became a senior dharma teacher in the Kwan Um School of Zen and began teaching Zen meditation retreats, while devoting herself to mothering her two sons, who are now successful, happy, kind, and compassionate young men. Currently she has offices in Bangor, Maine, and Cambridge, Massachusetts, and in 2005 she founded the Center for Studying Mindfulness in Work, Family, Health, & Relationship.

LIN JENSEN is the founding teacher of the Chico Zen Sangha, in Chico, California. He taught writing in colleges and universities for more than twenty years and continues to teach Buddhist ethics and practices at Chico State University. The essays excerpted here are from *Bad Dog*, a unique memoir of Jensen's journey from difficult childhood to teacher of Zen. His previous book, *Uncovering the Wisdom of the Heartmind*, received the award for Best Nonfiction/Spiritual Book from *Today's Librarian*.

CHARLES R. JOHNSON is a novelist, scholar, and essayist. He holds the S. Wilson and Grace M. Pollock Professorship for Excellence in English at the University of Washington in Seattle. He has been the recipient of many prestigious awards, including a Guggenheim Fellowship and a MacArthur Foundation grant. His novels include *Dreamer*, based on the life of Martin Luther King, Jr., and *Middle Passage*, for which he won a National Book Award. This selection in this anthology is from his recent short story collection, *Dr. King's Refrigerator*.

JON KABAT-ZINN, PH.D., is renowned as the founder of the Mindfulness-Based Stress Reduction movement, whose programs around the world have taught hundreds of thousands of people how to use mindfulness meditation to cope with illness, chronic pain, emotional difficulties, and stress. His major research pursuits lie in the emerging field of mind/body medicine, with a focus on the clinical, social, and human performance effects of mindfulness meditation training in various populations. He is the founder of the Center for Mindfulness in Medicine, Health Care, and Society at the University of Massachusetts Medical School and former director of its renowned Stress Reduction Clinic. Kabat-Zinn was one of the earliest students of the Korean Zen Master Seung Sahn and was a founding member of Cambridge Zen Center. His best-selling books include *Full Catastrophe Living* and *Wherever You Go There You Are*. His most recent book is *Coming to Our Senses: Healing Ourselves and the World Through Mindfulness*, excerpted here.

ROSHI BODHIN KJOLHEDE was formally installed as Philip Kapleau's dharma successor and abbot of the Rochester Zen Center in 1986. The appointment marked the culmination of a sixteen-year teacher-student relationship between Kjolhede and the famed author of *The Three Pillars of Zen*, the last decade working intimately together. He received a B.A. in psychology from the University of Michigan and was ordained as a Buddhist priest in 1976. After completing twelve years of koan training under Roshi Kapleau, while working closely with him on three of his books, he spent a year on pilgrimage in Japan, China, India, Tibet, and Taiwan. Since his installation, he has conducted some 150 retreats (*sesshin*). He now devotes most of his time to teaching at the Rochester Zen Center and its rural retreat facility.

DZIGAR KONGTRÜL was born in northern India, the son of the highly respected Buddhist lama, Neten Choling Rinpoche. After being recognized as a reincarnation of the nonsectarian master Jamgön Kongtrül Lodro Thaye, he received extensive traditional training in all aspects of Tibetan Buddhist doctrine. Yet, born in India to Tibetan refugee parents, his life evolved in ways that stretched far beyond a traditional setting. Sleeping on hemp roadside cots along the highways of India, with only a sack of belongings, he traveled to study with different Buddhist masters. Later, he married his wife Elizabeth, a surprising turn of events which led them to make America their home. In 1990, he began a five-year tenure as a professor of Buddhist philosophy at Naropa University in Boulder, Colorado. He also founded Mangala Shri Bhuti, his own teaching organization, during this period. He has established a mountain re-treat center, Longchen Jigme Samten Ling, in southern Colorado. When not guiding students in long-term retreats or in retreat him-self, he travels throughout the world teaching and furthering his own education.

DAVID R. LOY returned to the United States in 2006 after twenty-eight years in Asia to become Besl Professor of ethics/religion and society at Xavier University in Cincinnati. He is the author of nu-merous books and articles on Buddhism and comparative philoso-phy, including *Nonduality: A Study in Comparative Philosophy, Lack and Transcendence: The Problem of Death and Life in Psychotherapy, Existentialism, and Buddhism*, and the ground-breaking *A Buddhist History of the West: Studies in Lack*. Loy started Zen practice in 1971 with Robert Aitken Roshi and Yamada-Koun Roshi, who invited him to Kamakura, Japan, to undertake intensive Zen practice. He is qualified as a sensei in the Sanbo Kyodan tradition.

MARK MAGILL feels he has yet to take the first Panchen Lama's in-junction to heart: "Inspire me to grasp life's essential meaning and not be distracted by pointless activities." Magill divides his time be-tween New York City and the Catskill mountains. Aside from his work as a writer, Magill keeps bees and is a member of the North Branch Volunteer Fire Department. Magill's first encounter with Buddhism was a course on koans in college. He went on to a screen-writing career that resulted in winning the Sundance Film Festival with a feature called *Waiting for the Moon*. In an effort to pitch yet another film, he agreed to meet his story editor for dinner at a Zen monastery near his home in the Catskills. The editor never showed up, but Magill wound up meditating with the monks after a bowl of rice and vegetables. Since then, Magill has served as a contributing editor for *Tricycle* magazine. His nonfiction work includes *Why Is the Buddha Smiling?* and *A Voice at the Borders of Silence,* a biography of painter William Segal published in conjunction with three short films by Ken Burns. He also served as a co-author with Gehlek Rinpoche on his book *Good Life, Good Death.*

SAKYONG MIPHAM RINPOCHE is the spiritual leader of Shambhala, an international network of meditation centers. He is eldest son of the late Chögyam Trungpa Rinpoche, who was instrumental in bringing Buddhism to the West, and received training from many of the great Tibetan Buddhist teachers of the twentieth century. In 1995 he was recognized as the incarnation of the revered Tibetan teacher Mipham the Great. Sakyong Mipham continually maintains his personal meditation, study, and writing practice. He travels extensively, teaching throughout the world, and supports a number of humanitarian and religious projects in Tibet. He is a poet and an artist, who also enjoys golf, running, horseback riding, and yoga. His first book, *Turning the Mind into an Ally,* was published in 2003. His most recent book is *Ruling Your World,* excerpted here.

ANDREW OLENDZKI, PH.D., is the executive director of the Barre Center for Buddhist Studies and the editor of Insight Journal. He is a scholar of early Buddhist thought and literature who has trained at Lancaster University in England, the University of Sri Lanka, and Harvard. He was the executive director of the Insight Meditation Society in Barre, and has taught at several New England colleges, including Harvard and Brandeis.

NOELLE OXENHANDLER was a graduate student at the University of Toronto when she lost the term paper she had just completed on "non-attachment." Plunged instantly into a state of panic, she remembered the signs in Canadian subways: "Mind the Gap!" Clearly, the gap between thinking and being had grown too great in her life—and so she left graduate school and got herself to a Zen Buddhist monastery in northern California. There, while shoveling snow and hosing down goat manure, she worked on "minding the gap." Oxenhandler still lives in northern California, but not in a monastery. She teaches creative writing at Sonoma State University and her essays have appeared in many national and literary magazines. She is the author of *The Eros of Parenthood* and is currently at work on her third book, *An Experiment in Desire.*

THE DZOGCHEN PONLOP RINPOCHE is one of a group of impressive young Tibetan teachers born and trained in the Tibetan Diaspora. Highly learned, fluent in English, and familiar with the ways of the modern world, these teachers are a bridge between the ancient traditions of Tibet and the needs of contemporary students. Ponlop Rinpoche is founder and president of Nalandabodhi and Nitartha International, executive director of Nitartha Institute, and publisher of *Bodhi* magazine. His most recent books are *Penetrating Wisdom* and *Wild Awakening: The Heart of Mahamudra and Dzogchen.* A renowned scholar, poet, and meditation master, he is also a member of the official Rolling Stones Fan Club.

SHARON SALZBERG experienced a childhood involving considerable loss and turmoil, but an early realization of the power of meditation to overcome personal suffering determined her life direction. Her teaching and writing now communicate that power to a worldwide audience of practitioners. She offers non-sectarian retreat and study opportunities for participants from widely diverse backgrounds. Salzberg attended her first intensive meditation course in India in 1971 and spent the next three years engaged in intensive study with Buddhist teachers in the Theravadan and Tibetan traditions. She returned to America in 1974 and began teaching Vipassana (insight) meditation. In 1976, she established, together with Joseph Goldstein and Jack Kornfield, the Insight Meditation Society (IMS) in Barre, Massachusetts. One of Western Buddhism's best-known teachers and writers, she resides in Barre and New York City.

JOAN SUTHERLAND is a Zen teacher and the founder of The Open Source, a collaborative network of communities and individuals in the western United States. She was the first American woman to receive transmission in her koan lineage, and she is deeply involved in re-imagining the koan tradition and exploring its relationship to creativity. She also integrates mythopoetics and contemporary mind and consciousness discoveries with meditation. Sutherland has a Master of Arts in East Asian languages and cultures and translates Chan and Zen texts into English; she also apprenticed in mythoarchaeology with the late Marija Gimbutas. For some time she has lived among the redwoods in the coastal hills of northern California, where she has been active in environmental work.

JUDITH TOY was ordained by Thich Nhat Hanh in 1997, and with her husband, Philip Toy, has founded three sanghas in Pennsylvania and North Carolina, one in a medium security prison. Cloud Cottage Sangha meets four times weekly in a meditation hall adjacent to the couple's Appalachian cottage. She is a devoted grandmother who teaches, gardens, makes giant puppets, writes, and guides the sangha. Her giant Buddha puppet appears at Asheville's annual Wesak celebration and at interfaith events. The story in this anthology is from her book in progress, *Minding the Fire: Zen Essays on Forgiveness.*

POLLY TROUT is the founder and director of Seattle Education Access, a nonprofit that helps homeless youth transition successfully to college, so they can escape poverty through the power of education. She has a Ph.D. in religious studies from Boston University and is the author of *Eastern Seeds, Western Soil: Three Gurus in America.* A mother and activist, her passions include social and economic justice, sex positive spirituality, and art as a path to freedom. Her faith is inspired by earth-centered traditions and Asian traditions, especially Vipassana and Shaktism. "I am not a Buddhist, but I pay attention to what the Buddha had to say," says Polly. "He rocked."

TULKU URGYEN RINPOCHE (1920–1996) was one of the outstanding Tibetan Buddhist teachers of his generation. Leaving Tibet in the face of the Chinese invasion in 1959, he settled in the hermitage of

Nagi Gompa, on the northern slopes of Nepal's Kathmandu Valley. There he lived quietly as a true Dzogchen yogi, visited by a steady stream of scholars, students, and practitioners from around the world. Though spending over twenty-five years in retreat, he not only taught extensively but also founded numerous monasteries and retreat centers. Tulku Urgyen was famed for his profound meditative realization and for the concise, lucid, and humorous style with which he imparted the essence of the Dzogchen teachings. He was the author of such popular books as *Rainbow Painting* and *As It Is*.

JOHN WELWOOD, PH.D., is a clinical psychologist, psychotherapist, teacher, and author. He originally studied philosophy at Bowdoin College and spent two years at the Sorbonne in Paris studying existentialist thought. As a graduate student he trained in existential psychology and worked closely with Eugene Gendlin at the University of Chicago, where he received his Ph.D. in clinical psychology in 1974. In the 1980's Welwood emerged as a major figure in the leading-edge fields of transpersonal psychology and East/West psychology. He is currently associate editor of the *Journal of Transpersonal Psychology* and leads workshops on psychospiritual work and conscious relationship throughout the world. Among his books are the classics *Journey of the Heart* and *Toward a Psychology of Awakening*. His most recent book, *Perfect Love, Imperfect Relationships*, excerpted here, is the winner of a Books for a Better Life Award.

Credits

Peter Conradi, "The Mystic and the Cynic": From *Going Buddhist: Panic and Emptiness, the Buddha and Me*, by Peter J Conradi. Published by Short Books.

George Crane, "A Saint Beyond My Understanding": From *Beyond the House of the False Lama* by George Crane. Copyright © 2005 by George Crane. Reprinted by permission of HarperCollins Publishers.

Anne Cushman, "What Is Death, Mommy?": From the December 2005 issue of the *Shambhala Sun*.

Christina Feldman, "Listening to the Cries of the World": Excerpted from *Compassion: Listening to the Cries of the World*. Copyright © 2005 by Christina Feldman. Reprinted by permission of Rodmell Press (www.rodmellpress.com).

Norman Fischer, "Wash Your Bowls": From *Hooked: Buddhist Writings on Greed, Desire, and the Urge to Consume* edited by Stephanie Kaza. Copyright © 2005 by Norman Fischer. Published by Shambhala Publications, Inc., www.shambhala.com.

Carolyn Rose Gimian, "The Three Lords of Materialism": From the September 2005 issue of the *Shambhala Sun*.

Tenzin Gyatso, "Studying Mind from the Inside": From *The Universe in a Single Atom: The Convergence of Science and Spirituality* by His Holiness The Dalai Lama. Copyright © 2005 The Dalai Lama. Used by permission of an imprint of The Doubleday Broadway Publishing, a division of Random House, Inc.

Thich Nhat Hanh, "A Century of Spirituality": From *Calming the Fearful Mind: A Zen Response to Terrorism* by Thich Nhat Hanh. Copyright © 2005 by Unified Buddhist Church. With permission from Parallax Press, www.parallax.org.

Mark Magill, "Passing It On": From the Fall 2005 issue of *Tricycle: The Buddhist Review.*

Sakyong Mipham: "The Dragon's Mind and the Power of Non-Self": From *Ruling Your World: Ancient Strategies for Modern Life* by Sakyong Mipham. Copyright © 2005 by Sakyong Mipham. Used by permission of Broadway Books, a division of Random House, Inc.

Andrew Olendzki, "Removing the Thorn": From the Fall 2005 issue of *Tricycle: The Buddhist Review.*

Noelle Oxenhandler, "To Drink a Glass of Water": From the Summer 2005 issue of *Tricycle: The Buddhist Review.*

The Dzogchen Ponlop Rinpoche, "Contemplating Emptiness": Adapted from talks presented at Nalandabodhi Open Retreat, Santa Sabina California, and published in *Bodhi* magazine. Copyright © 2005 by The Dzogchen Ponlop Rinpoche.

Sharon Salzberg, "Surprised by Joy": From *The Force of Kindness,* published by Sounds True. Copyright © 2005 by Sharon Salzberg. Reprinted here by permission of the author.

Nyogen Senzaki, "As a wanderer in this strange land . . .": From *Like a Dream, Like a Fantasy: The Zen Teachings and Translations of Nyogen Senzaki.* Copyright © 2005 Zen Studies Society. Reprinted with the permission of Wisdom Publications, www.wisdompubs.org.

Joan Sutherland, "This Floating World": From the March 2005 issue of the *Shambhala Sun.*

Judith Toy, "Murder as a Call to Love": From the Summer 2005 issue of *The Mindfulness Bell.*